D1110758

Good Ol' CHARLIE BROWN

Titan Facsimile Editions by Charles M. Schulz

On sale now:
Peanuts
More Peanuts
Good Grief, More Peanuts!

Coming soon:
Snoopy
You're Out of Your Mind, Charlie Brown!
But We Love You, Charlie Brown
Peanuts Revisited
Go Fly a Kite, Charlie Brown
Peanuts Every Sunday

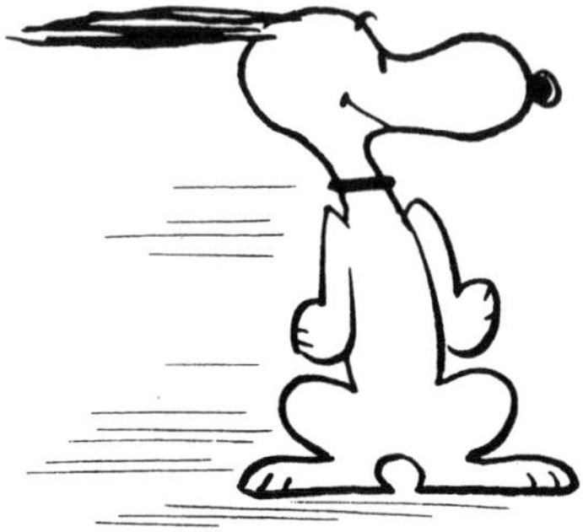

Good Ol'
CHARLIE BROWN

A NEW PEANUTS BOOK

by Charles M. Schulz

TITAN COMICS

GOOD OL' CHARLIE BROWN

ISBN: 9781782761587

PUBLISHED BY TITAN COMICS, A DIVISION OF TITAN PUBLISHING GROUP LTD,

144 SOUTHWARK ST, LONDON SE1 0UP. TCN 303.

COPYRIGHT © 2015 BY PEANUTS WORLDWIDE LLC.

PRINTED IN INDIA.

10 9 8 7 6 5 4 3

WWW.TITAN-COMICS.COM

WWW.PEANUTS.COM

ORIGINALLY PUBLISHED IN 1957 BY RHINEHART & CO. INCORPORATED

NEW YORK & TORONTO

A CIP CATALOGUE RECORD FOR THIS TITLE

IS AVAILABLE FROM THE BRITISH LIBRARY.

THIS EDITION FIRST PUBLISHED: SEPTEMBER 2015

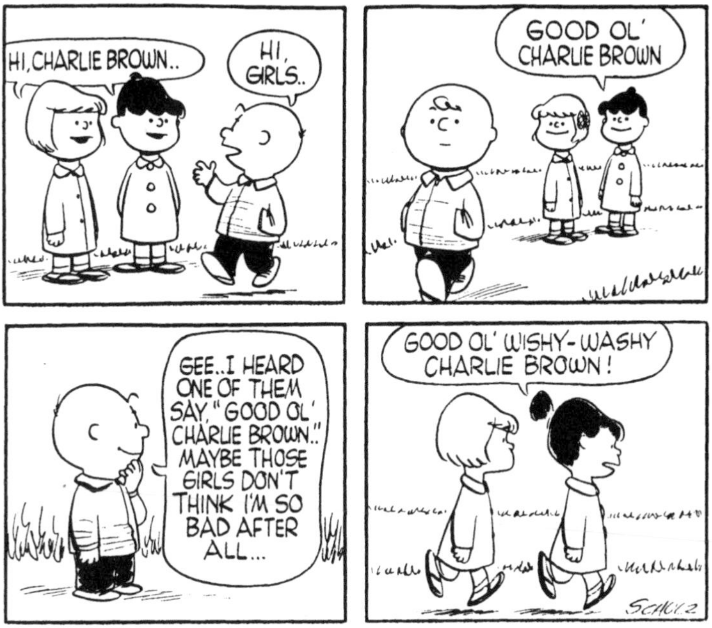
HI, CHARLIE BROWN..
HI, GIRLS..
GOOD OL' CHARLIE BROWN
GEE..I HEARD ONE OF THEM SAY, "GOOD OL' CHARLIE BROWN.." MAYBE THOSE GIRLS DON'T THINK I'M SO BAD AFTER ALL...
GOOD OL' WISHY-WASHY CHARLIE BROWN!
SCHULZ

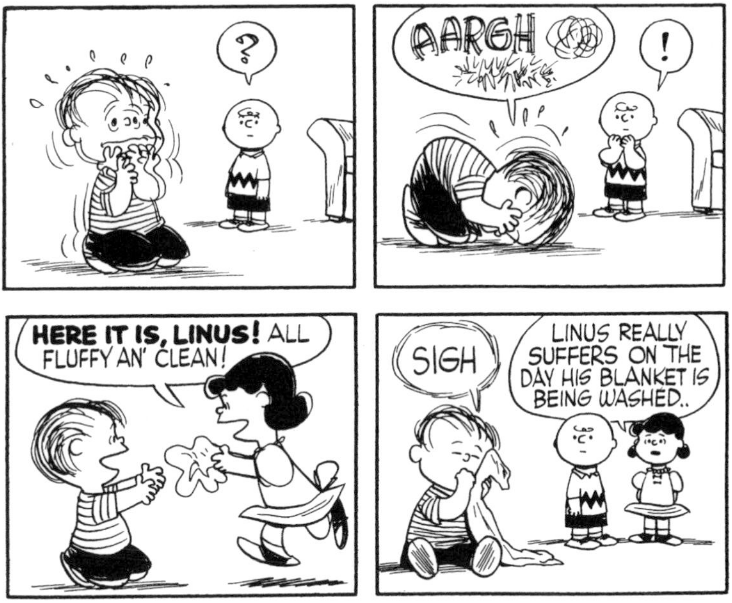
?
AARGH
!
HERE IT IS, LINUS! ALL FLUFFY AN' CLEAN!
SIGH
LINUS REALLY SUFFERS ON THE DAY HIS BLANKET IS BEING WASHED..

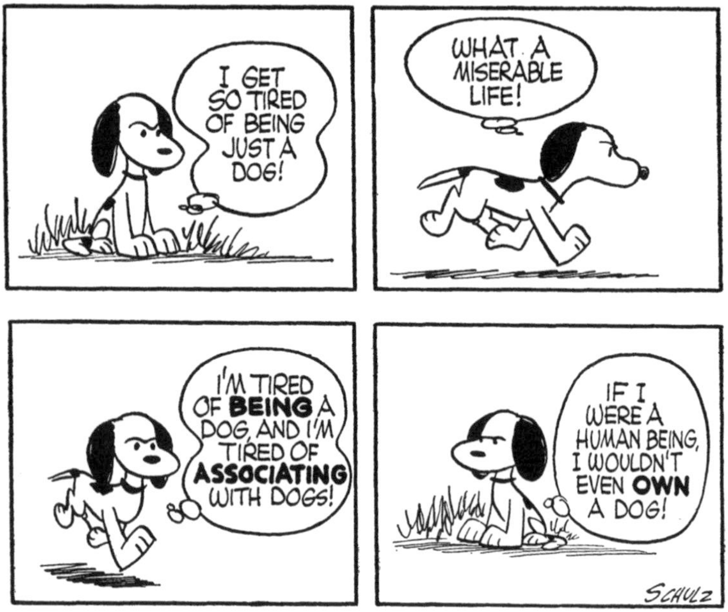
I GET SO TIRED OF BEING JUST A DOG!
WHAT A MISERABLE LIFE!
I'M TIRED OF BEING A DOG, AND I'M TIRED OF ASSOCIATING WITH DOGS!
IF I WERE A HUMAN BEING, I WOULDN'T EVEN OWN A DOG!
SCHULZ

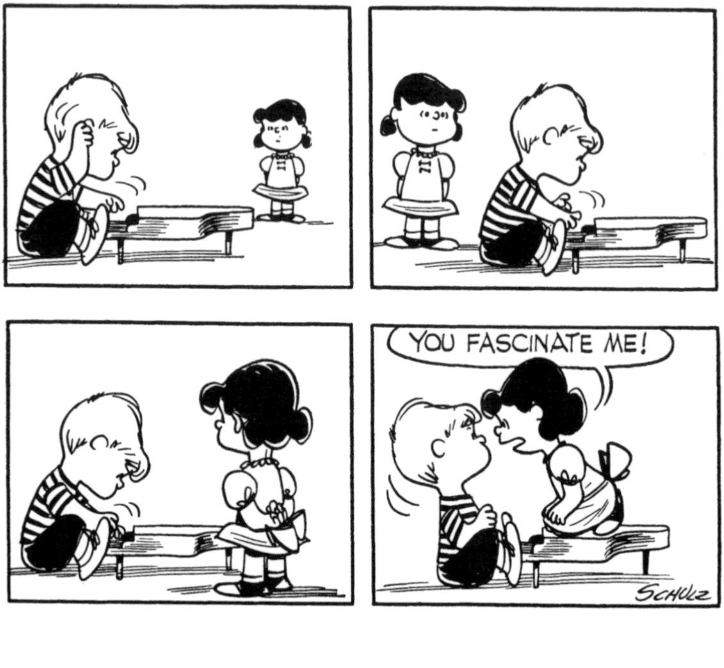
YOU FASCINATE ME!
SCHULZ

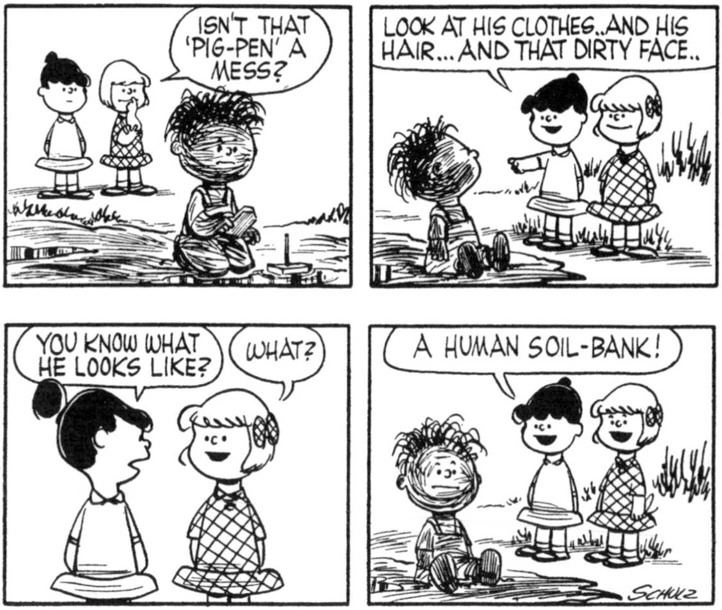
ISN'T THAT 'PIG-PEN' A MESS?
LOOK AT HIS CLOTHES..AND HIS HAIR...AND THAT DIRTY FACE..
YOU KNOW WHAT HE LOOKS LIKE?
WHAT?
A HUMAN SOIL-BANK!
SCHULZ

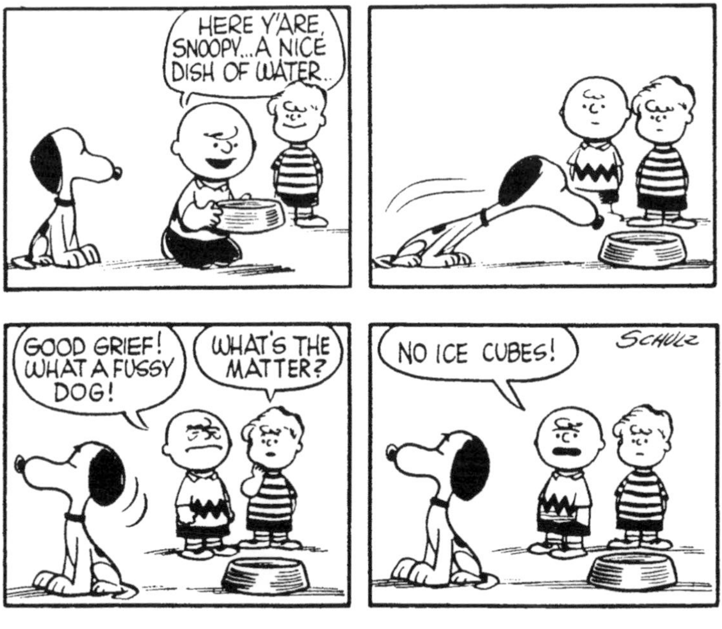
HERE Y'ARE, SNOOPY...A NICE DISH OF WATER..
GOOD GRIEF! WHAT A FUSSY DOG!
WHAT'S THE MATTER?
NO ICE CUBES!
SCHULZ

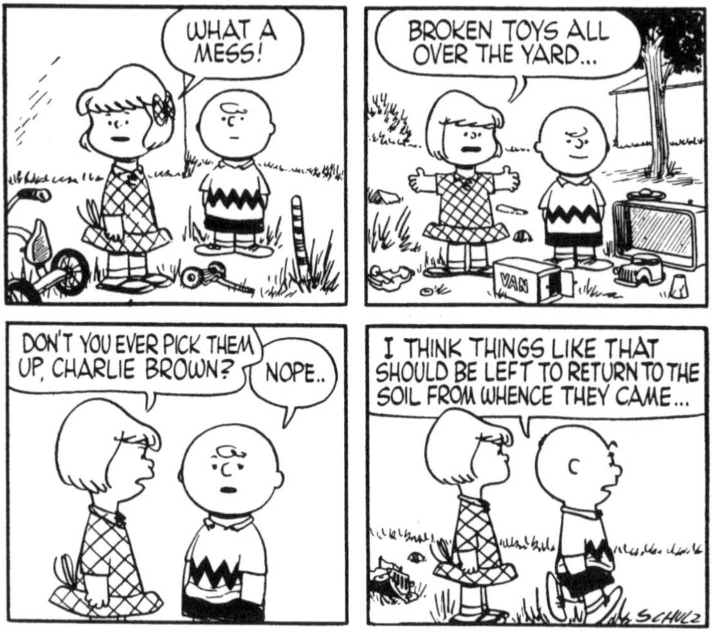
WHAT A MESS!
BROKEN TOYS ALL OVER THE YARD...
VAN
DON'T YOU EVER PICK THEM UP, CHARLIE BROWN?
NOPE..
I THINK THINGS LIKE THAT SHOULD BE LEFT TO RETURN TO THE SOIL FROM WHENCE THEY CAME...
SCHULZ

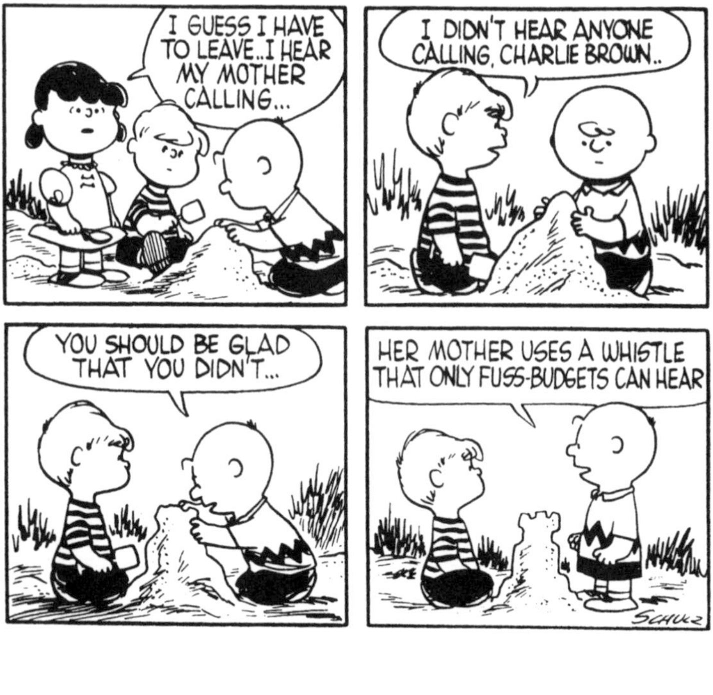
I GUESS I HAVE TO LEAVE..I HEAR MY MOTHER CALLING...
I DIDN'T HEAR ANYONE CALLING, CHARLIE BROWN..
YOU SHOULD BE GLAD THAT YOU DIDN'T...
HER MOTHER USES A WHISTLE THAT ONLY FUSS-BUDGETS CAN HEAR
SCHULZ

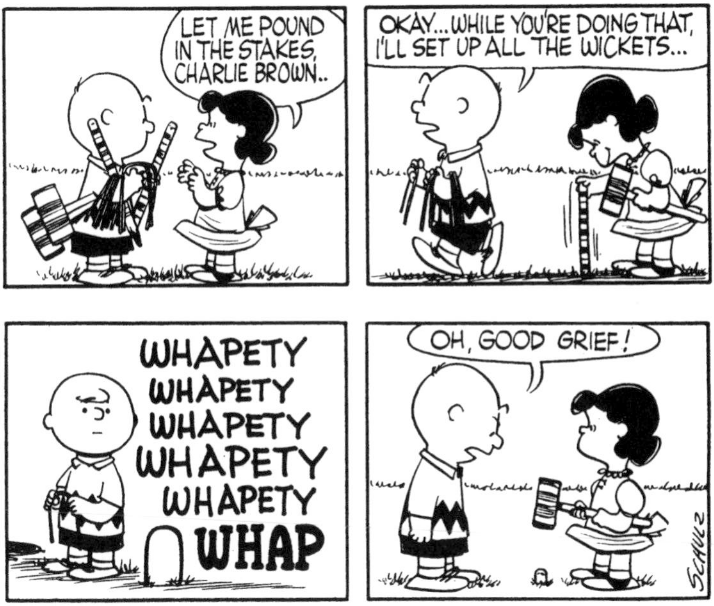
LET ME POUND IN THE STAKES, CHARLIE BROWN..
OKAY...WHILE YOU'RE DOING THAT, I'LL SET UP ALL THE WICKETS...
WHAPETY WHAPETY WHAPETY WHAPETY WHAPETY WHAP
OH, GOOD GRIEF!
SCHULZ

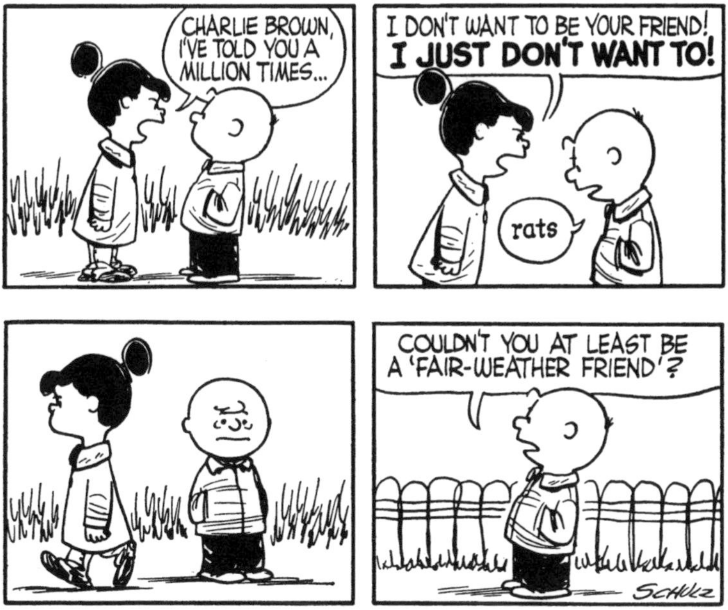
CHARLIE BROWN, I'VE TOLD YOU A MILLION TIMES...
I DON'T WANT TO BE YOUR FRIEND! I JUST DON'T WANT TO!
rats
COULDN'T YOU AT LEAST BE A 'FAIR-WEATHER FRIEND'?
SCHULZ

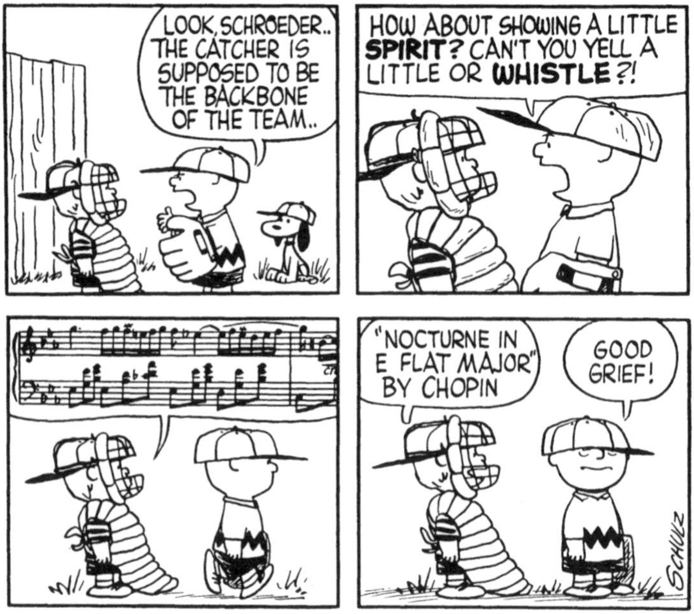
LOOK, SCHROEDER.. THE CATCHER IS SUPPOSED TO BE THE BACKBONE OF THE TEAM..
HOW ABOUT SHOWING A LITTLE **SPIRIT?** CAN'T YOU YELL A LITTLE OR **WHISTLE**?!
"NOCTURNE IN E FLAT MAJOR" BY CHOPIN
GOOD GRIEF!
SCHULZ

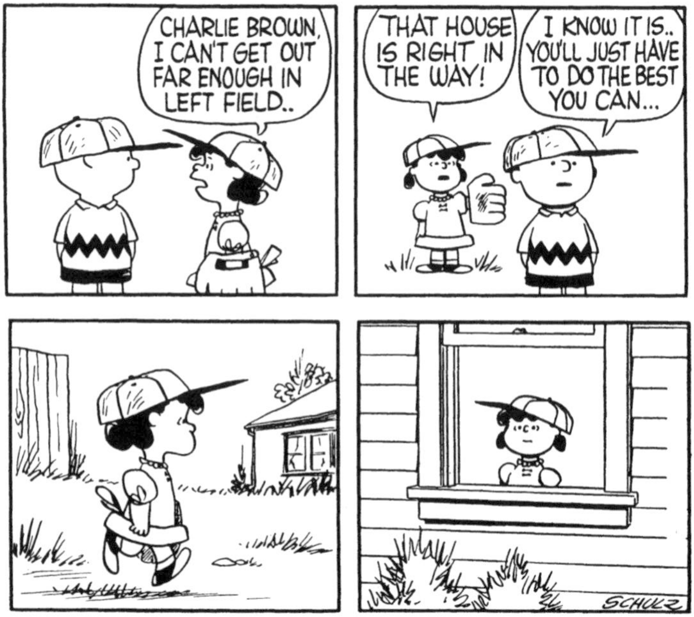
CHARLIE BROWN, I CAN'T GET OUT FAR ENOUGH IN LEFT FIELD..
THAT HOUSE IS RIGHT IN THE WAY!
I KNOW IT IS.. YOU'LL JUST HAVE TO DO THE BEST YOU CAN...
SCHULZ

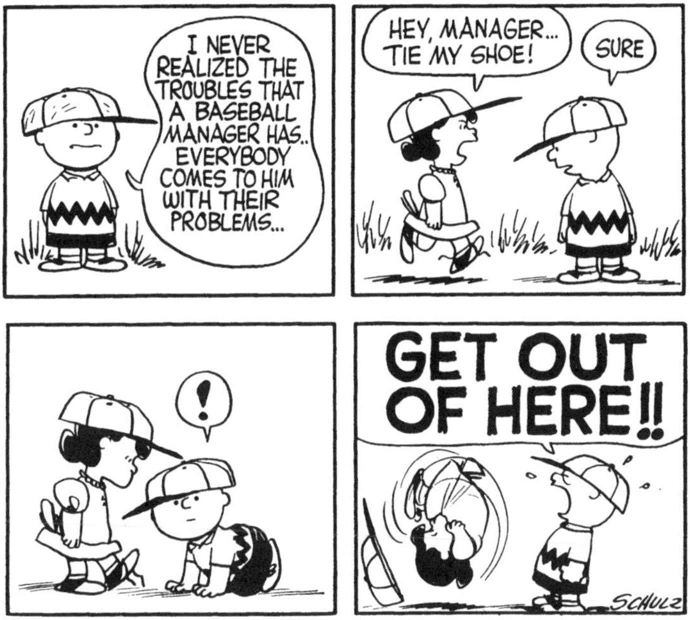
I NEVER REALIZED THE TROUBLES THAT A BASEBALL MANAGER HAS.. EVERYBODY COMES TO HIM WITH THEIR PROBLEMS...
HEY, MANAGER... TIE MY SHOE!
SURE
!
GET OUT OF HERE!!
SCHULZ

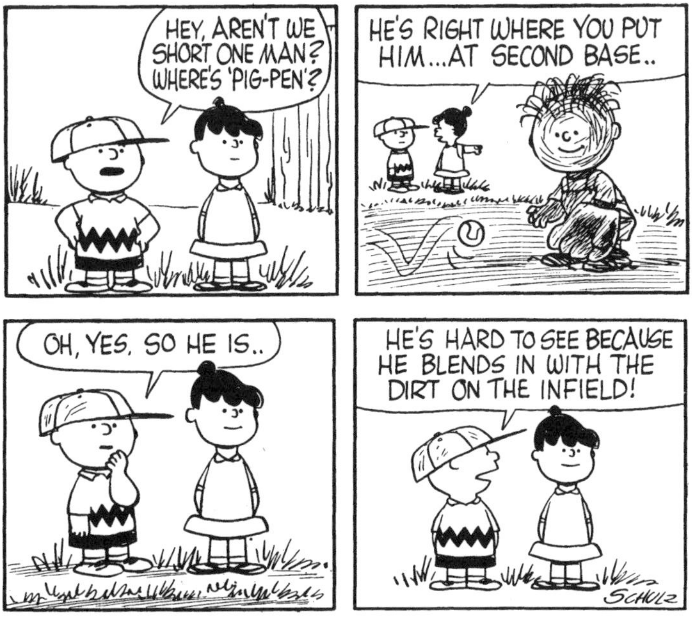
HEY, AREN'T WE SHORT ONE MAN? WHERE'S 'PIG-PEN'?
HE'S RIGHT WHERE YOU PUT HIM...AT SECOND BASE..
OH, YES, SO HE IS..
HE'S HARD TO SEE BECAUSE HE BLENDS IN WITH THE DIRT ON THE INFIELD!
SCHULZ

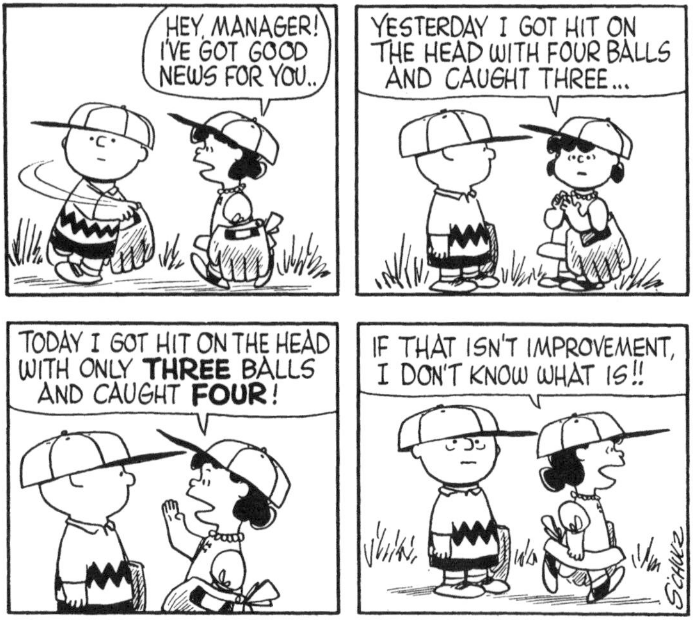
HEY, MANAGER! I'VE GOT GOOD NEWS FOR YOU..
YESTERDAY I GOT HIT ON THE HEAD WITH FOUR BALLS AND CAUGHT THREE...
TODAY I GOT HIT ON THE HEAD WITH ONLY **THREE** BALLS AND CAUGHT **FOUR**!
IF THAT ISN'T IMPROVEMENT, I DON'T KNOW WHAT IS!!
SCHULZ

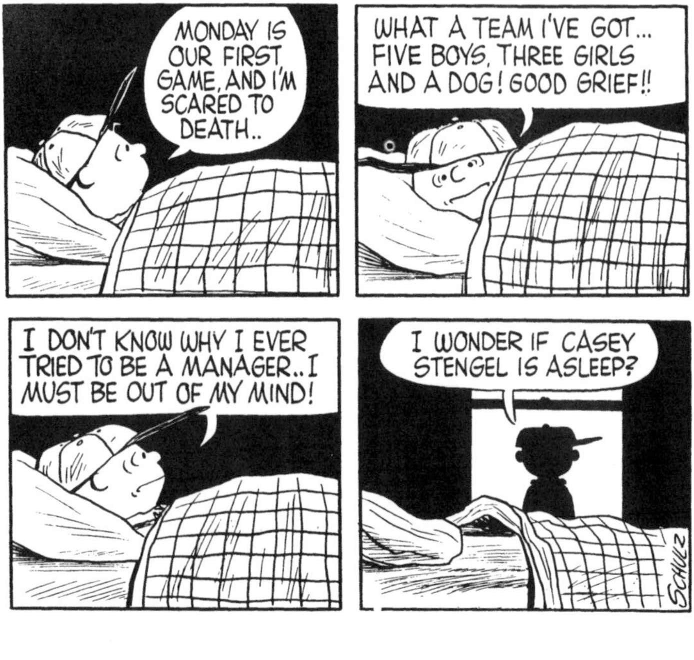
MONDAY IS OUR FIRST GAME, AND I'M SCARED TO DEATH..
WHAT A TEAM I'VE GOT... FIVE BOYS, THREE GIRLS AND A DOG! GOOD GRIEF!!
I DON'T KNOW WHY I EVER TRIED TO BE A MANAGER.. I MUST BE OUT OF MY MIND!
I WONDER IF CASEY STENGEL IS ASLEEP?
SCHULZ

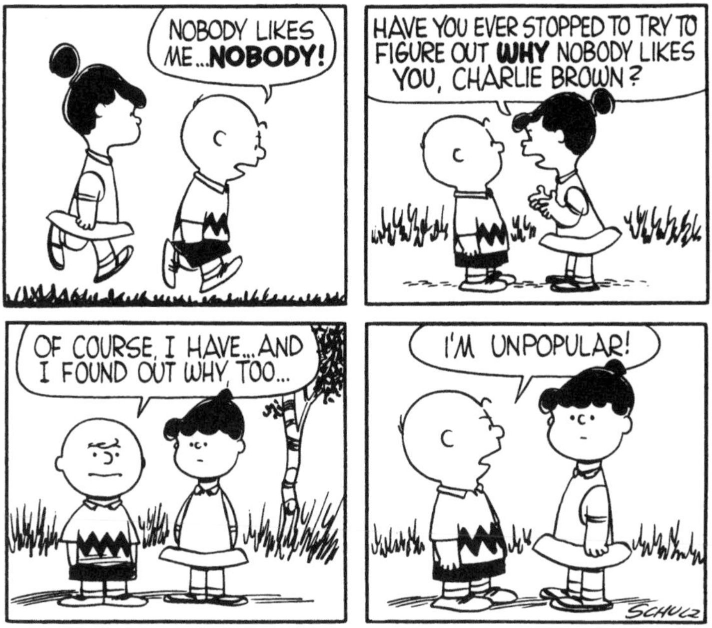
NOBODY LIKES ME...**NOBODY!**
HAVE YOU EVER STOPPED TO TRY TO FIGURE OUT **WHY** NOBODY LIKES YOU, CHARLIE BROWN?
OF COURSE, I HAVE...AND I FOUND OUT WHY, TOO...
I'M UNPOPULAR!
SCHULZ

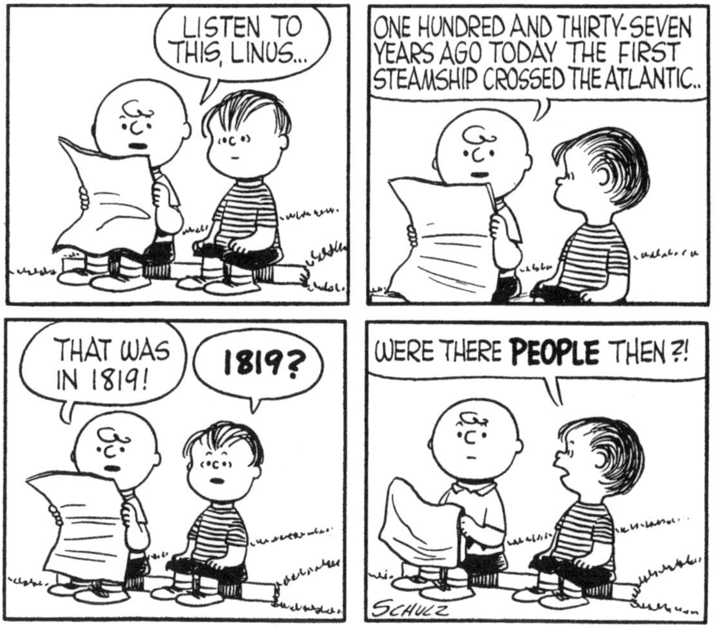
LISTEN TO THIS, LINUS...
ONE HUNDRED AND THIRTY-SEVEN YEARS AGO TODAY THE FIRST STEAMSHIP CROSSED THE ATLANTIC..
THAT WAS IN 1819!
1819?
WERE THERE **PEOPLE** THEN?!
SCHULZ

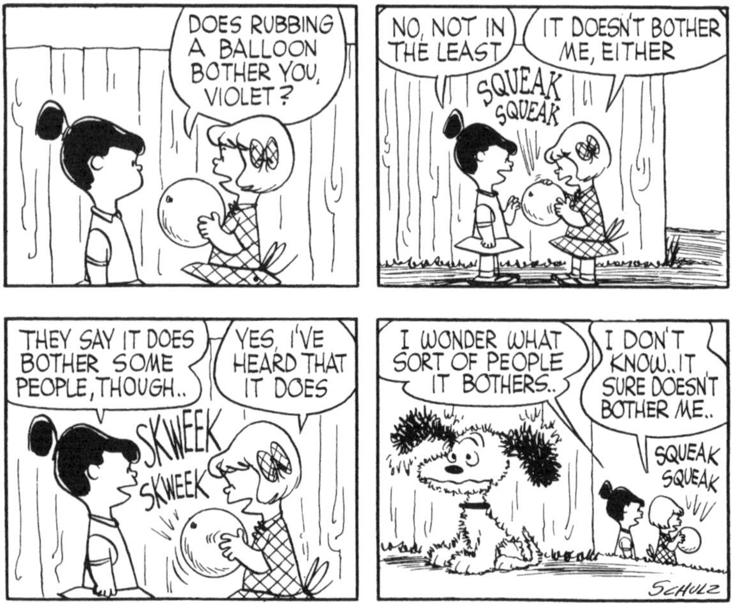
DOES RUBBING A BALLOON BOTHER YOU, VIOLET?
NO, NOT IN THE LEAST
IT DOESN'T BOTHER ME, EITHER
SQUEAK SQUEAK
THEY SAY IT DOES BOTHER SOME PEOPLE, THOUGH..
YES, I'VE HEARD THAT IT DOES
SKWEEK SKWEEK
I WONDER WHAT SORT OF PEOPLE IT BOTHERS..
I DON'T KNOW..IT SURE DOESN'T BOTHER ME..
SQUEAK SQUEAK
SCHULZ

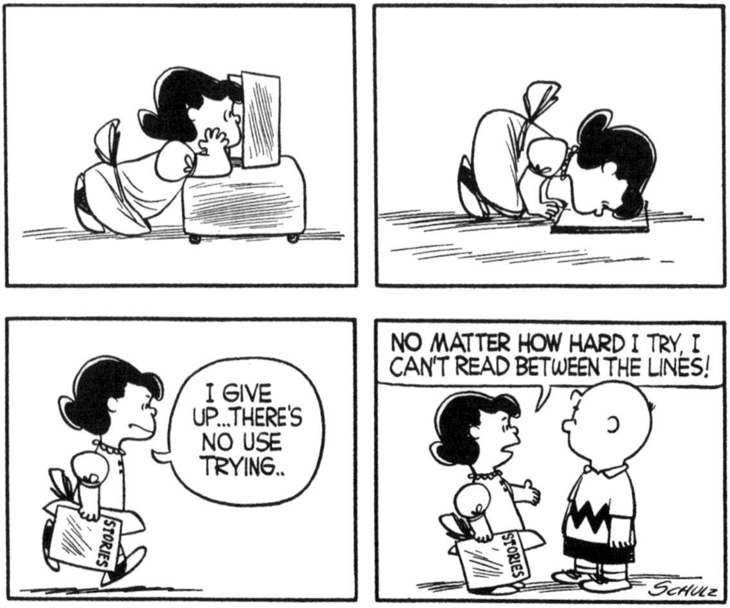
I GIVE UP...THERE'S NO USE TRYING..
STORIES
NO MATTER HOW HARD I TRY, I CAN'T READ BETWEEN THE LINES!
STORIES
SCHULZ

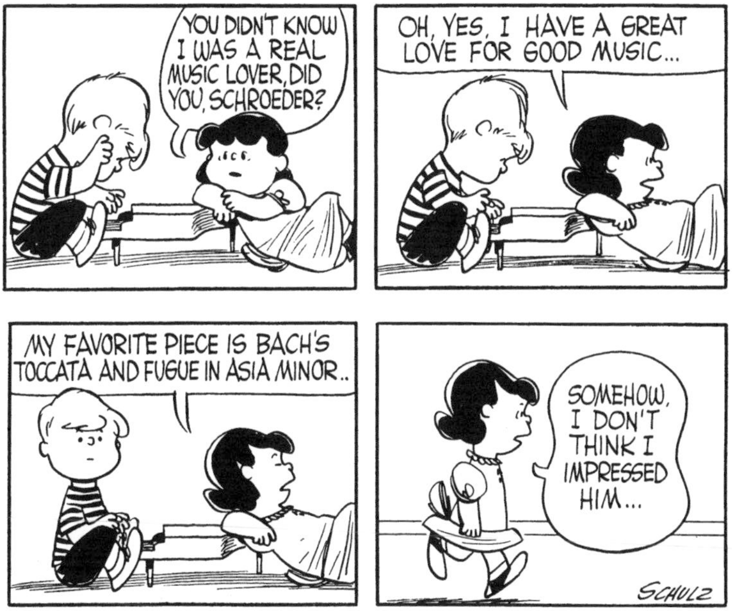
YOU DIDN'T KNOW I WAS A REAL MUSIC LOVER, DID YOU, SCHROEDER?
OH, YES, I HAVE A GREAT LOVE FOR GOOD MUSIC...
MY FAVORITE PIECE IS BACH'S TOCCATA AND FUGUE IN ASIA MINOR..
SOMEHOW, I DON'T THINK I IMPRESSED HIM...
SCHULZ

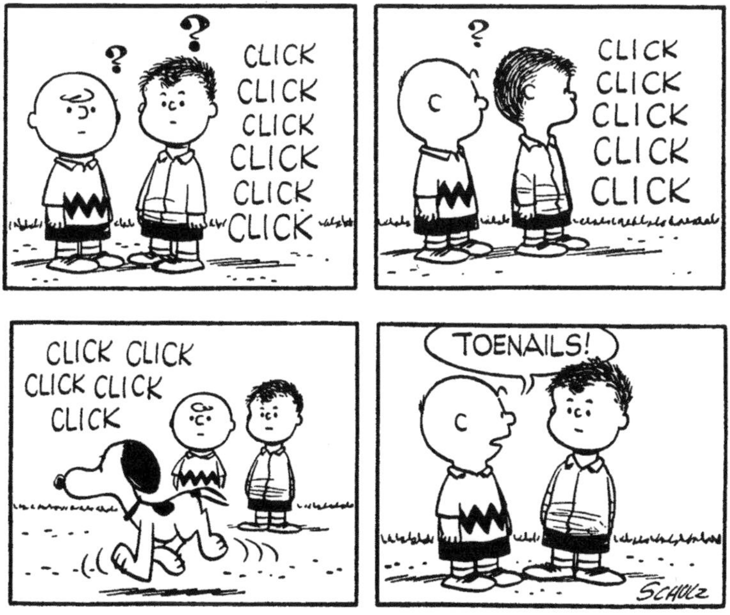
CLICK CLICK CLICK CLICK CLICK CLICK
CLICK CLICK CLICK CLICK CLICK
CLICK CLICK CLICK CLICK CLICK
TOENAILS!
SCHULZ

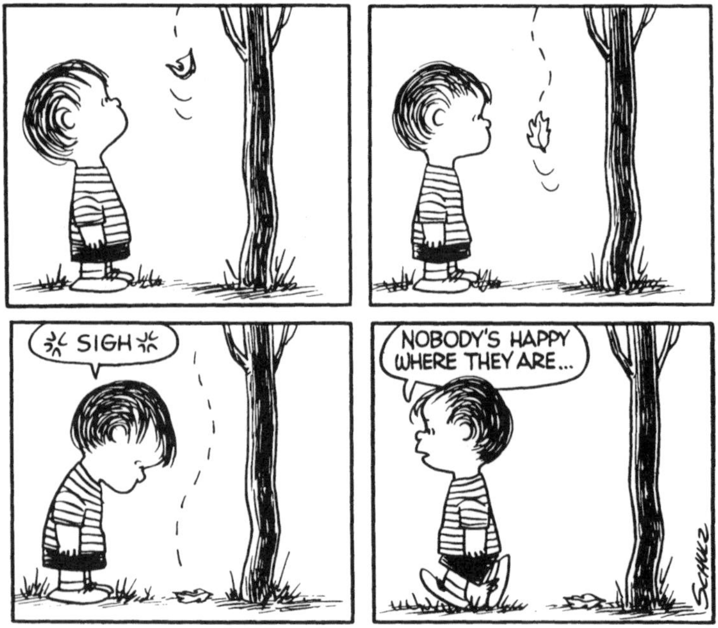
SIGH
NOBODY'S HAPPY WHERE THEY ARE...
SCHULZ

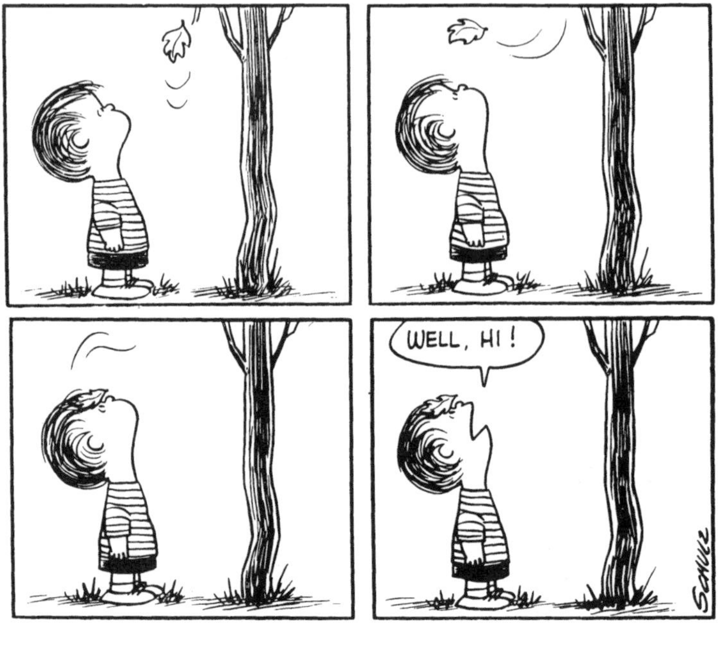
WELL, HI!
SCHULZ

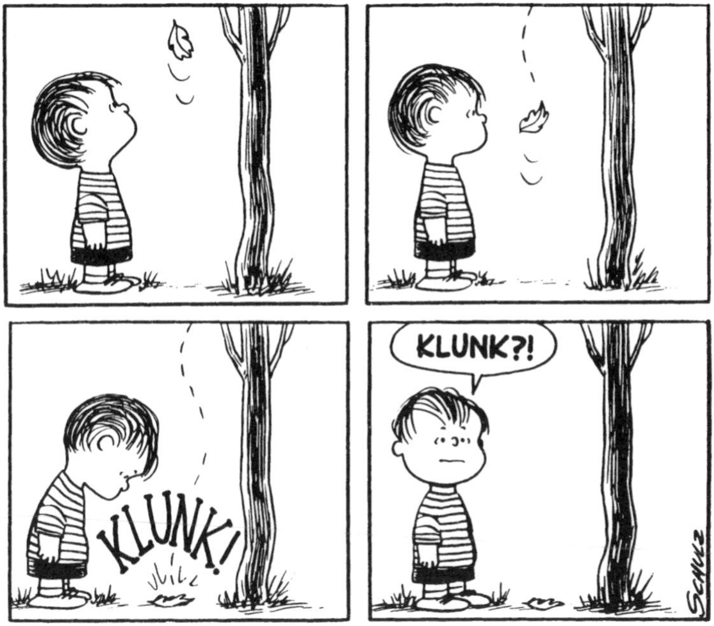
KLUNK!
KLUNK?!
SCHULZ

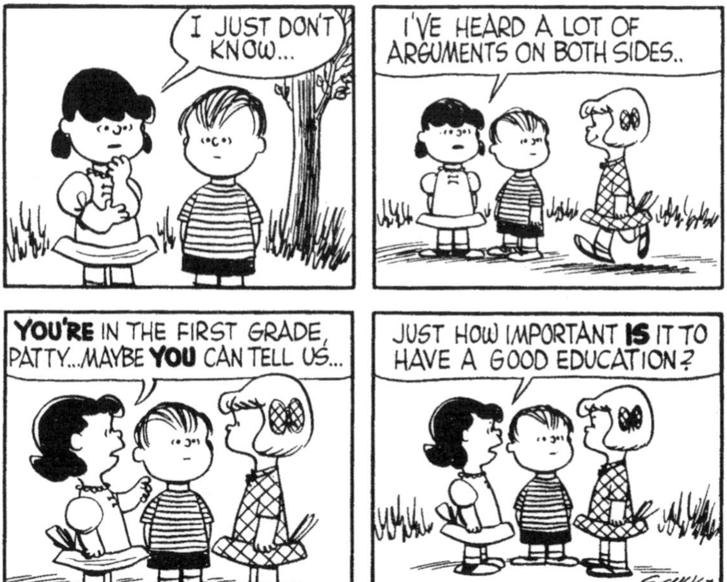
I JUST DON'T KNOW...
I'VE HEARD A LOT OF ARGUMENTS ON BOTH SIDES..
YOU'RE IN THE FIRST GRADE, PATTY...MAYBE YOU CAN TELL US...
JUST HOW IMPORTANT IS IT TO HAVE A GOOD EDUCATION?
SCHULZ

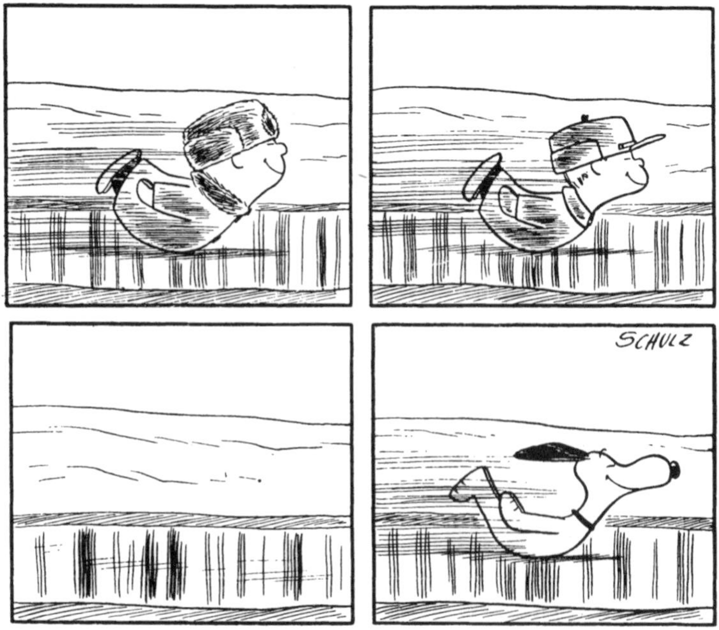
SCHULZ

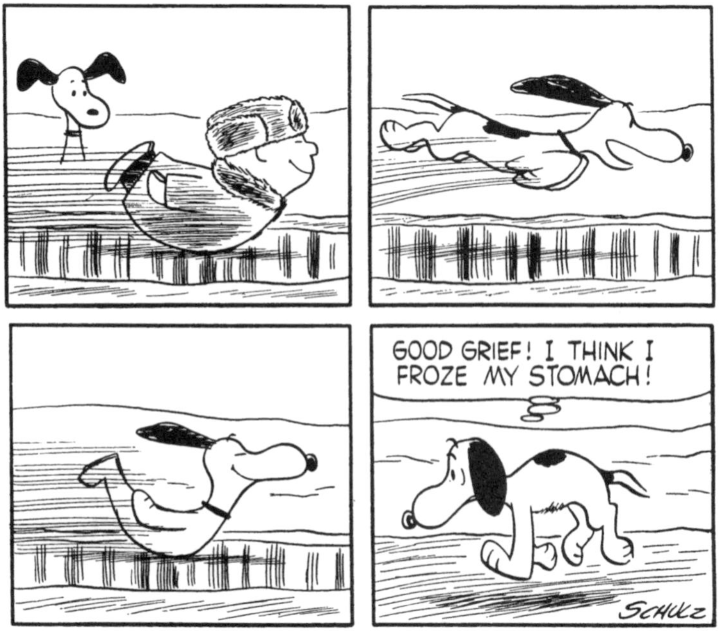
GOOD GRIEF! I THINK I FROZE MY STOMACH!
SCHULZ

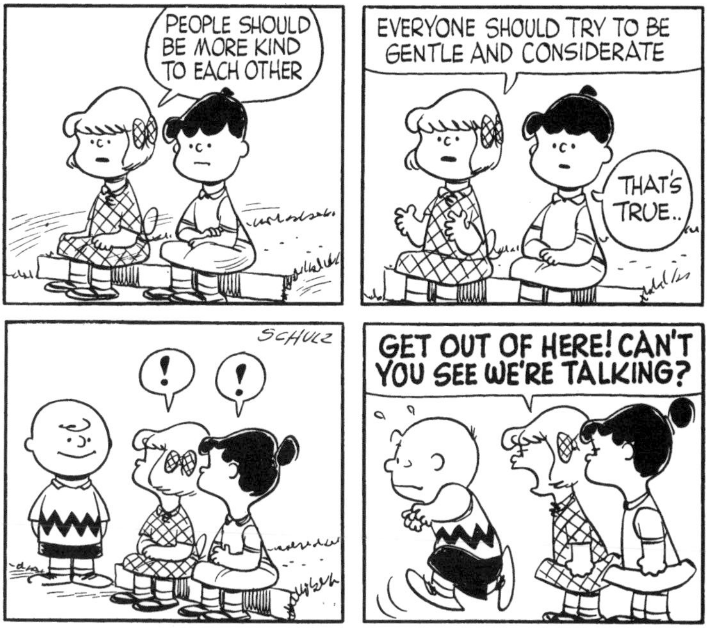
PEOPLE SHOULD BE MORE KIND TO EACH OTHER
EVERYONE SHOULD TRY TO BE GENTLE AND CONSIDERATE
THAT'S TRUE..
SCHULZ
!
!
GET OUT OF HERE! CAN'T YOU SEE WE'RE TALKING?

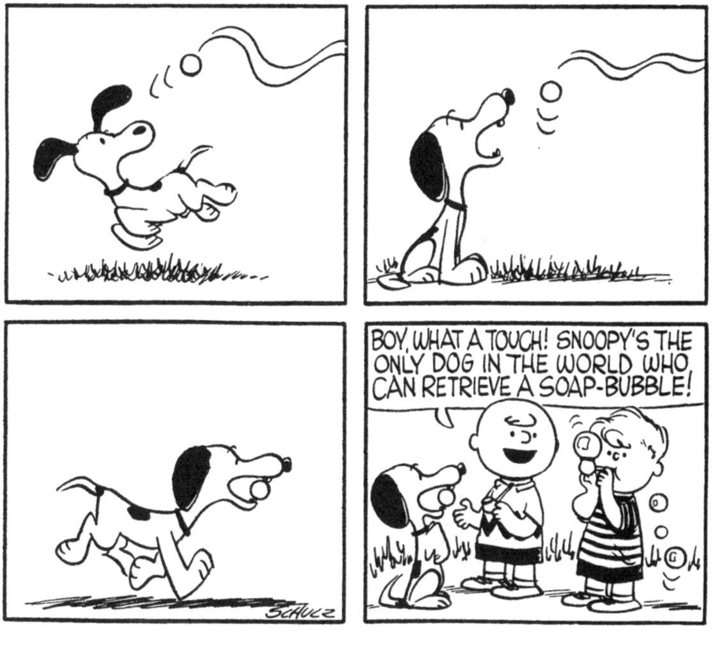
SCHULZ
BOY, WHAT A TOUCH! SNOOPY'S THE ONLY DOG IN THE WORLD WHO CAN RETRIEVE A SOAP-BUBBLE!

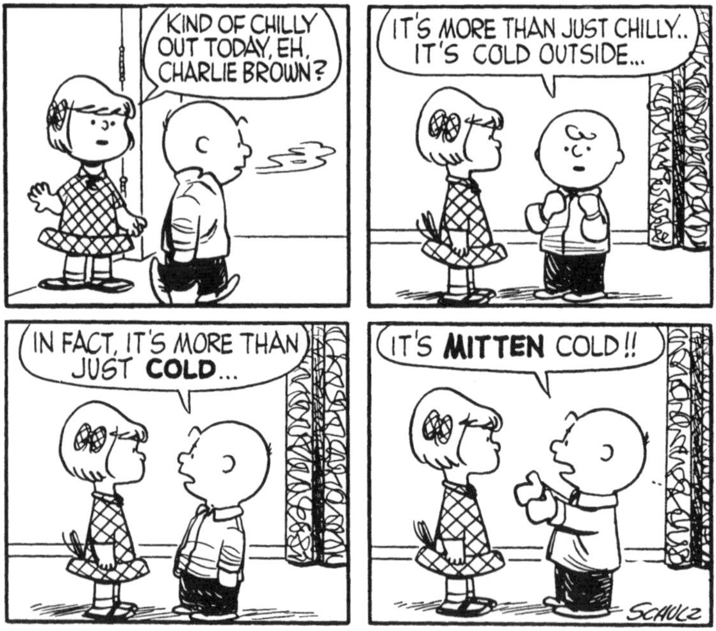
KIND OF CHILLY OUT TODAY, EH, CHARLIE BROWN?
IT'S MORE THAN JUST CHILLY.. IT'S COLD OUTSIDE...
IN FACT, IT'S MORE THAN JUST **COLD**...
IT'S **MITTEN** COLD!!
SCHULZ

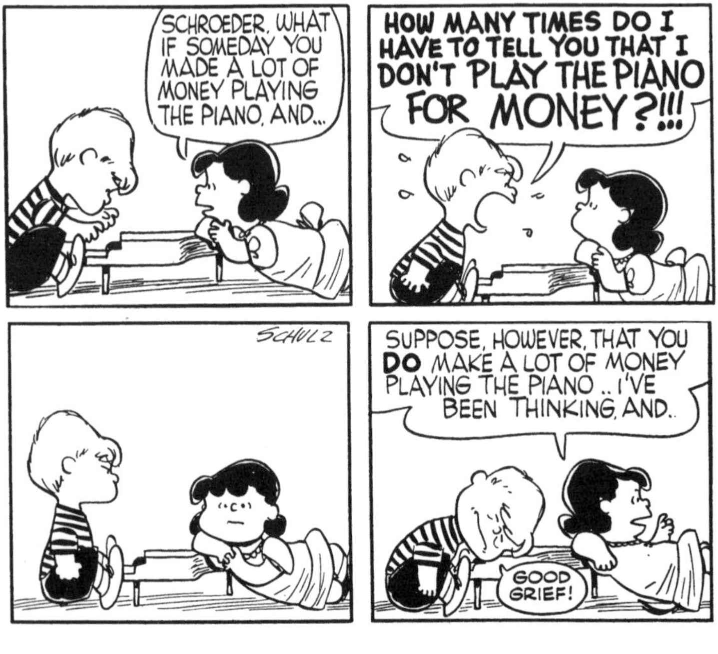
SCHROEDER, WHAT IF SOMEDAY YOU MADE A LOT OF MONEY PLAYING THE PIANO, AND...
HOW MANY TIMES DO I HAVE TO TELL YOU THAT I DON'T PLAY THE PIANO FOR MONEY?!!!
SCHULZ
SUPPOSE, HOWEVER, THAT YOU **DO** MAKE A LOT OF MONEY PLAYING THE PIANO .. I'VE BEEN THINKING, AND..
GOOD GRIEF!

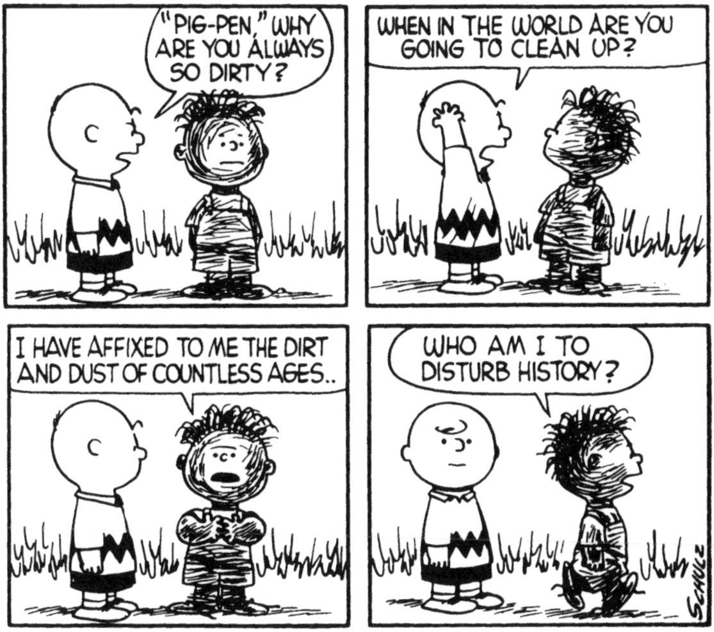
"PIG-PEN," WHY ARE YOU ALWAYS SO DIRTY?
WHEN IN THE WORLD ARE YOU GOING TO CLEAN UP?
I HAVE AFFIXED TO ME THE DIRT AND DUST OF COUNTLESS AGES..
WHO AM I TO DISTURB HISTORY?
SCHULZ

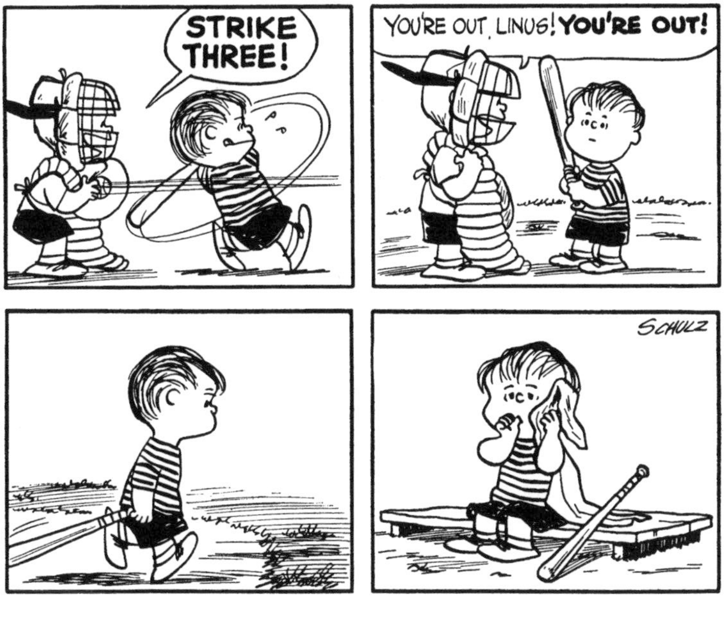
STRIKE THREE!
YOU'RE OUT, LINUS! **YOU'RE OUT!**
SCHULZ

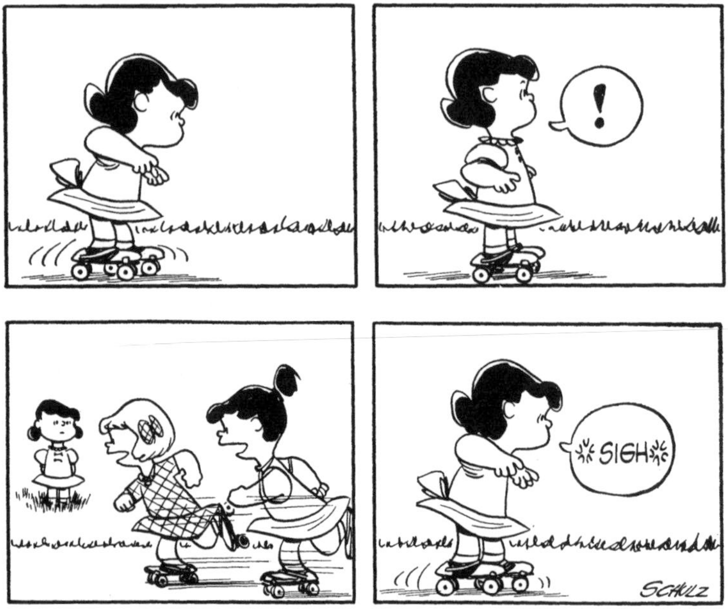
!
SIGH
SCHULZ

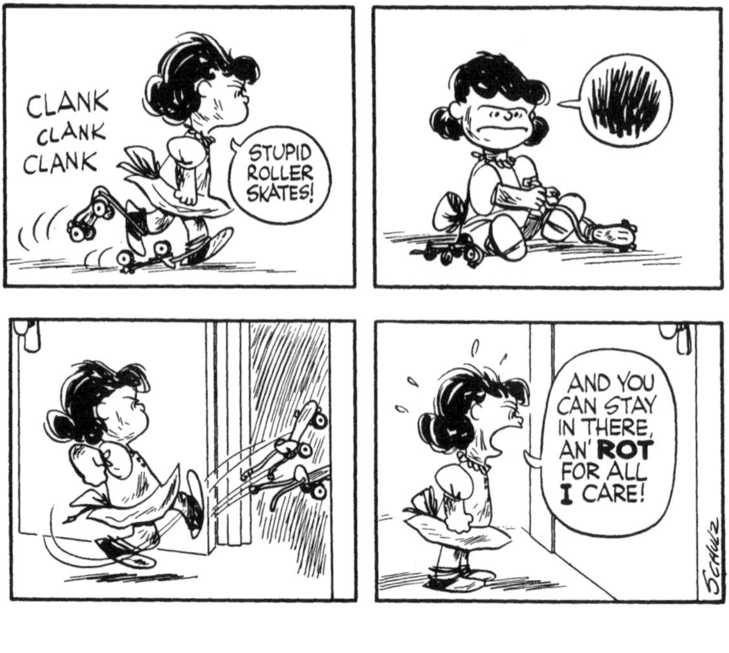
CLANK
CLANK
CLANK
STUPID ROLLER SKATES!
AND YOU CAN STAY IN THERE, AN' **ROT** FOR ALL **I** CARE!
SCHULZ

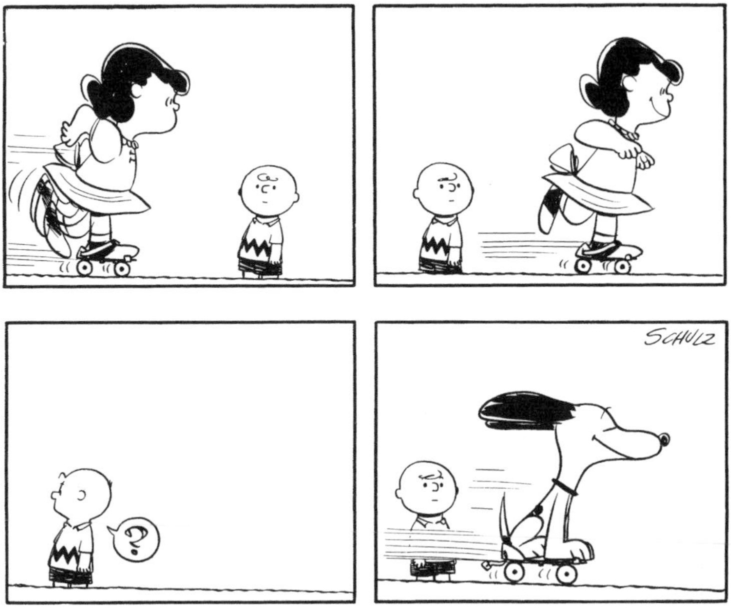
SCHULZ
?

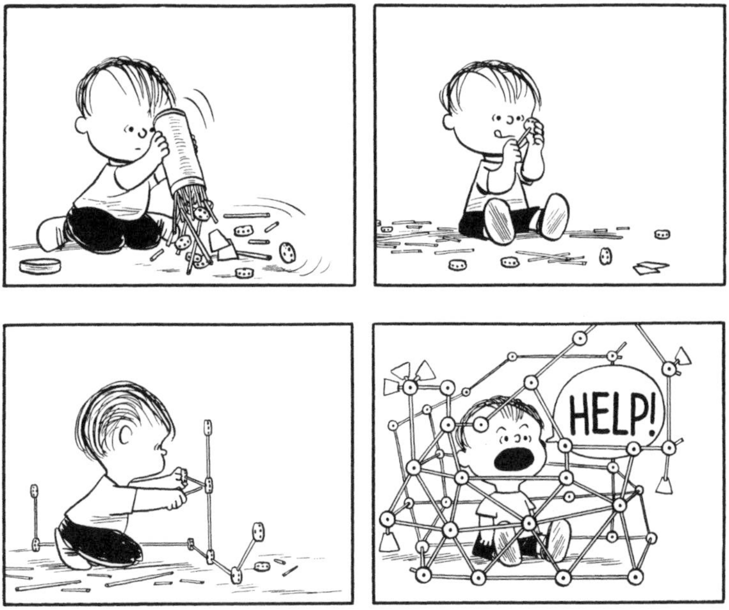
HELP!

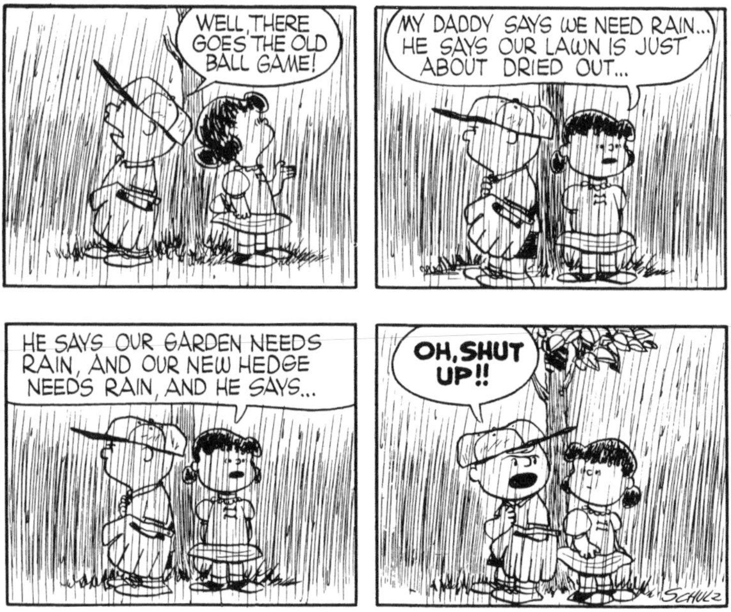
WELL, THERE GOES THE OLD BALL GAME!
MY DADDY SAYS WE NEED RAIN... HE SAYS OUR LAWN IS JUST ABOUT DRIED OUT...
HE SAYS OUR GARDEN NEEDS RAIN, AND OUR NEW HEDGE NEEDS RAIN, AND HE SAYS...
OH, SHUT UP!!
SCHULZ

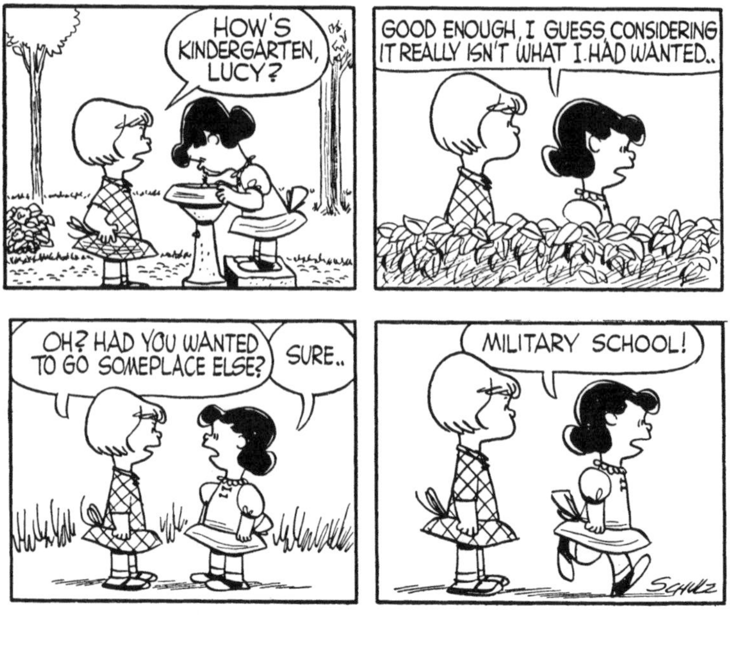
HOW'S KINDERGARTEN, LUCY?
GOOD ENOUGH, I GUESS, CONSIDERING IT REALLY ISN'T WHAT I HAD WANTED..
OH? HAD YOU WANTED TO GO SOMEPLACE ELSE?
SURE..
MILITARY SCHOOL!
SCHULZ

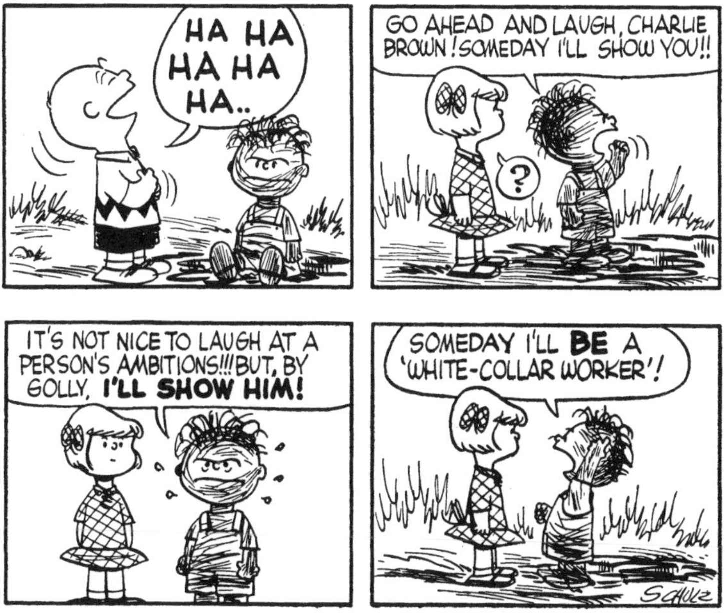
HA HA HA HA HA..
GO AHEAD AND LAUGH, CHARLIE BROWN! SOMEDAY I'LL SHOW YOU!!
?
IT'S NOT NICE TO LAUGH AT A PERSON'S AMBITIONS!!! BUT, BY GOLLY, I'LL SHOW HIM!
SOMEDAY I'LL BE A 'WHITE-COLLAR WORKER'!
SCHULZ

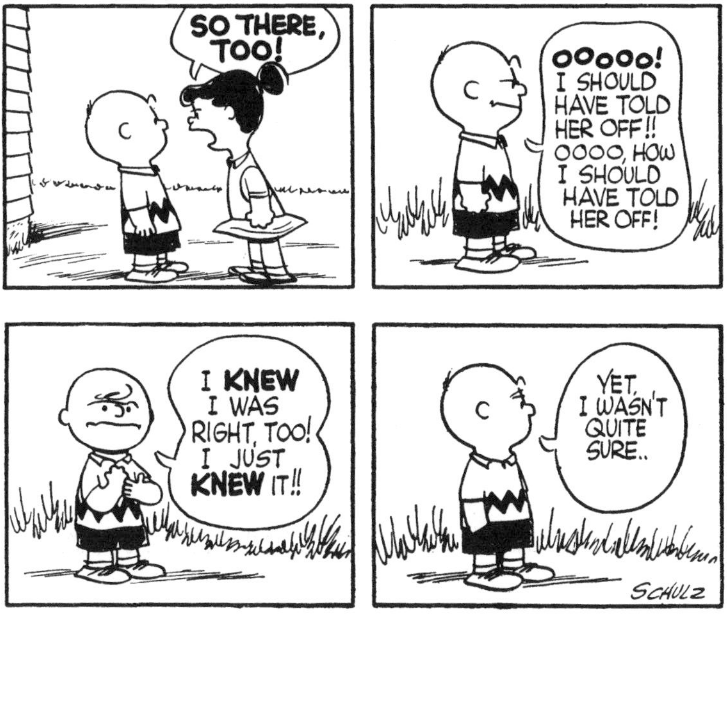
SO THERE, TOO!
OOOOO! I SHOULD HAVE TOLD HER OFF!! OOOO, HOW I SHOULD HAVE TOLD HER OFF!
I KNEW I WAS RIGHT, TOO! I JUST KNEW IT!!
YET, I WASN'T QUITE SURE..
SCHULZ

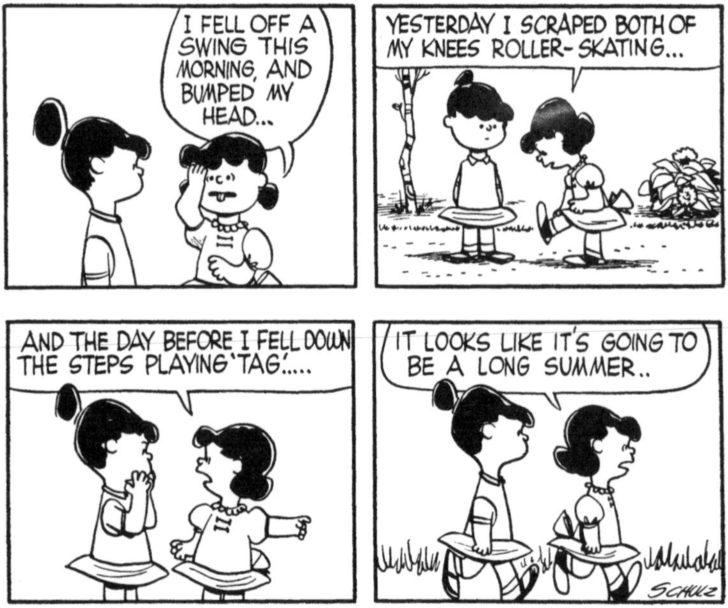
I FELL OFF A SWING THIS MORNING, AND BUMPED MY HEAD...
YESTERDAY I SCRAPED BOTH OF MY KNEES ROLLER-SKATING...
AND THE DAY BEFORE I FELL DOWN THE STEPS PLAYING 'TAG'.....
IT LOOKS LIKE IT'S GOING TO BE A LONG SUMMER..
SCHULZ

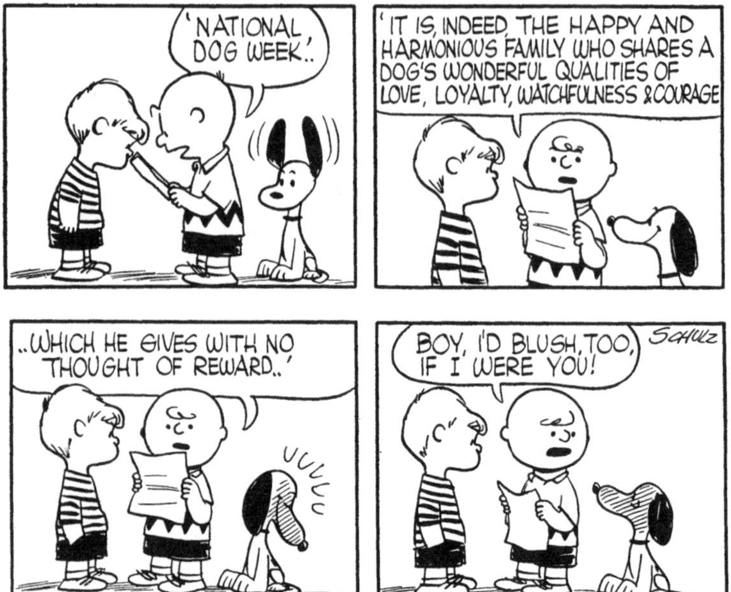
'NATIONAL DOG WEEK'..
'IT IS, INDEED, THE HAPPY AND HARMONIOUS FAMILY WHO SHARES A DOG'S WONDERFUL QUALITIES OF LOVE, LOYALTY, WATCHFULNESS & COURAGE
..WHICH HE GIVES WITH NO THOUGHT OF REWARD..'
UUUUU
BOY, I'D BLUSH, TOO, IF I WERE YOU!
SCHULZ

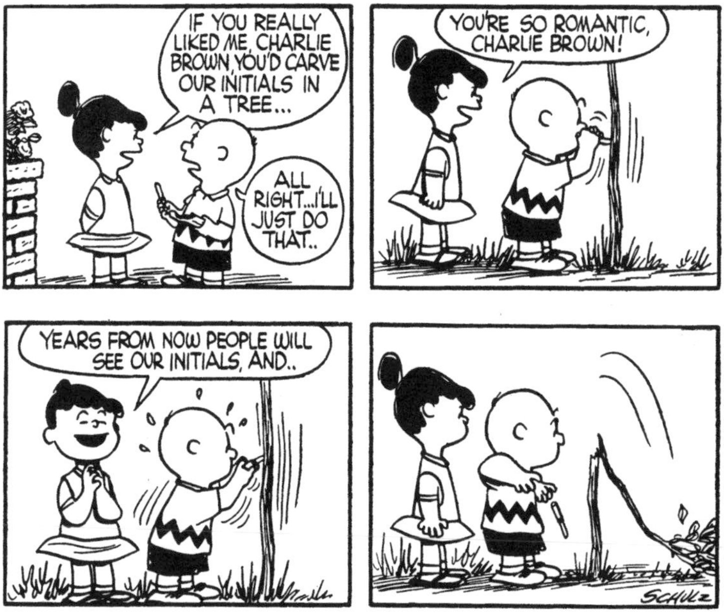
IF YOU REALLY LIKED ME, CHARLIE BROWN, YOU'D CARVE OUR INITIALS IN A TREE...
ALL RIGHT...I'LL JUST DO THAT..
YOU'RE SO ROMANTIC, CHARLIE BROWN!
YEARS FROM NOW PEOPLE WILL SEE OUR INITIALS, AND..
SCHULZ

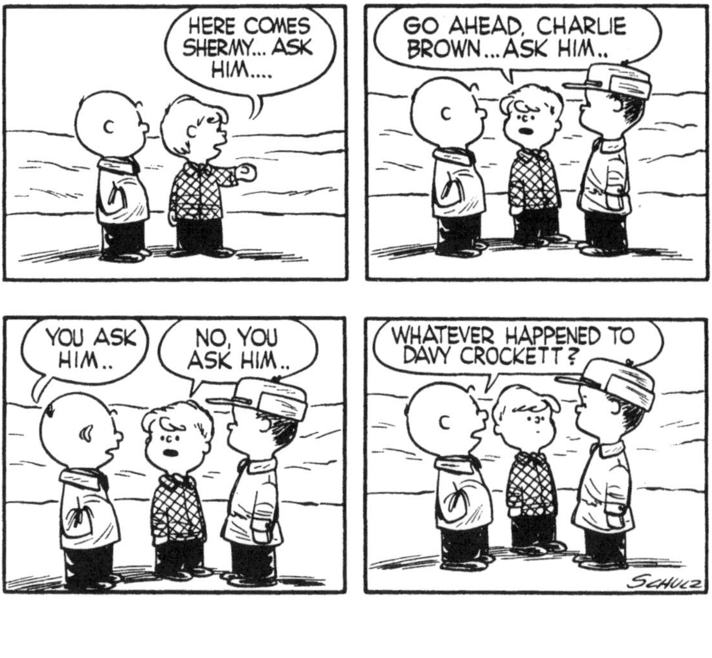
HERE COMES SHERMY... ASK HIM....
GO AHEAD, CHARLIE BROWN... ASK HIM..
YOU ASK HIM..
NO, YOU ASK HIM..
WHATEVER HAPPENED TO DAVY CROCKETT?
SCHULZ

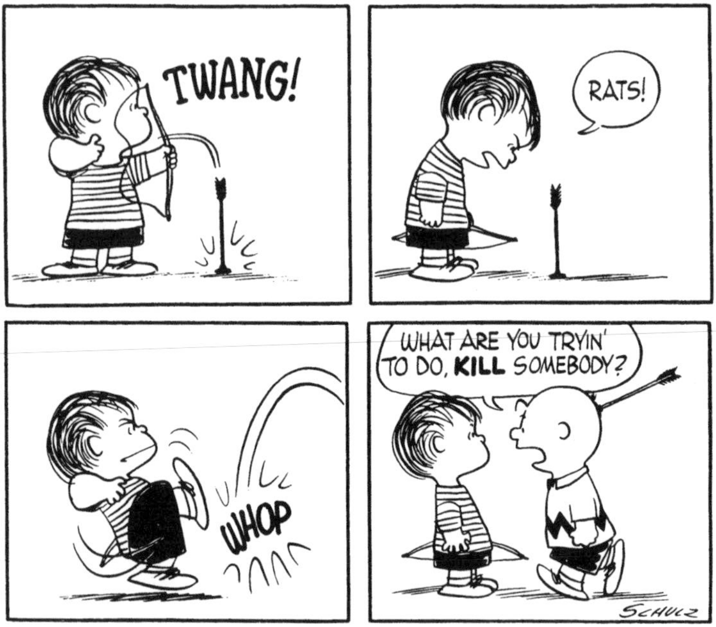
TWANG!
RATS!
WHOP
WHAT ARE YOU TRYIN' TO DO, **KILL** SOMEBODY?
SCHULZ

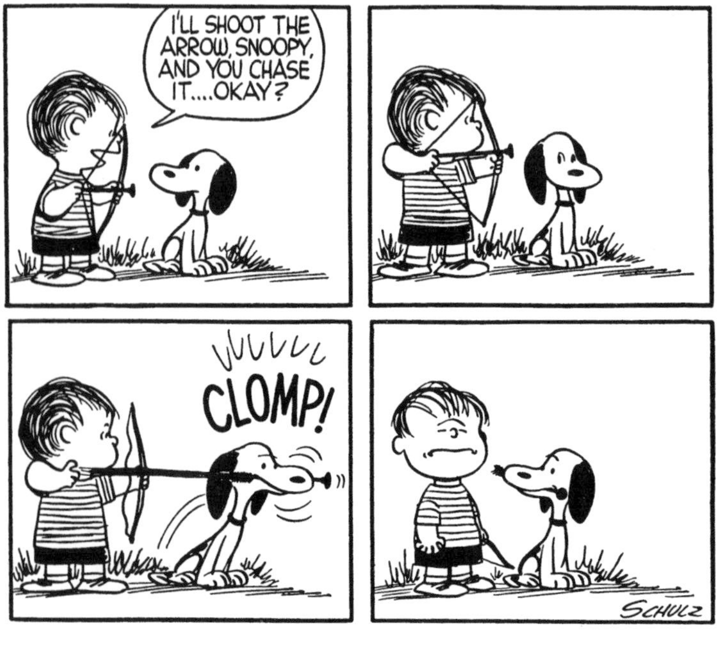
I'LL SHOOT THE ARROW, SNOOPY, AND YOU CHASE IT....OKAY?
CLOMP!
SCHULZ

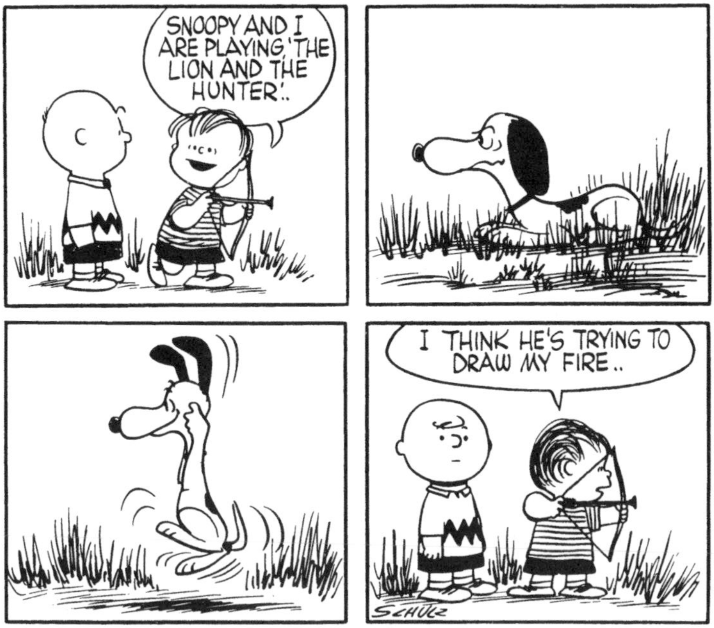
SNOOPY AND I ARE PLAYING 'THE LION AND THE HUNTER'..
I THINK HE'S TRYING TO DRAW MY FIRE..
SCHULZ

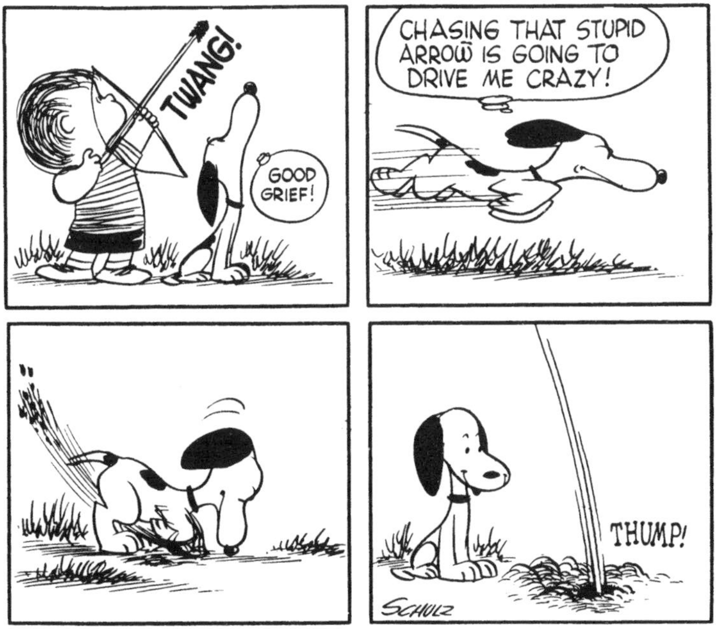
TWANG!
GOOD GRIEF!
CHASING THAT STUPID ARROW IS GOING TO DRIVE ME CRAZY!
THUMP!
SCHULZ

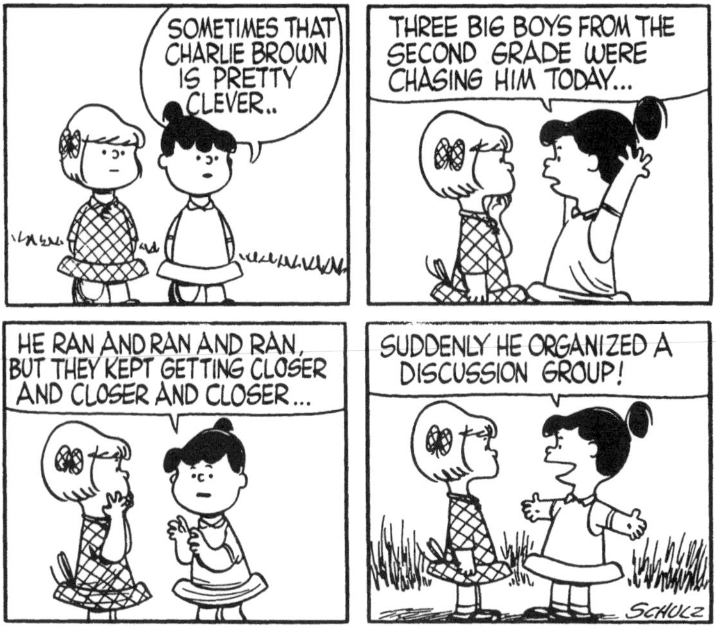
SOMETIMES THAT CHARLIE BROWN IS PRETTY CLEVER..
THREE BIG BOYS FROM THE SECOND GRADE WERE CHASING HIM TODAY...
HE RAN AND RAN AND RAN, BUT THEY KEPT GETTING CLOSER AND CLOSER AND CLOSER...
SUDDENLY HE ORGANIZED A DISCUSSION GROUP!
SCHULZ

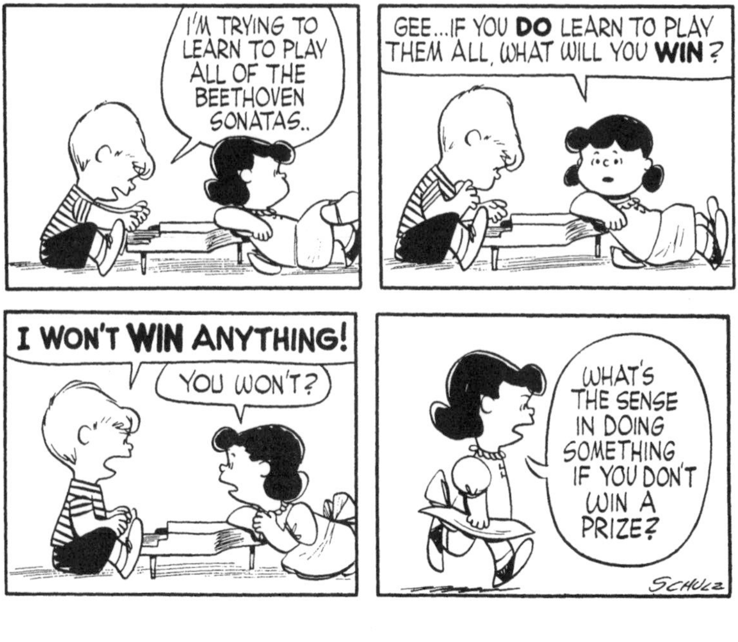
I'M TRYING TO LEARN TO PLAY ALL OF THE BEETHOVEN SONATAS..
GEE...IF YOU **DO** LEARN TO PLAY THEM ALL, WHAT WILL YOU **WIN**?
I WON'T **WIN** ANYTHING!
YOU WON'T?
WHAT'S THE SENSE IN DOING SOMETHING IF YOU DON'T WIN A PRIZE?
SCHULZ

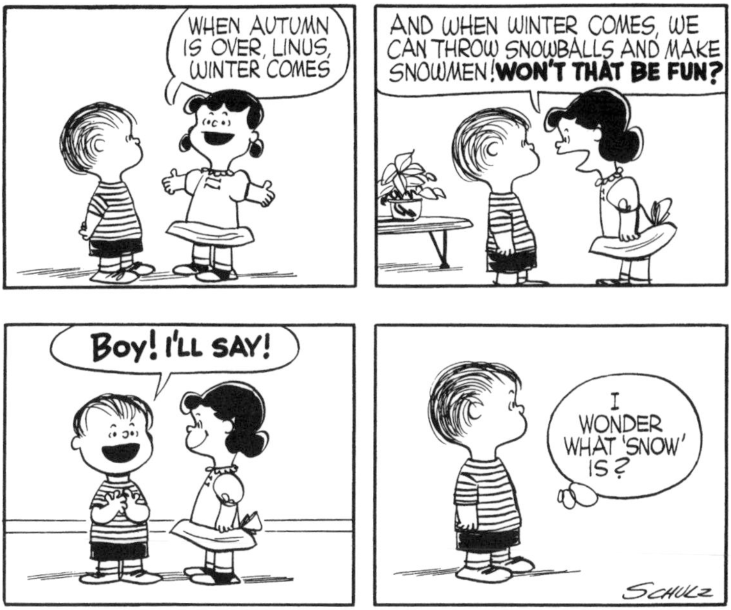

WHEN AUTUMN IS OVER, LINUS, WINTER COMES
AND WHEN WINTER COMES, WE CAN THROW SNOWBALLS AND MAKE SNOWMEN! WON'T THAT BE FUN?
BOY! I'LL SAY!
I WONDER WHAT 'SNOW' IS?
SCHULZ

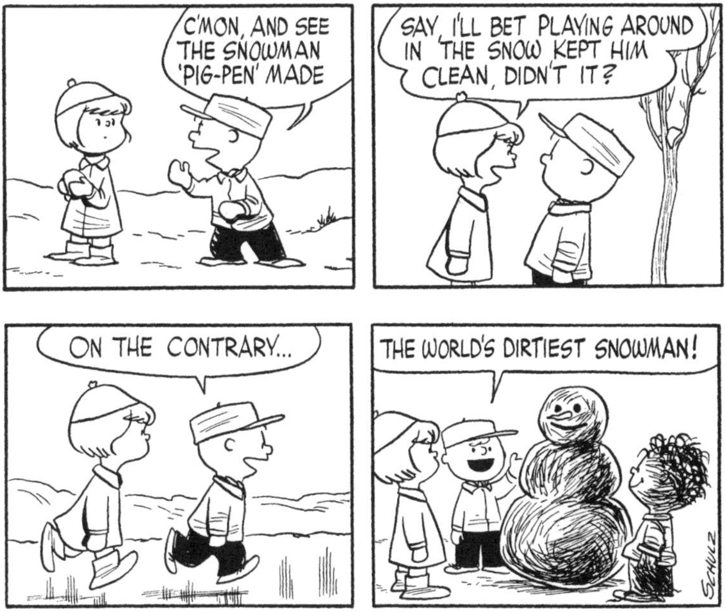

C'MON, AND SEE THE SNOWMAN 'PIG-PEN' MADE
SAY, I'LL BET PLAYING AROUND IN THE SNOW KEPT HIM CLEAN, DIDN'T IT?
ON THE CONTRARY...
THE WORLD'S DIRTIEST SNOWMAN!
SCHULZ

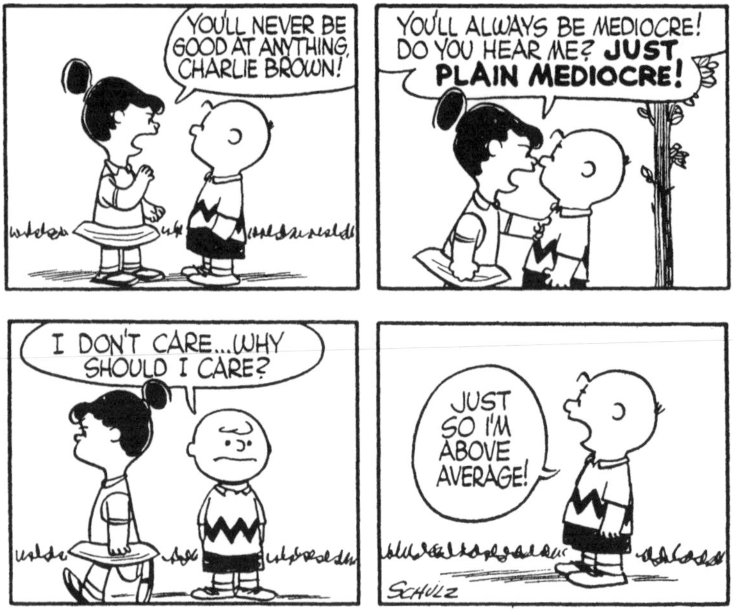
YOU'LL NEVER BE GOOD AT ANYTHING, CHARLIE BROWN!
YOU'LL ALWAYS BE MEDIOCRE! DO YOU HEAR ME? JUST PLAIN MEDIOCRE!
I DON'T CARE...WHY SHOULD I CARE?
JUST SO I'M ABOVE AVERAGE!
SCHULZ

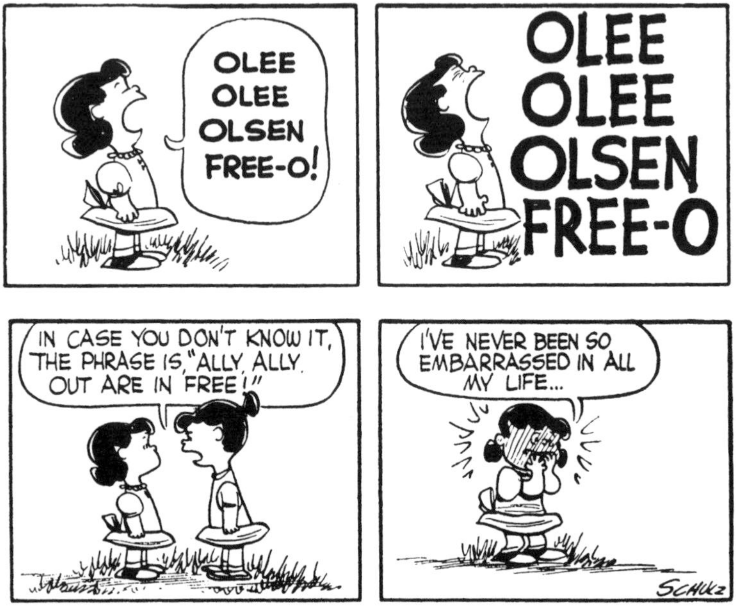
OLEE OLEE OLSEN FREE-O!
OLEE OLEE OLSEN FREE-O
IN CASE YOU DON'T KNOW IT, THE PHRASE IS, "ALLY, ALLY OUT ARE IN FREE!"
I'VE NEVER BEEN SO EMBARRASSED IN ALL MY LIFE...
SCHULZ

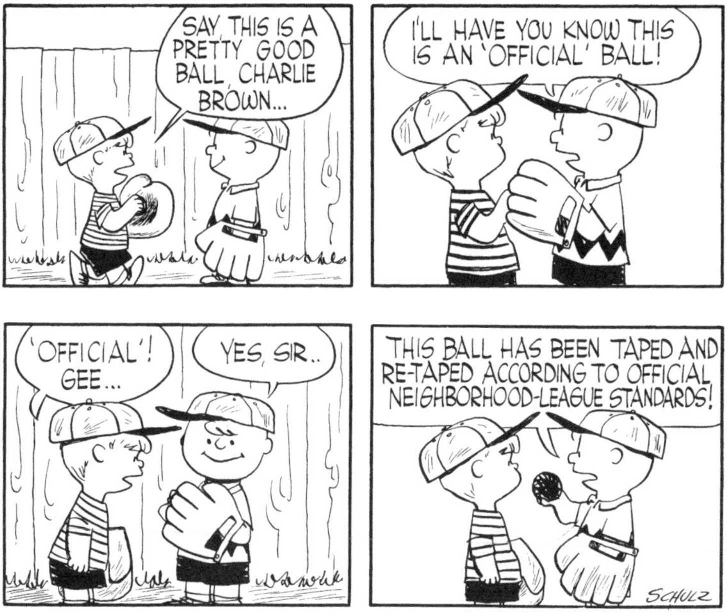
SAY, THIS IS A PRETTY GOOD BALL, CHARLIE BROWN...
I'LL HAVE YOU KNOW THIS IS AN 'OFFICIAL' BALL!
'OFFICIAL'! GEE...
YES, SIR..
THIS BALL HAS BEEN TAPED AND RE-TAPED ACCORDING TO OFFICIAL NEIGHBORHOOD-LEAGUE STANDARDS!
SCHULZ

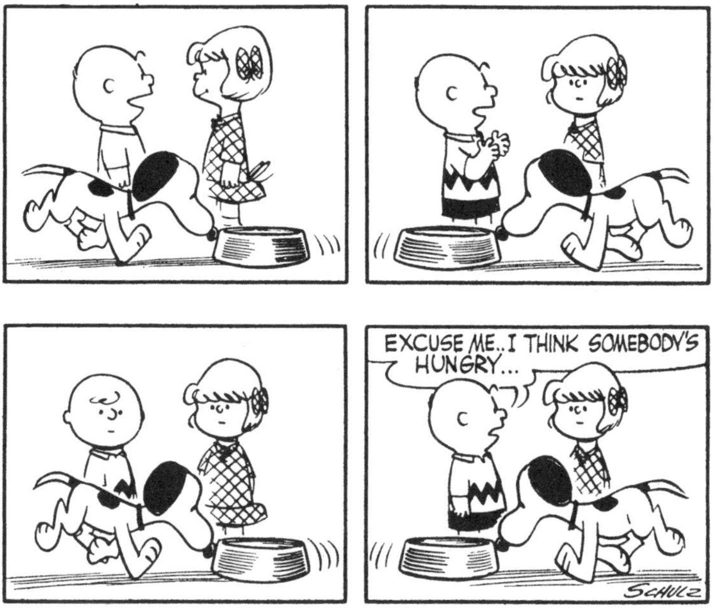
EXCUSE ME..I THINK SOMEBODY'S HUNGRY...
SCHULZ

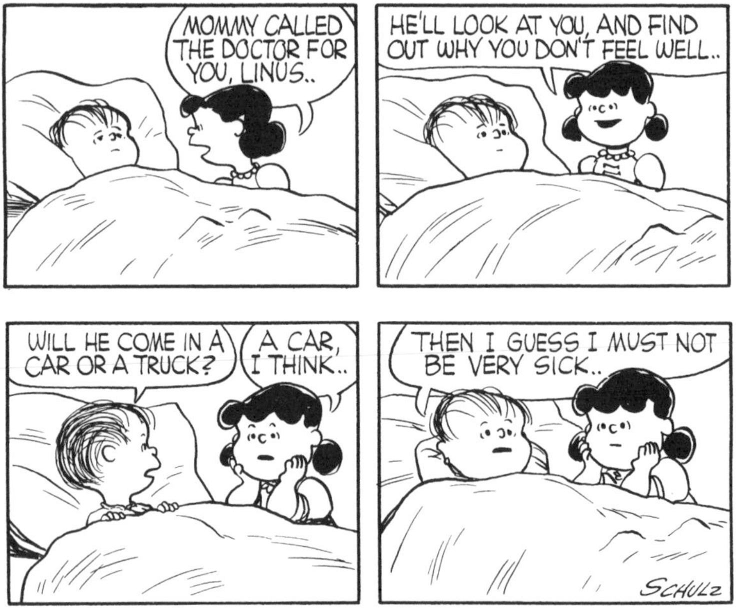
MOMMY CALLED THE DOCTOR FOR YOU, LINUS..
HE'LL LOOK AT YOU, AND FIND OUT WHY YOU DON'T FEEL WELL..
WILL HE COME IN A CAR OR A TRUCK?
A CAR, I THINK..
THEN I GUESS I MUST NOT BE VERY SICK..
SCHULZ

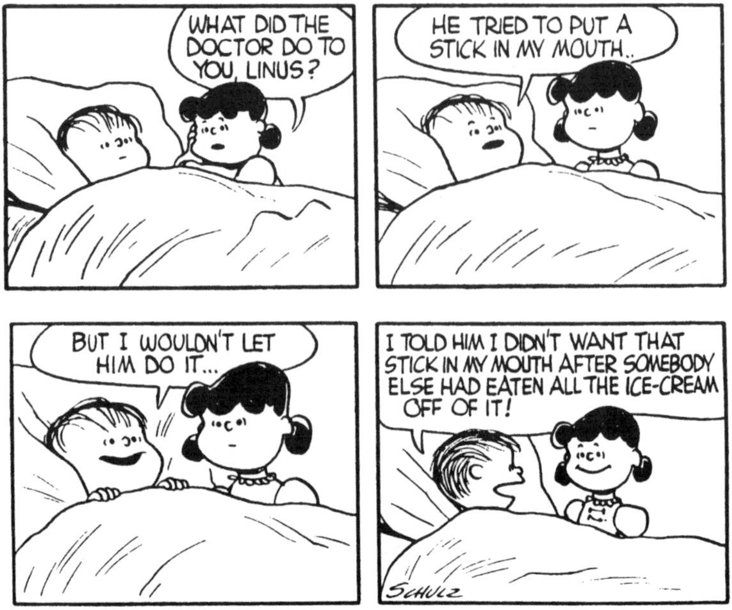
WHAT DID THE DOCTOR DO TO YOU, LINUS?
HE TRIED TO PUT A STICK IN MY MOUTH..
BUT I WOULDN'T LET HIM DO IT...
I TOLD HIM I DIDN'T WANT THAT STICK IN MY MOUTH AFTER SOMEBODY ELSE HAD EATEN ALL THE ICE-CREAM OFF OF IT!
SCHULZ

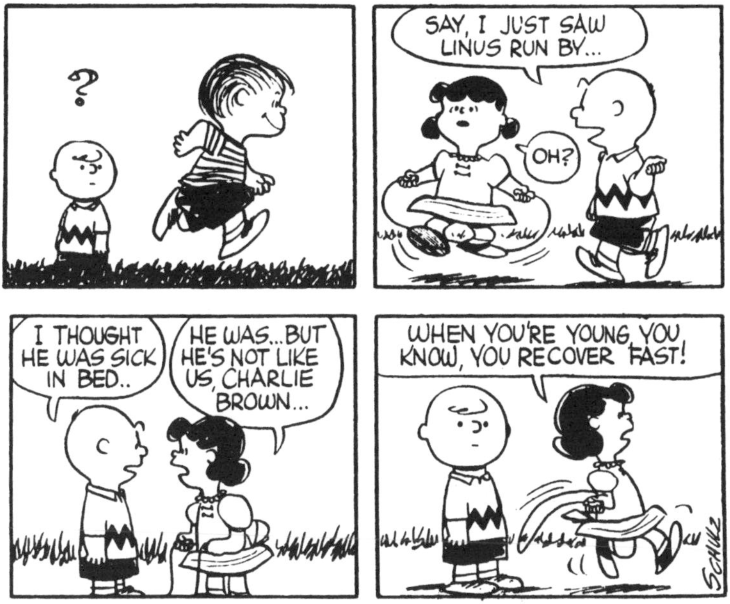
?
SAY, I JUST SAW LINUS RUN BY...
OH?
I THOUGHT HE WAS SICK IN BED..
HE WAS...BUT HE'S NOT LIKE US, CHARLIE BROWN...
WHEN YOU'RE YOUNG, YOU KNOW, YOU RECOVER FAST!
SCHULZ

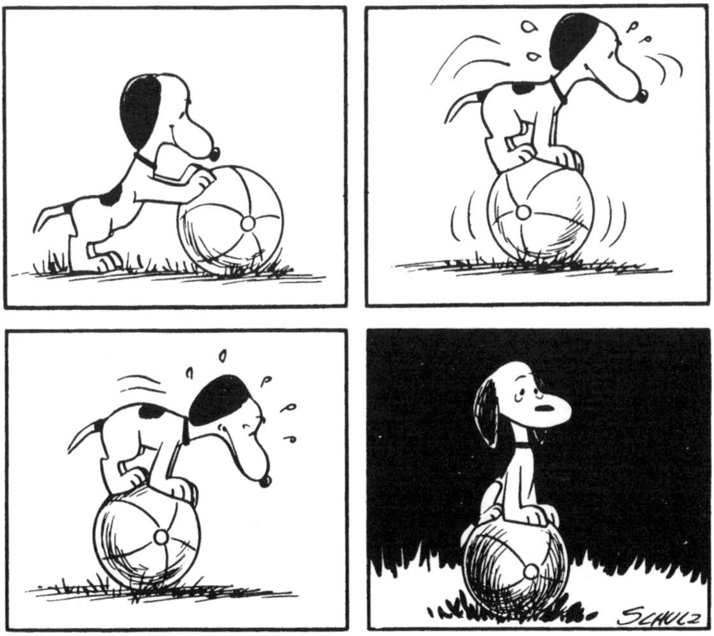
SCHULZ

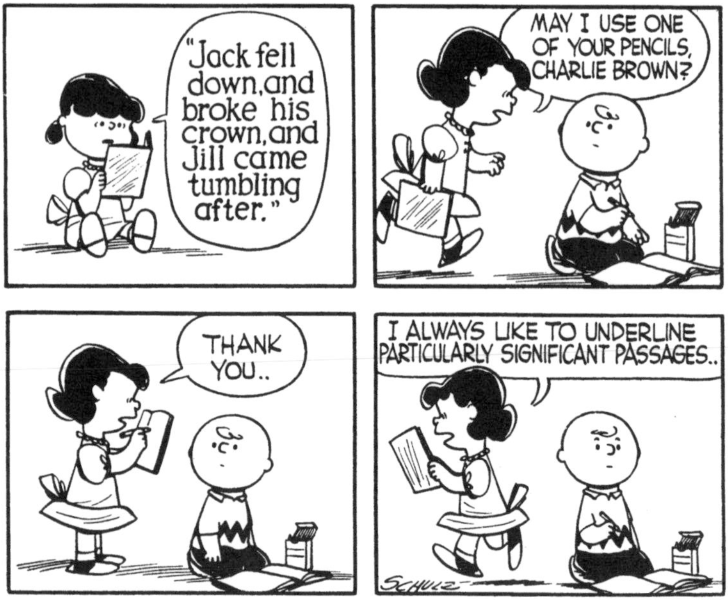

"Jack fell down, and broke his crown, and Jill came tumbling after."
MAY I USE ONE OF YOUR PENCILS, CHARLIE BROWN?
THANK YOU..
I ALWAYS LIKE TO UNDERLINE PARTICULARLY SIGNIFICANT PASSAGES..
SCHULZ

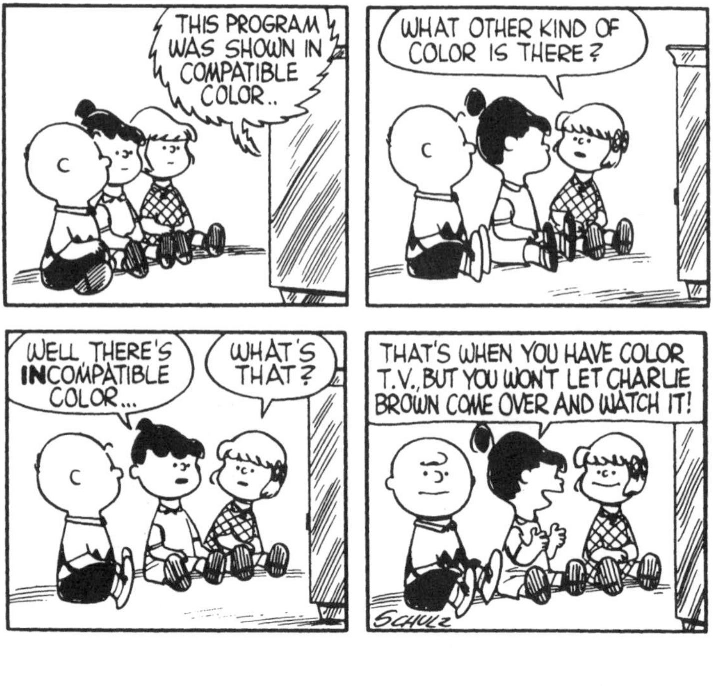

THIS PROGRAM WAS SHOWN IN COMPATIBLE COLOR..
WHAT OTHER KIND OF COLOR IS THERE?
WELL THERE'S INCOMPATIBLE COLOR...
WHAT'S THAT?
THAT'S WHEN YOU HAVE COLOR T.V., BUT YOU WON'T LET CHARLIE BROWN COME OVER AND WATCH IT!
SCHULZ

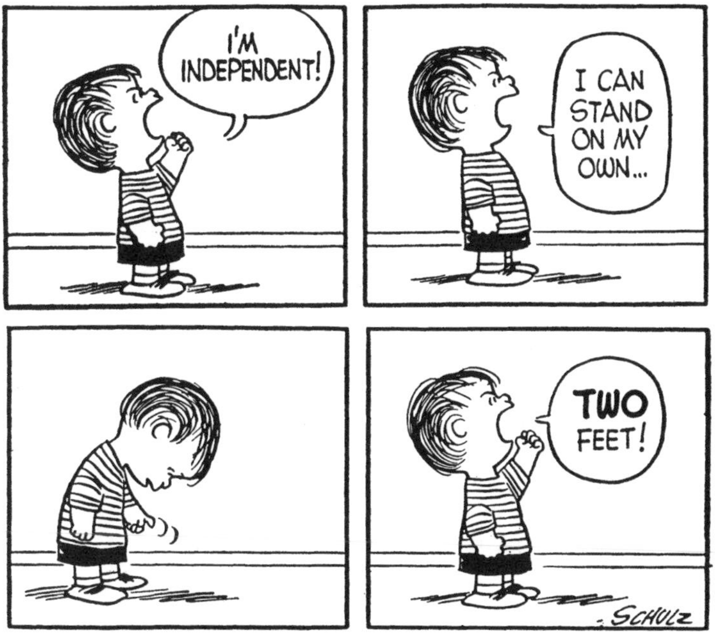
I'M INDEPENDENT!
I CAN STAND ON MY OWN...
TWO FEET!
SCHULZ

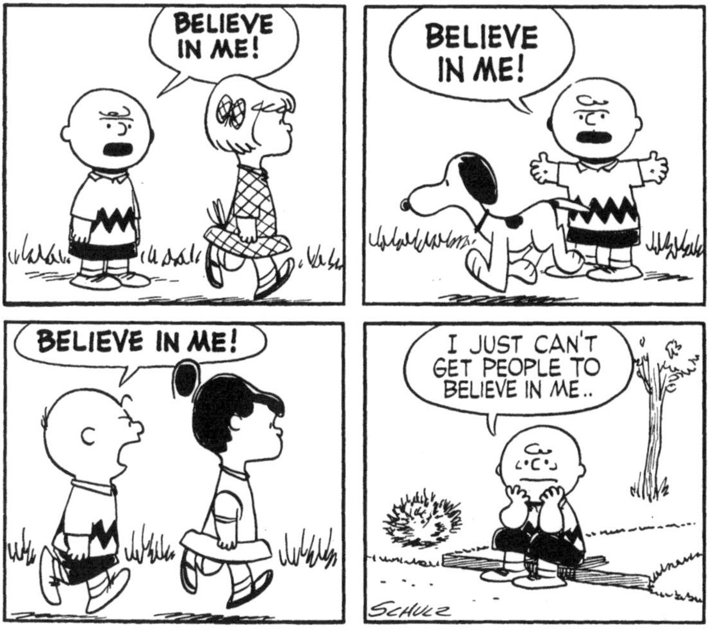
BELIEVE IN ME!
BELIEVE IN ME!
BELIEVE IN ME!
I JUST CAN'T GET PEOPLE TO BELIEVE IN ME..
SCHULZ

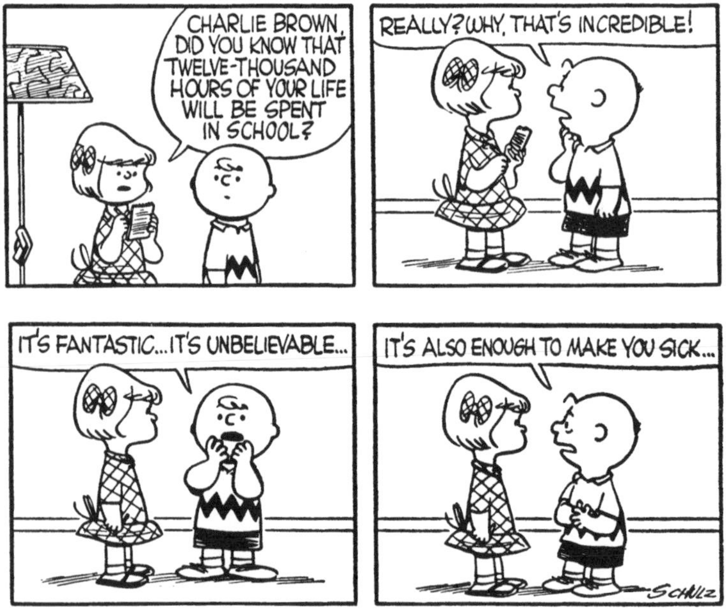
CHARLIE BROWN, DID YOU KNOW THAT TWELVE-THOUSAND HOURS OF YOUR LIFE WILL BE SPENT IN SCHOOL?
REALLY? WHY, THAT'S INCREDIBLE!
IT'S FANTASTIC...IT'S UNBELIEVABLE...
IT'S ALSO ENOUGH TO MAKE YOU SICK...
SCHULZ

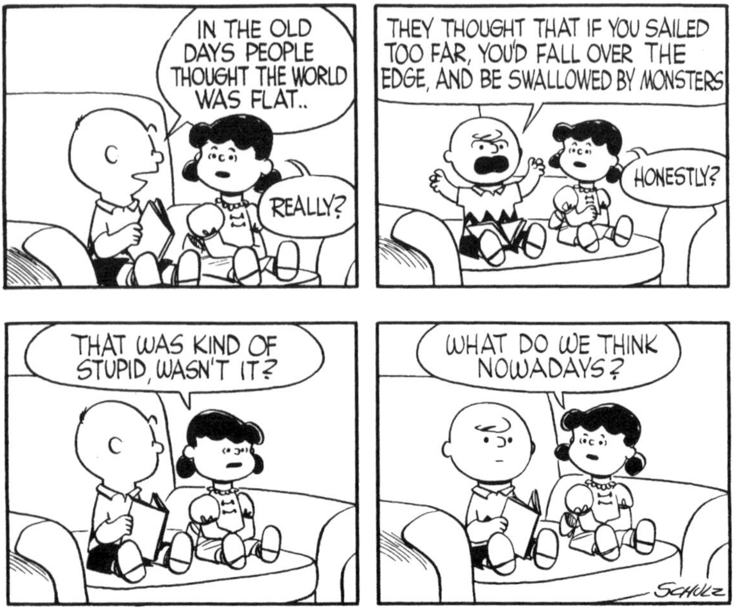
IN THE OLD DAYS PEOPLE THOUGHT THE WORLD WAS FLAT..
REALLY?
THEY THOUGHT THAT IF YOU SAILED TOO FAR, YOU'D FALL OVER THE EDGE, AND BE SWALLOWED BY MONSTERS
HONESTLY?
THAT WAS KIND OF STUPID, WASN'T IT?
WHAT DO WE THINK NOWADAYS?
SCHULZ

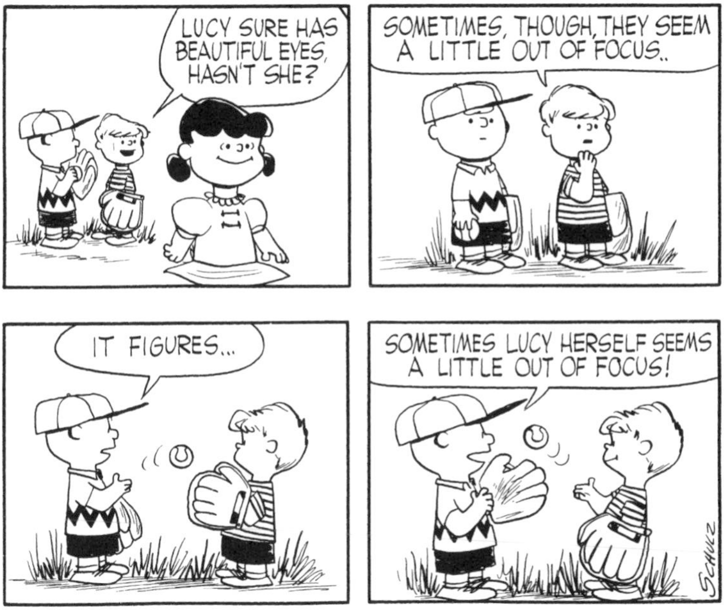
LUCY SURE HAS BEAUTIFUL EYES, HASN'T SHE?
SOMETIMES, THOUGH, THEY SEEM A LITTLE OUT OF FOCUS..
IT FIGURES...
SOMETIMES LUCY HERSELF SEEMS A LITTLE OUT OF FOCUS!
SCHULZ

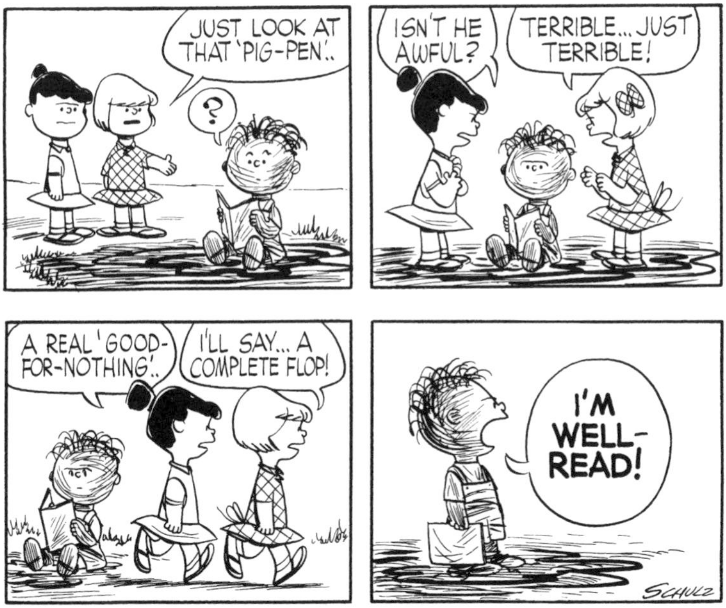
JUST LOOK AT THAT 'PIG-PEN'..
?
ISN'T HE AWFUL?
TERRIBLE... JUST TERRIBLE!
A REAL 'GOOD-FOR-NOTHING'..
I'LL SAY... A COMPLETE FLOP!
I'M WELL-READ!
SCHULZ

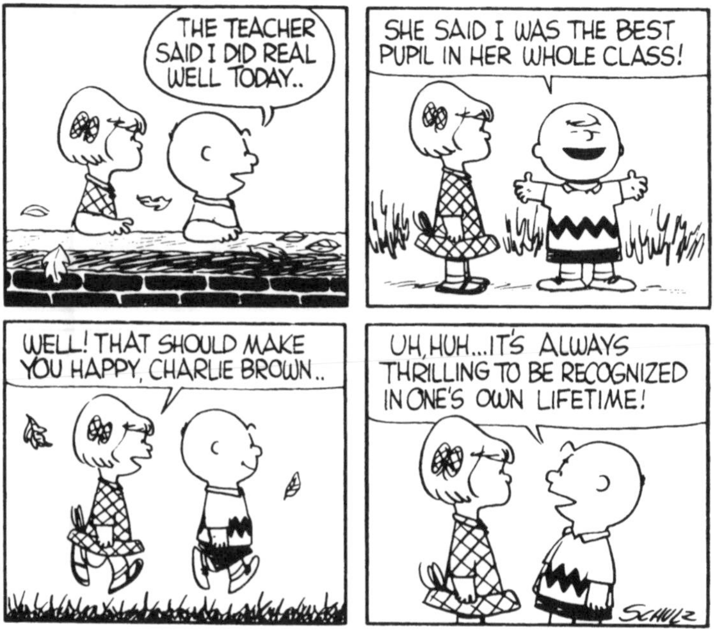
THE TEACHER SAID I DID REAL WELL TODAY..
SHE SAID I WAS THE BEST PUPIL IN HER WHOLE CLASS!
WELL! THAT SHOULD MAKE YOU HAPPY, CHARLIE BROWN..
UH, HUH...IT'S ALWAYS THRILLING TO BE RECOGNIZED IN ONE'S OWN LIFETIME!
SCHULZ

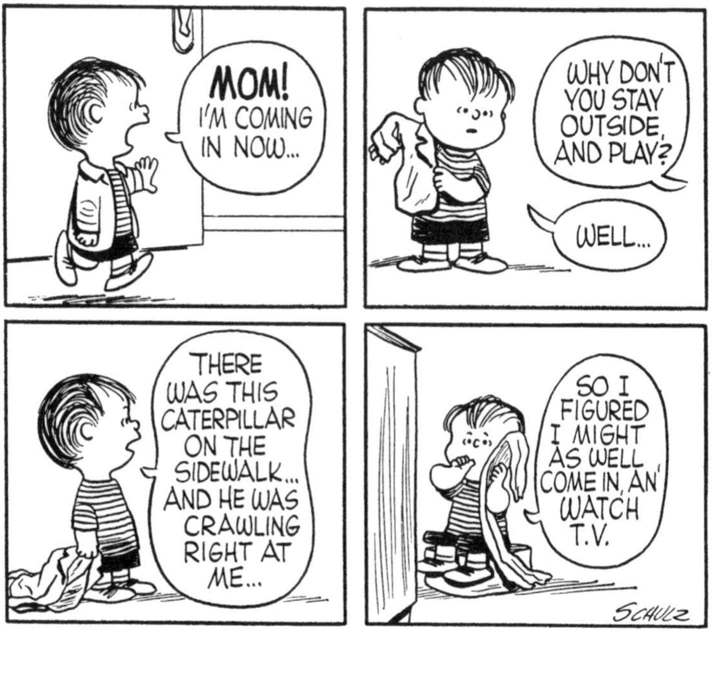
MOM! I'M COMING IN NOW...
WHY DON'T YOU STAY OUTSIDE, AND PLAY?
WELL...
THERE WAS THIS CATERPILLAR ON THE SIDEWALK... AND HE WAS CRAWLING RIGHT AT ME...
SO I FIGURED I MIGHT AS WELL COME IN, AN' WATCH T.V.
SCHULZ

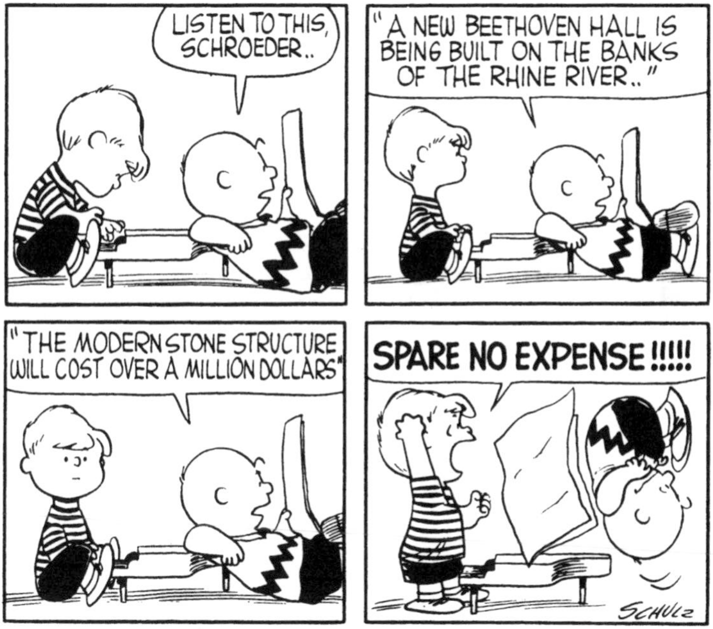
LISTEN TO THIS, SCHROEDER..
"A NEW BEETHOVEN HALL IS BEING BUILT ON THE BANKS OF THE RHINE RIVER.."
"THE MODERN STONE STRUCTURE WILL COST OVER A MILLION DOLLARS"
SPARE NO EXPENSE!!!!!
SCHULZ

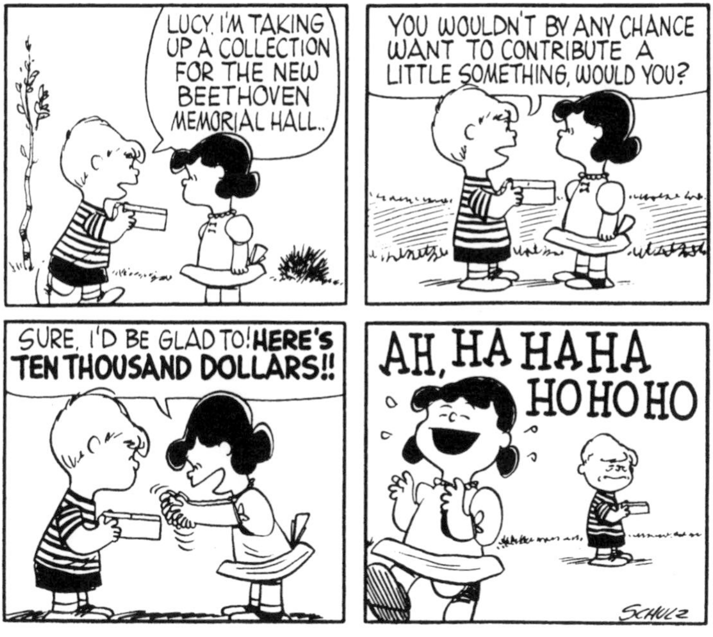
LUCY, I'M TAKING UP A COLLECTION FOR THE NEW BEETHOVEN MEMORIAL HALL..
YOU WOULDN'T BY ANY CHANCE WANT TO CONTRIBUTE A LITTLE SOMETHING, WOULD YOU?
SURE, I'D BE GLAD TO! HERE'S TEN THOUSAND DOLLARS!!
AH, HA HA HA HA
HO HO HO
SCHULZ

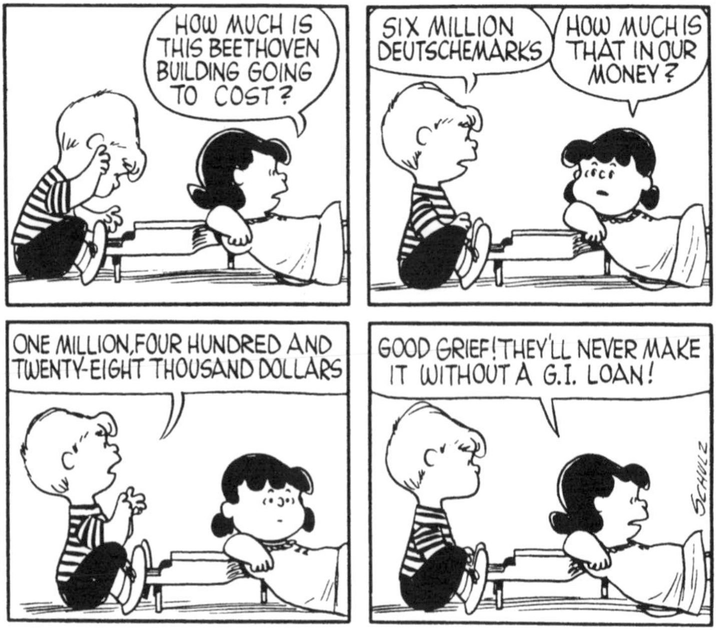
HOW MUCH IS THIS BEETHOVEN BUILDING GOING TO COST?
SIX MILLION DEUTSCHEMARKS
HOW MUCH IS THAT IN OUR MONEY?
ONE MILLION, FOUR HUNDRED AND TWENTY-EIGHT THOUSAND DOLLARS
GOOD GRIEF! THEY'LL NEVER MAKE IT WITHOUT A G.I. LOAN!
SCHULZ

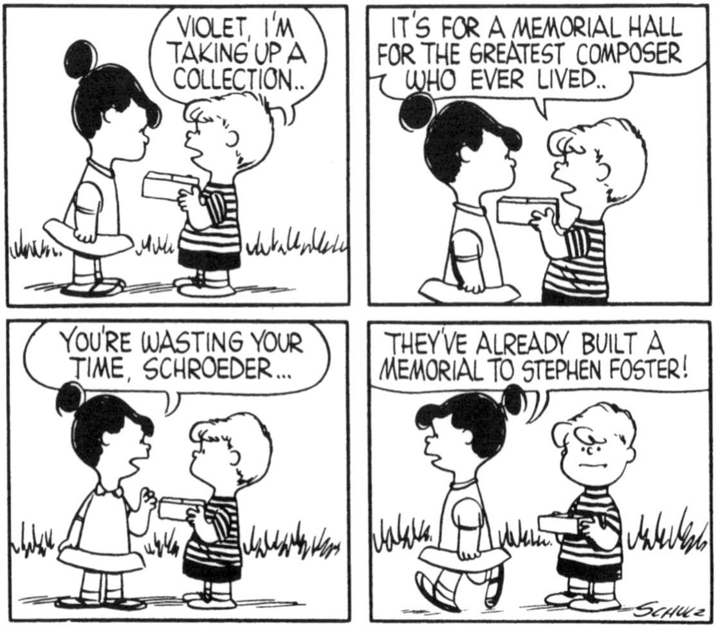
VIOLET, I'M TAKING UP A COLLECTION..
IT'S FOR A MEMORIAL HALL FOR THE GREATEST COMPOSER WHO EVER LIVED..
YOU'RE WASTING YOUR TIME, SCHROEDER...
THEY'VE ALREADY BUILT A MEMORIAL TO STEPHEN FOSTER!
SCHULZ

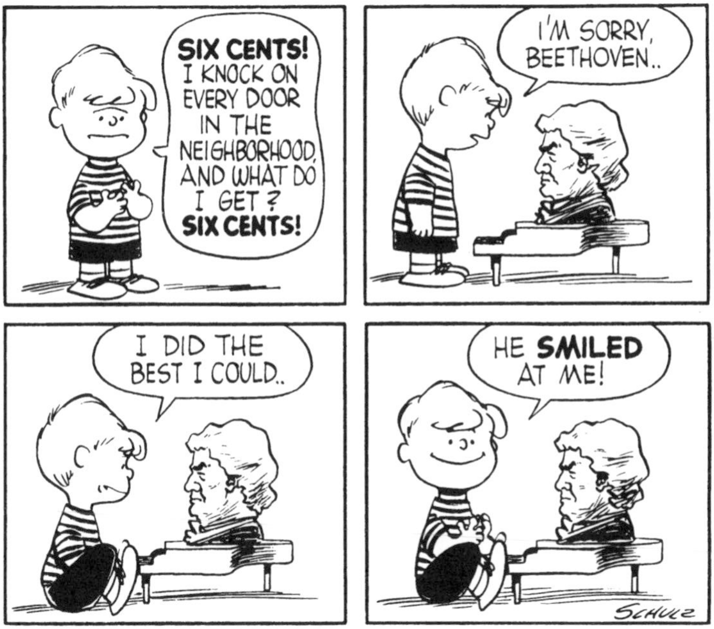
SIX CENTS! I KNOCK ON EVERY DOOR IN THE NEIGHBORHOOD, AND WHAT DO I GET? SIX CENTS!
I'M SORRY, BEETHOVEN..
I DID THE BEST I COULD..
HE SMILED AT ME!
SCHULZ

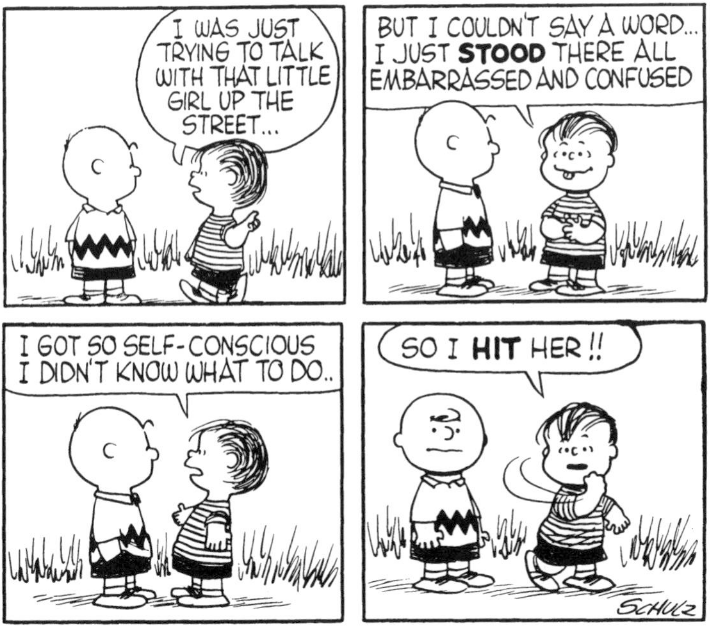
I WAS JUST TRYING TO TALK WITH THAT LITTLE GIRL UP THE STREET...
BUT I COULDN'T SAY A WORD... I JUST STOOD THERE ALL EMBARRASSED AND CONFUSED
I GOT SO SELF-CONSCIOUS I DIDN'T KNOW WHAT TO DO..
SO I HIT HER!!
SCHULZ

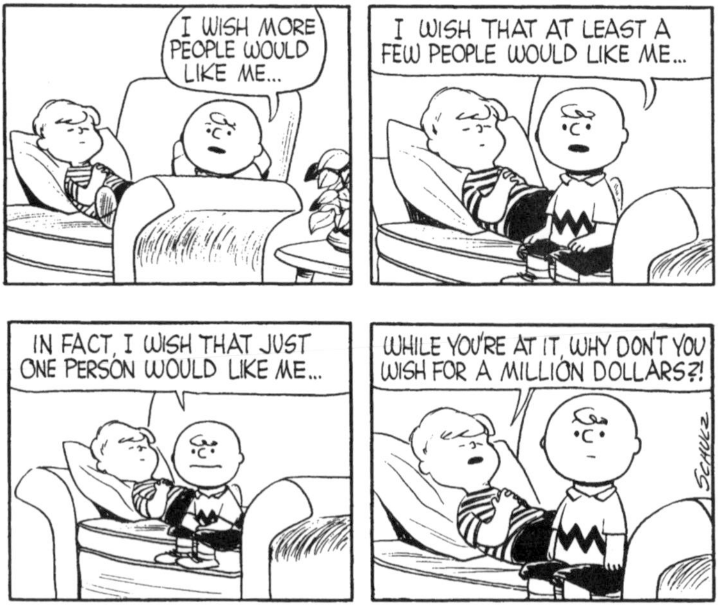
I WISH MORE PEOPLE WOULD LIKE ME...
I WISH THAT AT LEAST A FEW PEOPLE WOULD LIKE ME...
IN FACT, I WISH THAT JUST ONE PERSON WOULD LIKE ME...
WHILE YOU'RE AT IT, WHY DON'T YOU WISH FOR A MILLION DOLLARS?!
SCHULZ

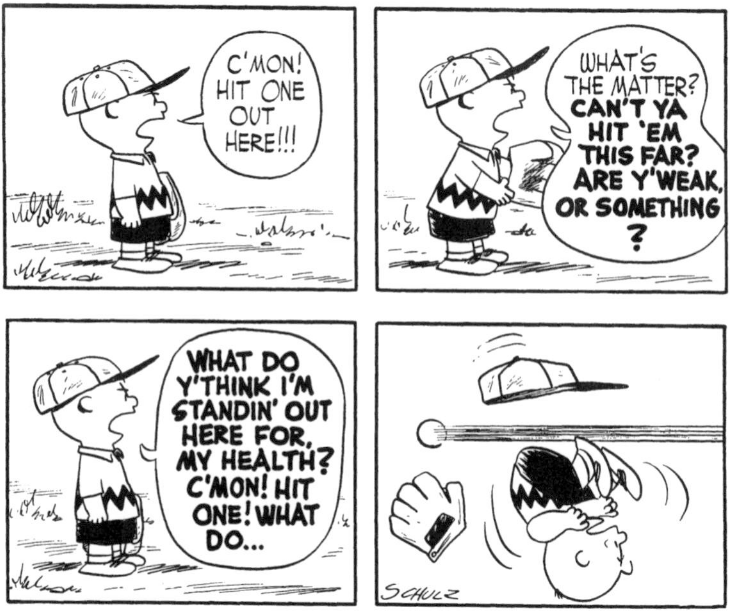
C'MON! HIT ONE OUT HERE!!!
WHAT'S THE MATTER? CAN'T YA HIT 'EM THIS FAR? ARE Y'WEAK, OR SOMETHING?
WHAT DO Y'THINK I'M STANDIN' OUT HERE FOR, MY HEALTH? C'MON! HIT ONE! WHAT DO...
SCHULZ

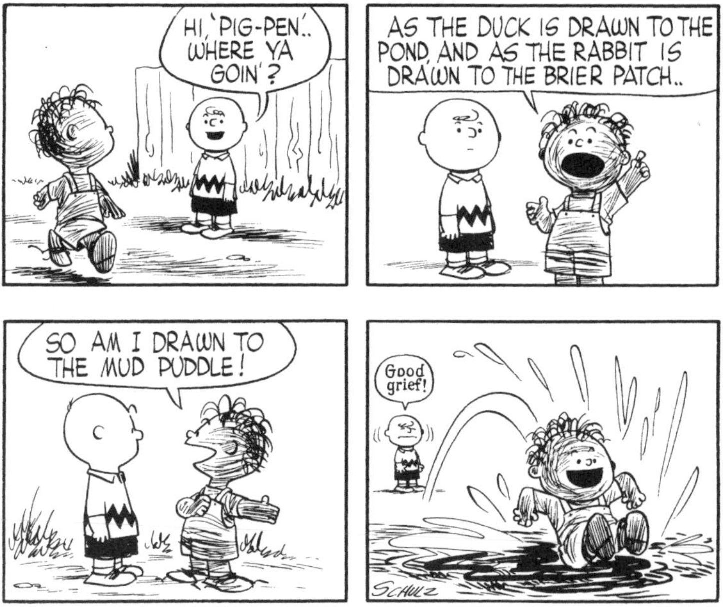
HI, 'PIG-PEN'.. WHERE YA GOIN'?
AS THE DUCK IS DRAWN TO THE POND, AND AS THE RABBIT IS DRAWN TO THE BRIER PATCH..
SO AM I DRAWN TO THE MUD PUDDLE!
Good grief!
SCHULZ

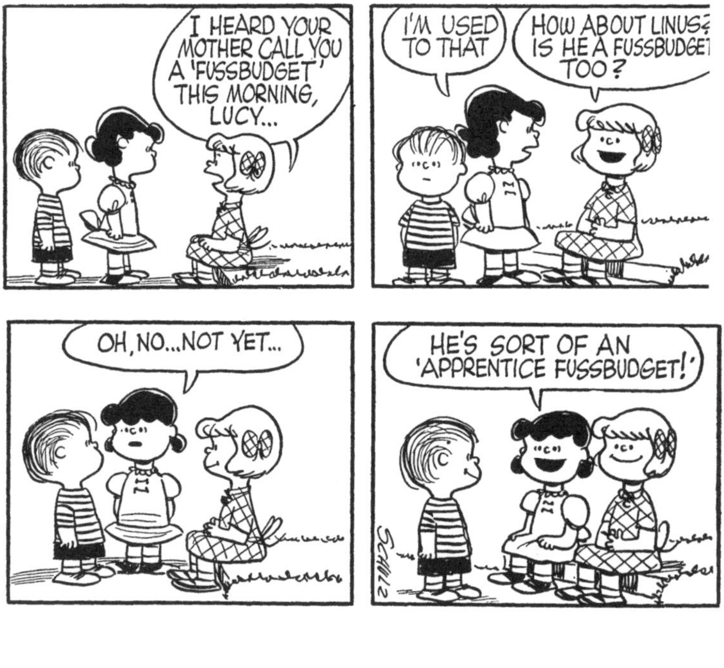
I HEARD YOUR MOTHER CALL YOU A 'FUSSBUDGET' THIS MORNING, LUCY...
I'M USED TO THAT
HOW ABOUT LINUS? IS HE A FUSSBUDGET TOO?
OH, NO...NOT YET...
HE'S SORT OF AN 'APPRENTICE FUSSBUDGET!'
SCHULZ

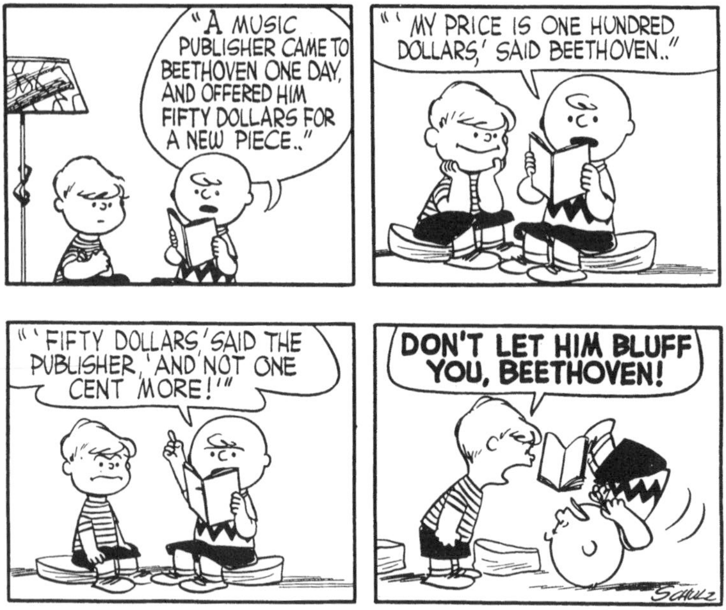
"A MUSIC PUBLISHER CAME TO BEETHOVEN ONE DAY, AND OFFERED HIM FIFTY DOLLARS FOR A NEW PIECE.."
"'MY PRICE IS ONE HUNDRED DOLLARS,' SAID BEETHOVEN.."
"'FIFTY DOLLARS,' SAID THE PUBLISHER, 'AND NOT ONE CENT MORE!'"
DON'T LET HIM BLUFF YOU, BEETHOVEN!
SCHULZ

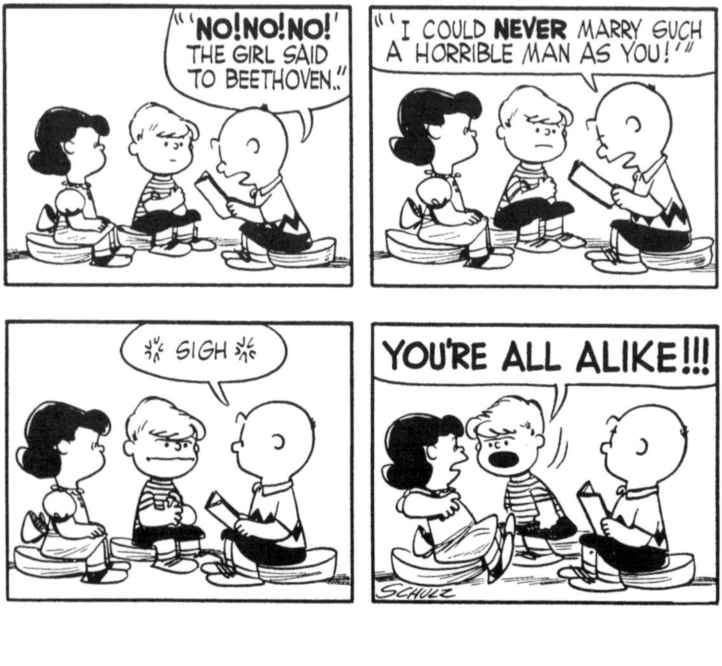
"'NO! NO! NO!' THE GIRL SAID TO BEETHOVEN."
"'I COULD NEVER MARRY SUCH A HORRIBLE MAN AS YOU!'"
SIGH
YOU'RE ALL ALIKE!!!
SCHULZ

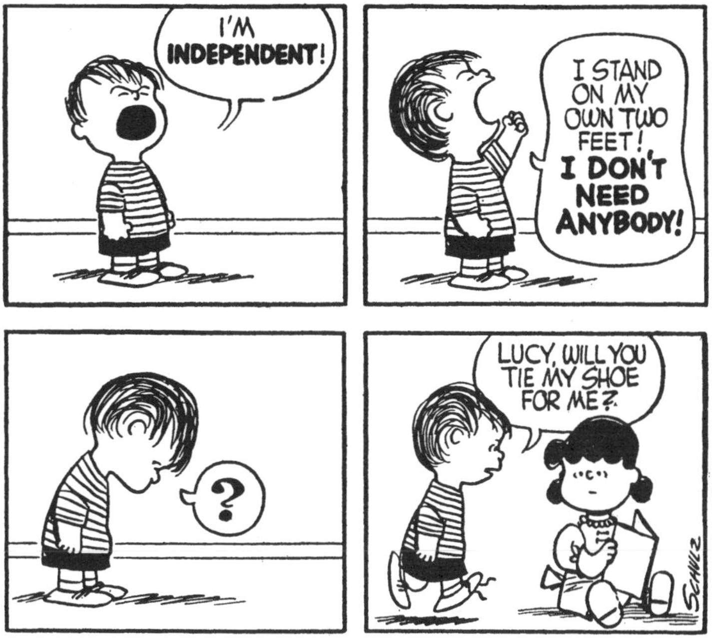
I'M INDEPENDENT!
I STAND ON MY OWN TWO FEET! I DON'T NEED ANYBODY!
?
LUCY, WILL YOU TIE MY SHOE FOR ME?
SCHULZ

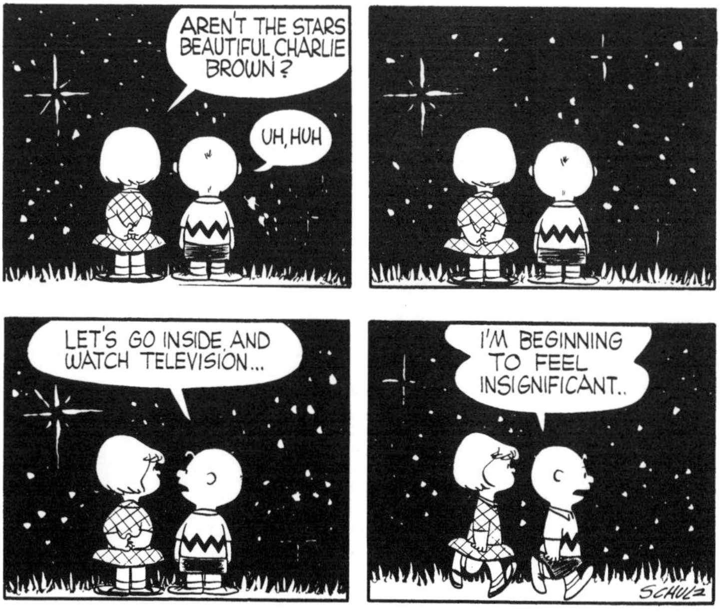
AREN'T THE STARS BEAUTIFUL, CHARLIE BROWN?
UH, HUH
LET'S GO INSIDE AND WATCH TELEVISION...
I'M BEGINNING TO FEEL INSIGNIFICANT..
SCHULZ

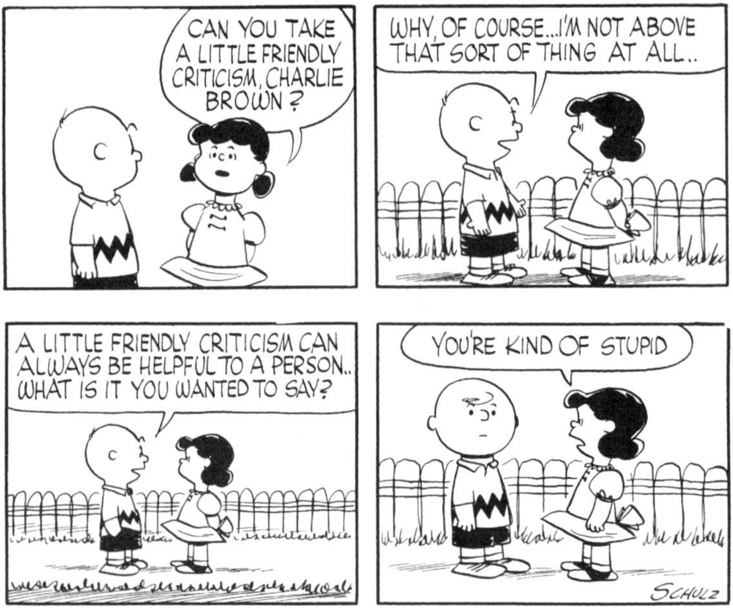
CAN YOU TAKE A LITTLE FRIENDLY CRITICISM, CHARLIE BROWN?
WHY, OF COURSE...I'M NOT ABOVE THAT SORT OF THING AT ALL..
A LITTLE FRIENDLY CRITICISM CAN ALWAYS BE HELPFUL TO A PERSON.. WHAT IS IT YOU WANTED TO SAY?
YOU'RE KIND OF STUPID
SCHULZ

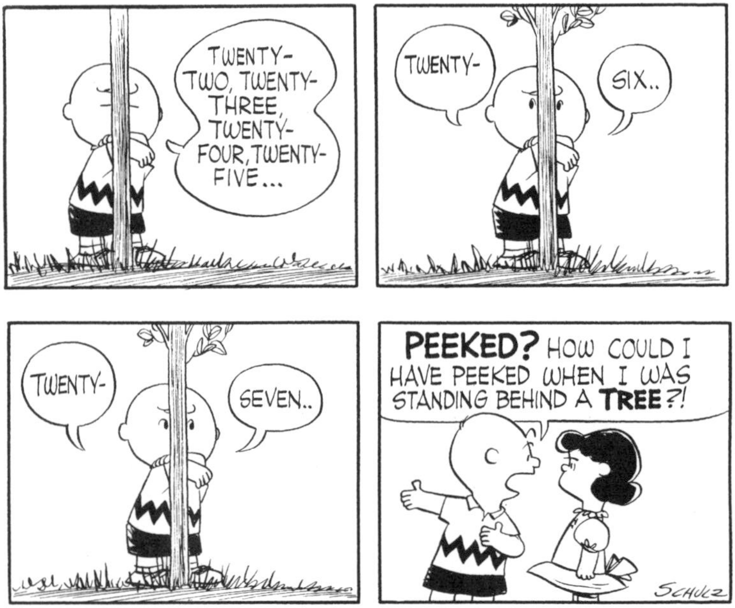
TWENTY-TWO, TWENTY-THREE, TWENTY-FOUR, TWENTY-FIVE...
TWENTY-
SIX..
TWENTY-
SEVEN..
PEEKED? HOW COULD I HAVE PEEKED WHEN I WAS STANDING BEHIND A **TREE**?!
SCHULZ

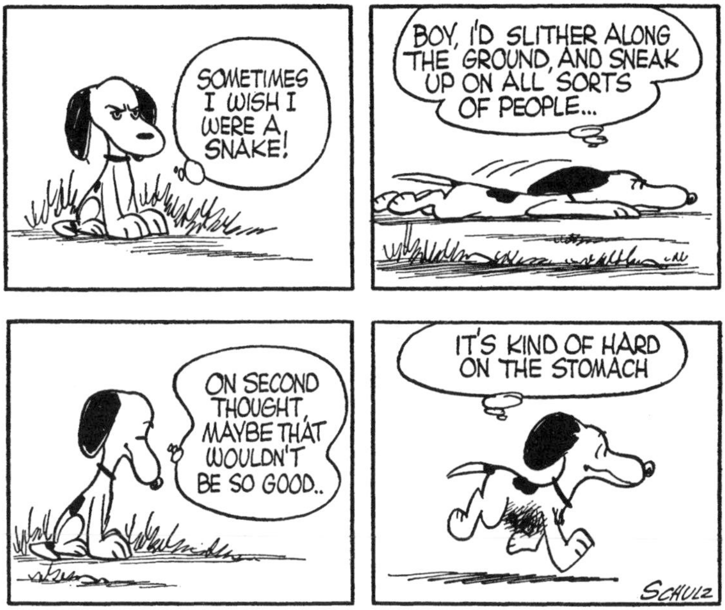

SOMETIMES I WISH I WERE A SNAKE!
BOY, I'D SLITHER ALONG THE GROUND, AND SNEAK UP ON ALL SORTS OF PEOPLE...
ON SECOND THOUGHT, MAYBE THAT WOULDN'T BE SO GOOD..
IT'S KIND OF HARD ON THE STOMACH
SCHULZ

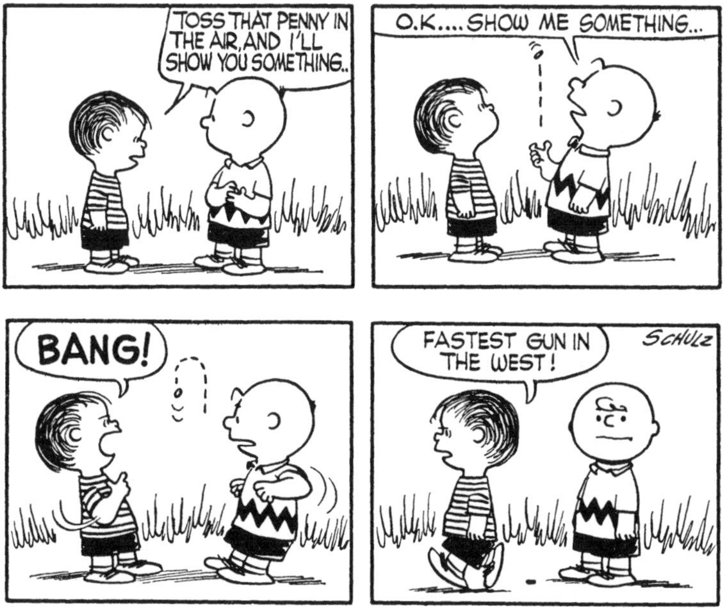

TOSS THAT PENNY IN THE AIR, AND I'LL SHOW YOU SOMETHING..
O.K.... SHOW ME SOMETHING...
BANG!
FASTEST GUN IN THE WEST!
SCHULZ

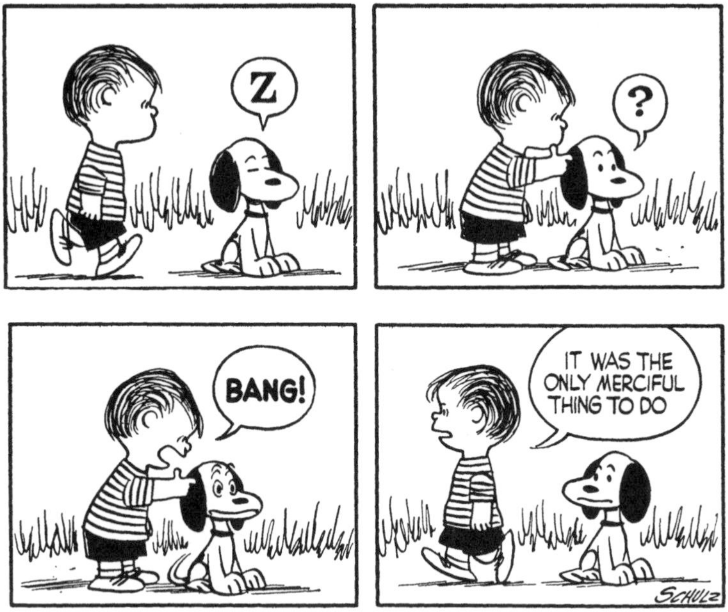
Z
?
BANG!
IT WAS THE ONLY MERCIFUL THING TO DO
SCHULZ

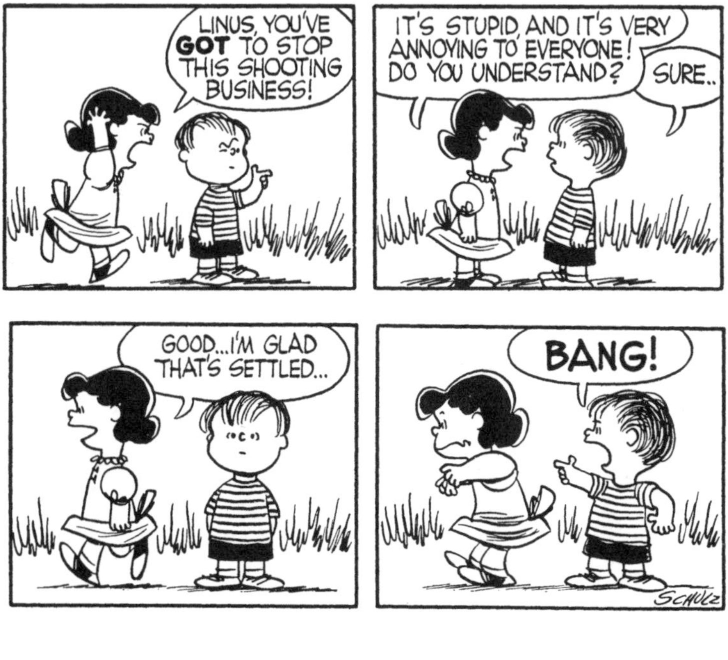
LINUS, YOU'VE **GOT** TO STOP THIS SHOOTING BUSINESS!
IT'S STUPID, AND IT'S VERY ANNOYING TO EVERYONE! DO YOU UNDERSTAND?
SURE..
GOOD...I'M GLAD THAT'S SETTLED...
BANG!
SCHULZ

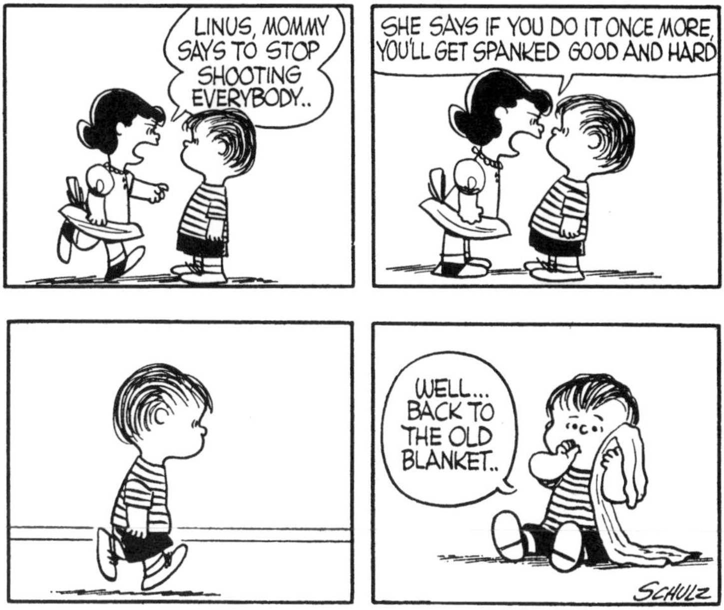
LINUS, MOMMY SAYS TO STOP SHOOTING EVERYBODY..
SHE SAYS IF YOU DO IT ONCE MORE, YOU'LL GET SPANKED GOOD AND HARD
WELL... BACK TO THE OLD BLANKET..
SCHULZ

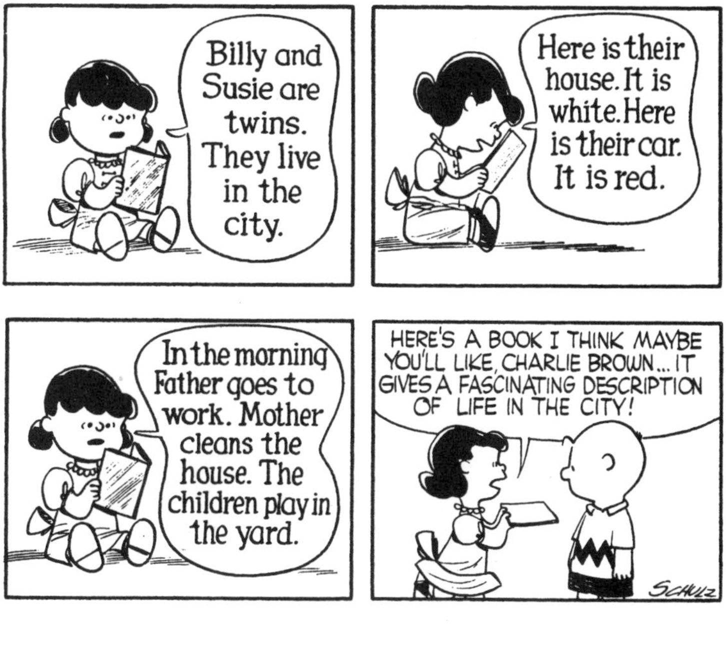
Billy and Susie are twins. They live in the city.
Here is their house. It is white. Here is their car. It is red.
In the morning Father goes to work. Mother cleans the house. The children play in the yard.
HERE'S A BOOK I THINK MAYBE YOU'LL LIKE, CHARLIE BROWN... IT GIVES A FASCINATING DESCRIPTION OF LIFE IN THE CITY!
SCHULZ

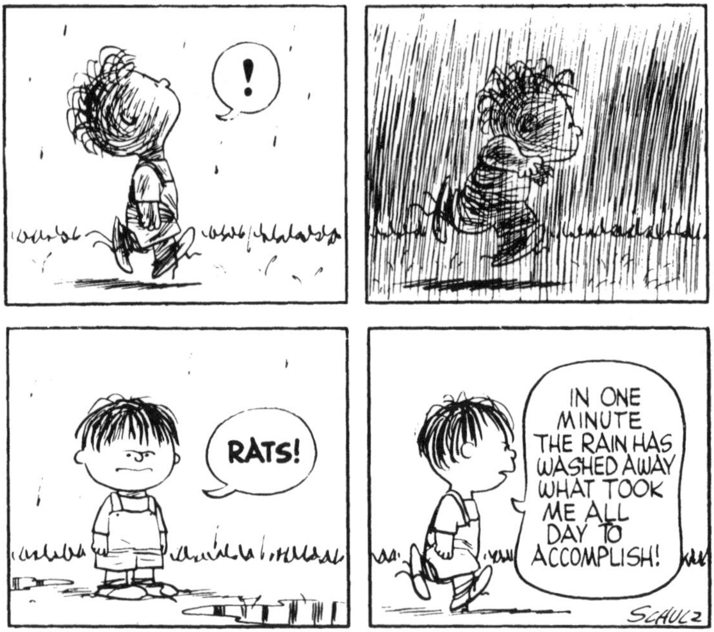
!
RATS!
IN ONE MINUTE THE RAIN HAS WASHED AWAY WHAT TOOK ME ALL DAY TO ACCOMPLISH!
SCHULZ

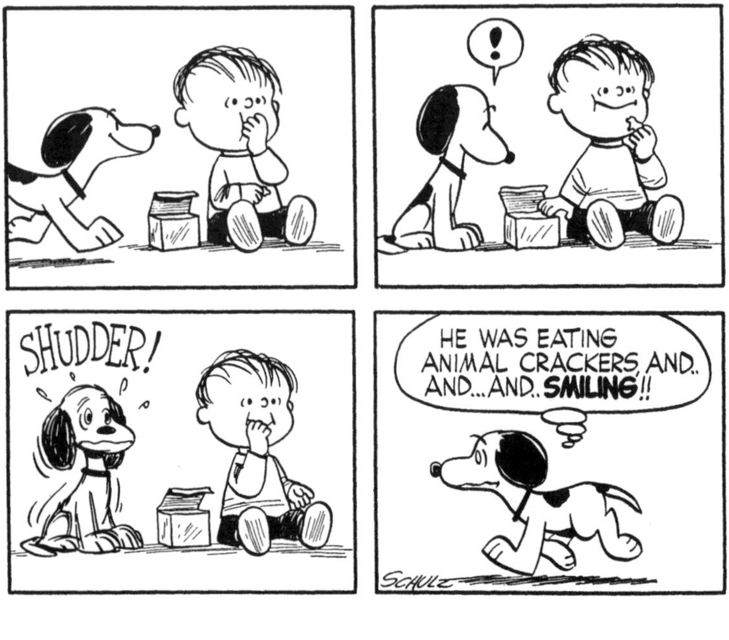
!
SHUDDER!
HE WAS EATING ANIMAL CRACKERS, AND.. AND...AND..SMILING!!
SCHULZ

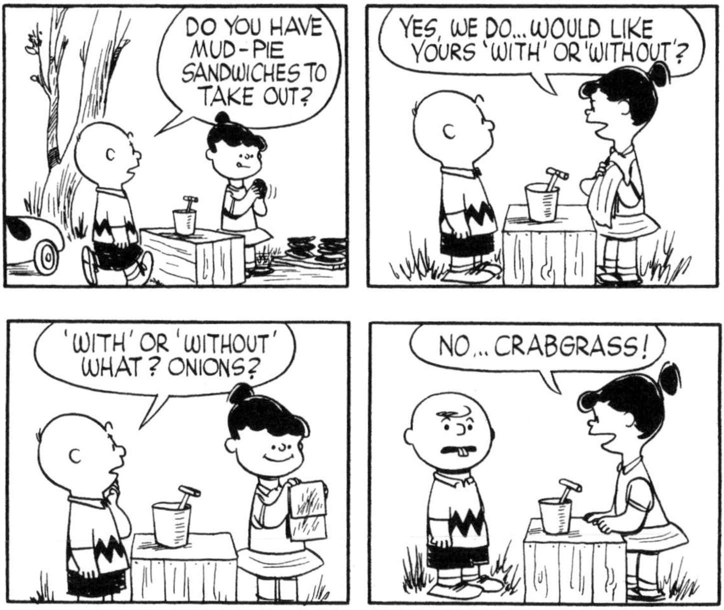
DO YOU HAVE MUD-PIE SANDWICHES TO TAKE OUT?
YES, WE DO... WOULD LIKE YOURS 'WITH' OR 'WITHOUT'?
'WITH' OR 'WITHOUT' WHAT? ONIONS?
NO... CRABGRASS!

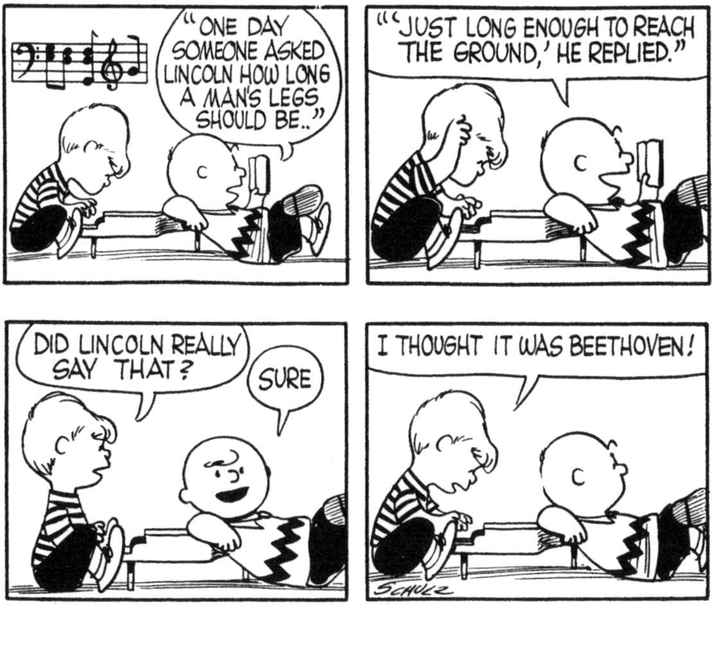
"ONE DAY SOMEONE ASKED LINCOLN HOW LONG A MAN'S LEGS SHOULD BE.."
"'JUST LONG ENOUGH TO REACH THE GROUND,' HE REPLIED."
DID LINCOLN REALLY SAY THAT?
SURE
I THOUGHT IT WAS BEETHOVEN!
SCHULZ

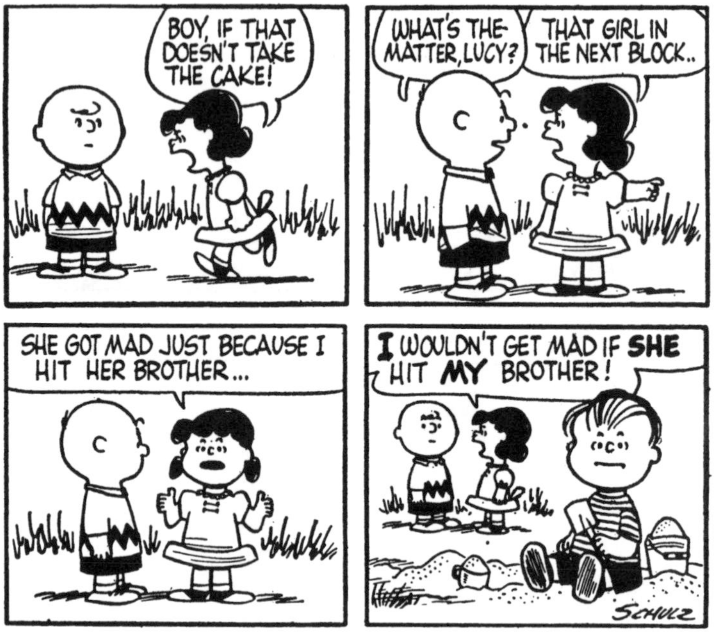
BOY, IF THAT DOESN'T TAKE THE CAKE!
WHAT'S THE MATTER, LUCY?
THAT GIRL IN THE NEXT BLOCK..
SHE GOT MAD JUST BECAUSE I HIT HER BROTHER...
I WOULDN'T GET MAD IF SHE HIT MY BROTHER!
SCHULZ

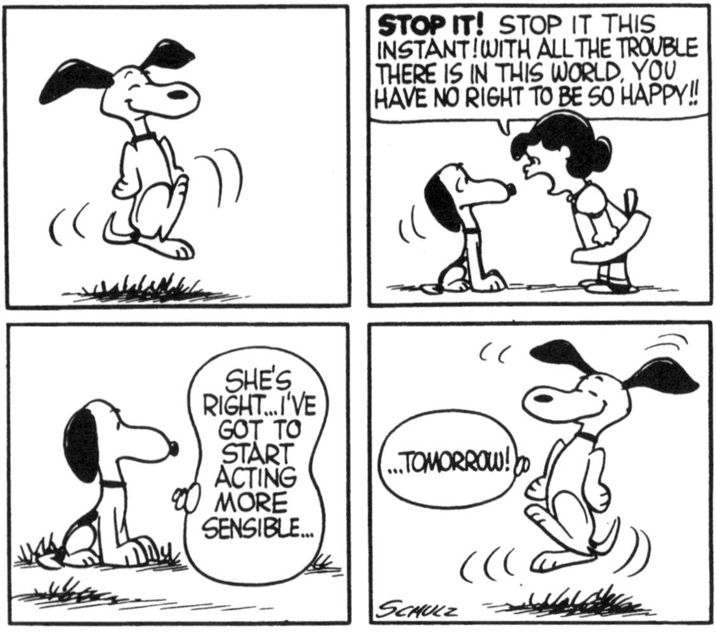
STOP IT! STOP IT THIS INSTANT! WITH ALL THE TROUBLE THERE IS IN THIS WORLD, YOU HAVE NO RIGHT TO BE SO HAPPY!!
SHE'S RIGHT...I'VE GOT TO START ACTING MORE SENSIBLE...
...TOMORROW!
SCHULZ

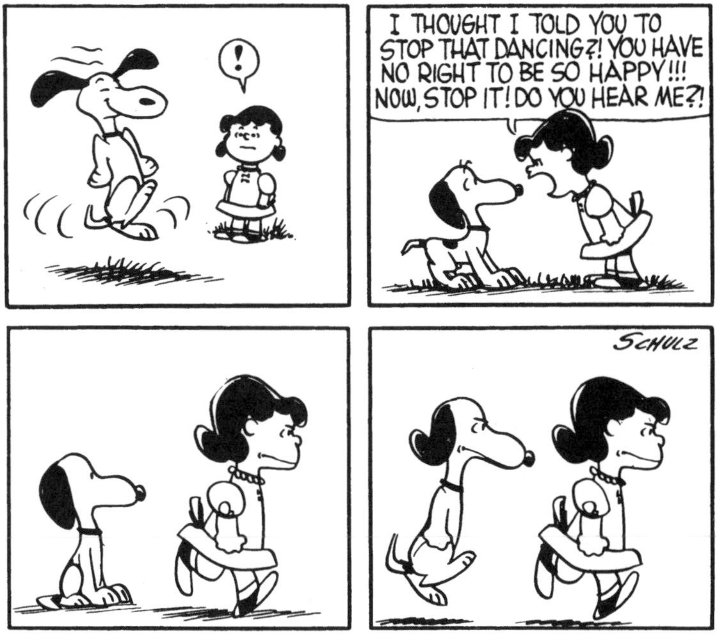
!
I THOUGHT I TOLD YOU TO STOP THAT DANCING?! YOU HAVE NO RIGHT TO BE SO HAPPY!!! NOW, STOP IT! DO YOU HEAR ME?!
SCHULZ

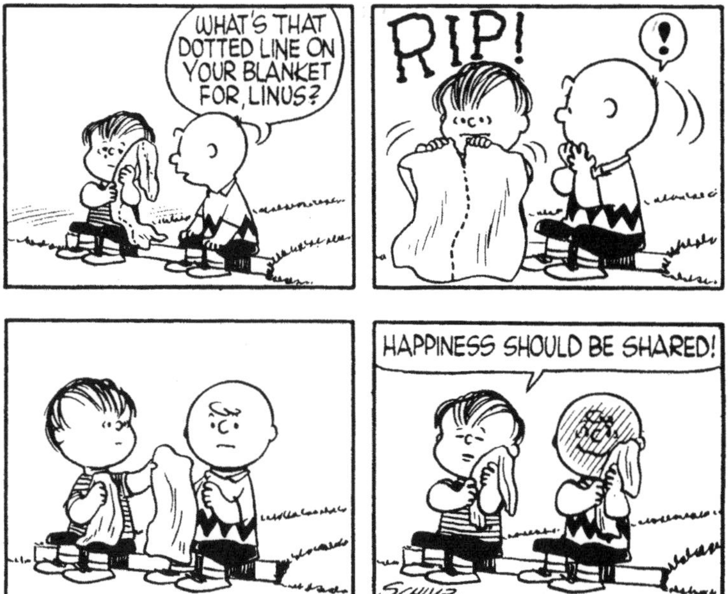
WHAT'S THAT DOTTED LINE ON YOUR BLANKET FOR, LINUS?
RIP!
!
HAPPINESS SHOULD BE SHARED!
SCHULZ

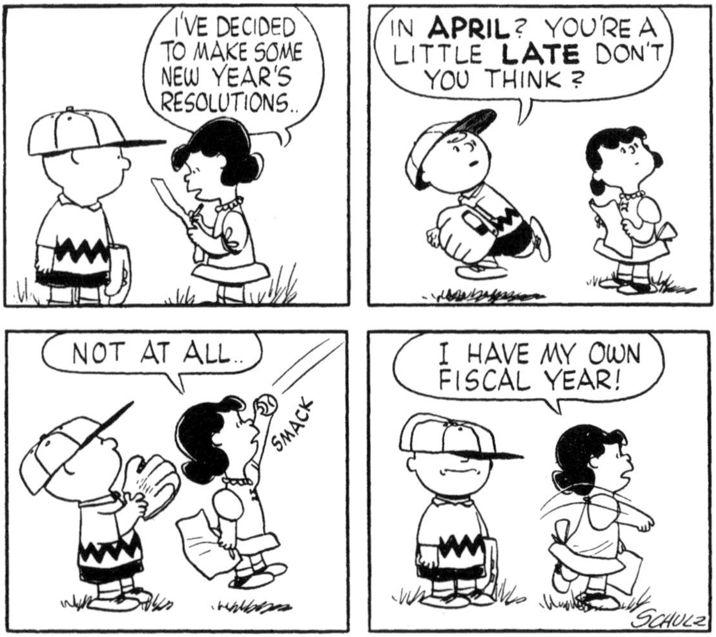
I'VE DECIDED TO MAKE SOME NEW YEAR'S RESOLUTIONS..
IN **APRIL**? YOU'RE A LITTLE **LATE** DON'T YOU THINK?
NOT AT ALL..
SMACK
I HAVE MY OWN FISCAL YEAR!
SCHULZ

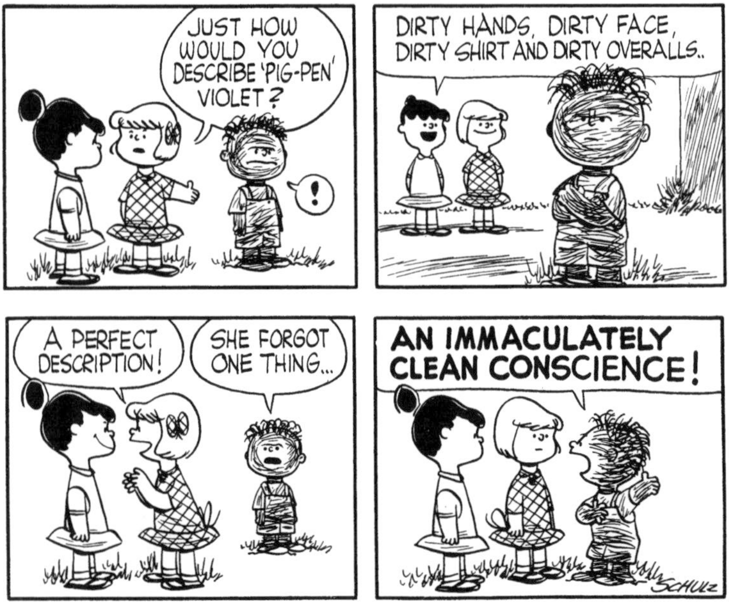
JUST HOW WOULD YOU DESCRIBE 'PIG-PEN' VIOLET?
!
DIRTY HANDS, DIRTY FACE, DIRTY SHIRT AND DIRTY OVERALLS..
A PERFECT DESCRIPTION!
SHE FORGOT ONE THING...
AN IMMACULATELY CLEAN CONSCIENCE!
SCHULZ

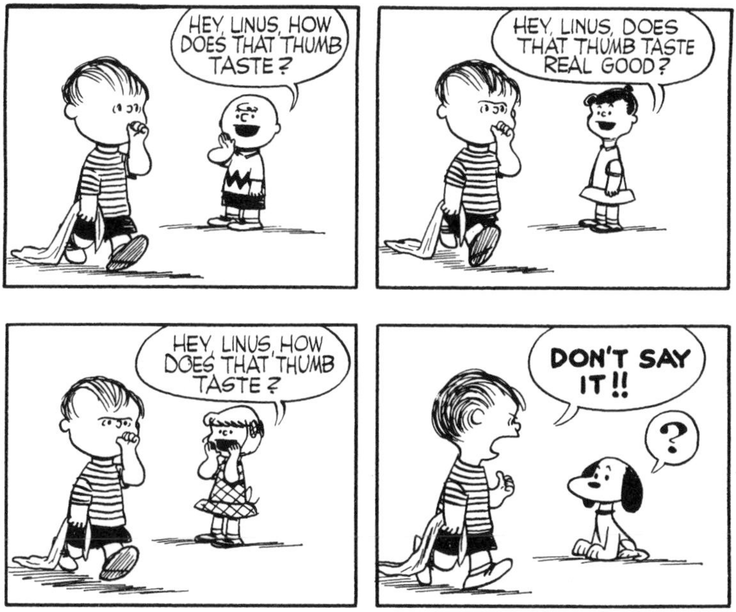
HEY, LINUS, HOW DOES THAT THUMB TASTE?
HEY, LINUS, DOES THAT THUMB TASTE REAL GOOD?
HEY, LINUS, HOW DOES THAT THUMB TASTE?
DON'T SAY IT!!
?

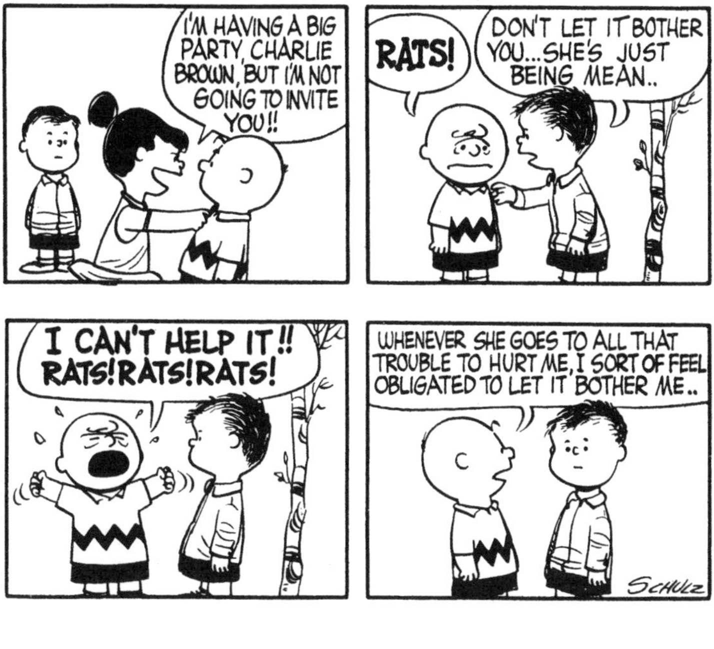
I'M HAVING A BIG PARTY, CHARLIE BROWN, BUT I'M NOT GOING TO INVITE YOU!!
RATS!
DON'T LET IT BOTHER YOU...SHE'S JUST BEING MEAN..
I CAN'T HELP IT!! RATS! RATS! RATS!
WHENEVER SHE GOES TO ALL THAT TROUBLE TO HURT ME, I SORT OF FEEL OBLIGATED TO LET IT BOTHER ME..
SCHULZ

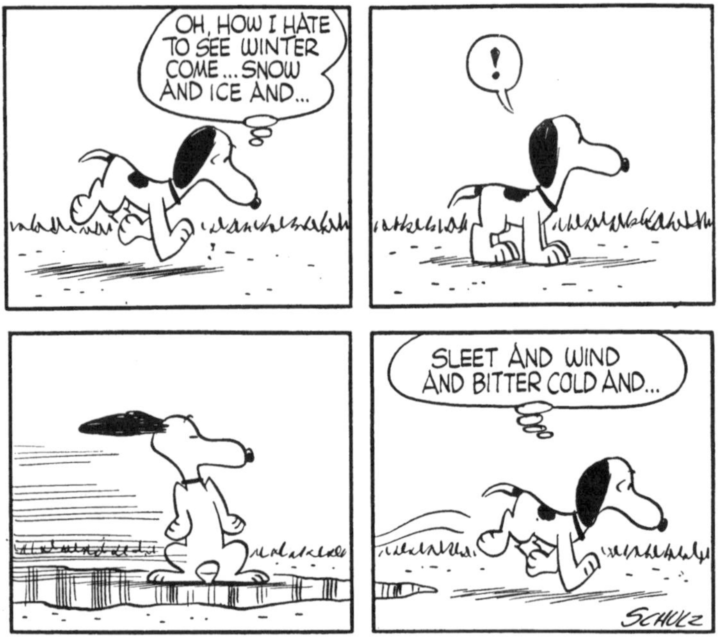
OH, HOW I HATE TO SEE WINTER COME... SNOW AND ICE AND...
!
SLEET AND WIND AND BITTER COLD AND...
SCHULZ

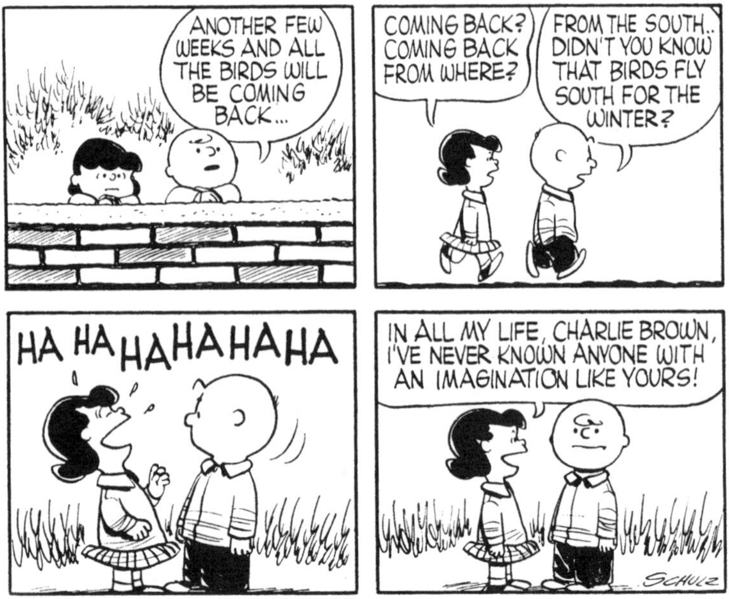
ANOTHER FEW WEEKS AND ALL THE BIRDS WILL BE COMING BACK...
COMING BACK? COMING BACK FROM WHERE?
FROM THE SOUTH.. DIDN'T YOU KNOW THAT BIRDS FLY SOUTH FOR THE WINTER?
HA HA HAHAHAHAHA
IN ALL MY LIFE, CHARLIE BROWN, I'VE NEVER KNOWN ANYONE WITH AN IMAGINATION LIKE YOURS!
SCHULZ

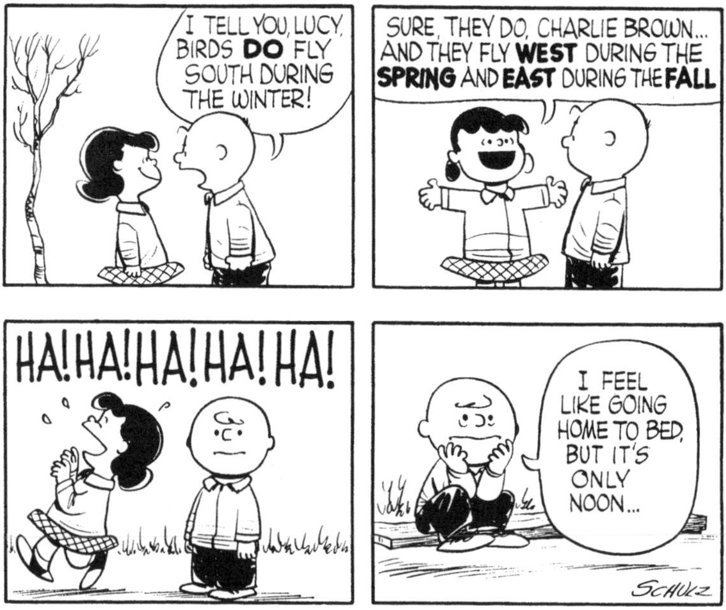
I TELL YOU, LUCY, BIRDS DO FLY SOUTH DURING THE WINTER!
SURE, THEY DO, CHARLIE BROWN... AND THEY FLY WEST DURING THE SPRING AND EAST DURING THE FALL
HA! HA! HA! HA! HA!
I FEEL LIKE GOING HOME TO BED, BUT IT'S ONLY NOON...
SCHULZ

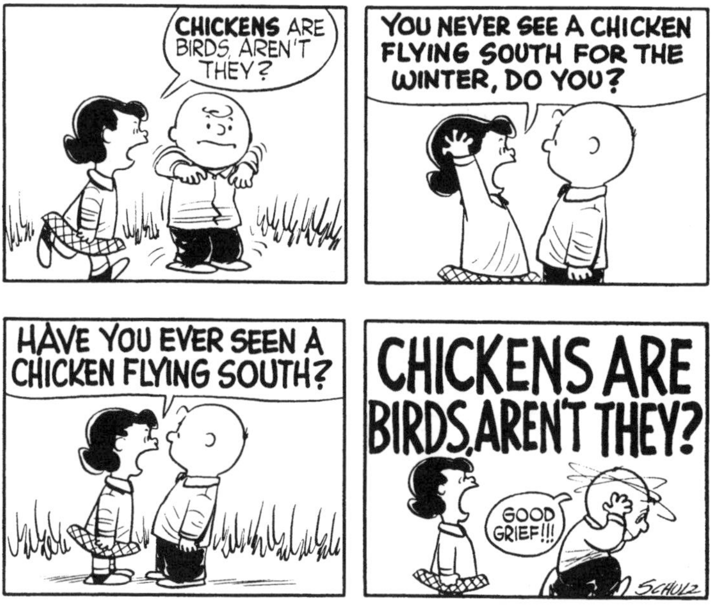
CHICKENS ARE BIRDS, AREN'T THEY?
YOU NEVER SEE A CHICKEN FLYING SOUTH FOR THE WINTER, DO YOU?
HAVE YOU EVER SEEN A CHICKEN FLYING SOUTH?
CHICKENS ARE BIRDS, AREN'T THEY?
GOOD GRIEF!!!
SCHULZ

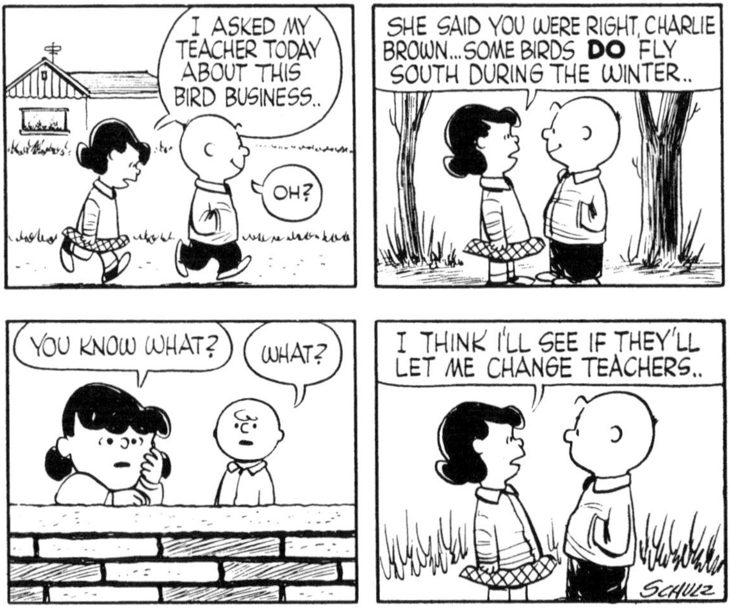
I ASKED MY TEACHER TODAY ABOUT THIS BIRD BUSINESS..
OH?
SHE SAID YOU WERE RIGHT, CHARLIE BROWN...SOME BIRDS **DO** FLY SOUTH DURING THE WINTER..
YOU KNOW WHAT?
WHAT?
I THINK I'LL SEE IF THEY'LL LET ME CHANGE TEACHERS..
SCHULZ

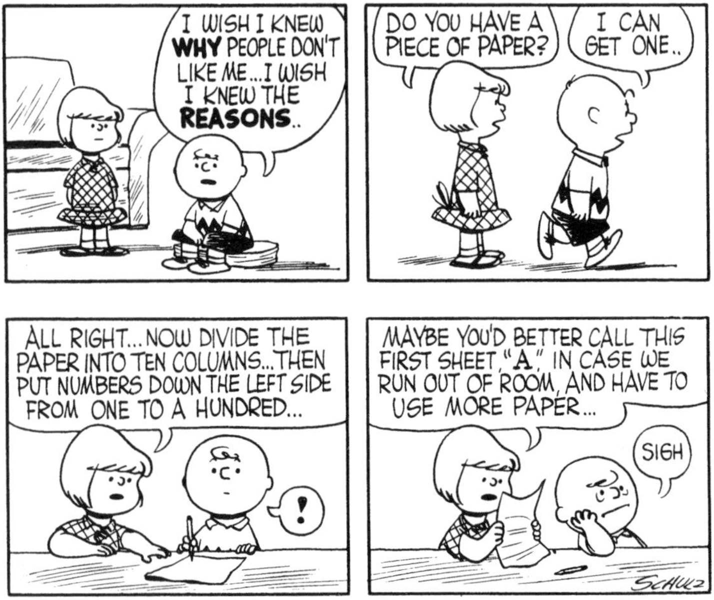
I WISH I KNEW **WHY** PEOPLE DON'T LIKE ME...I WISH I KNEW THE **REASONS**..
DO YOU HAVE A PIECE OF PAPER?
I CAN GET ONE..
ALL RIGHT...NOW DIVIDE THE PAPER INTO TEN COLUMNS...THEN PUT NUMBERS DOWN THE LEFT SIDE FROM ONE TO A HUNDRED...
!
MAYBE YOU'D BETTER CALL THIS FIRST SHEET, "**A**," IN CASE WE RUN OUT OF ROOM, AND HAVE TO USE MORE PAPER...
SIGH
SCHULZ

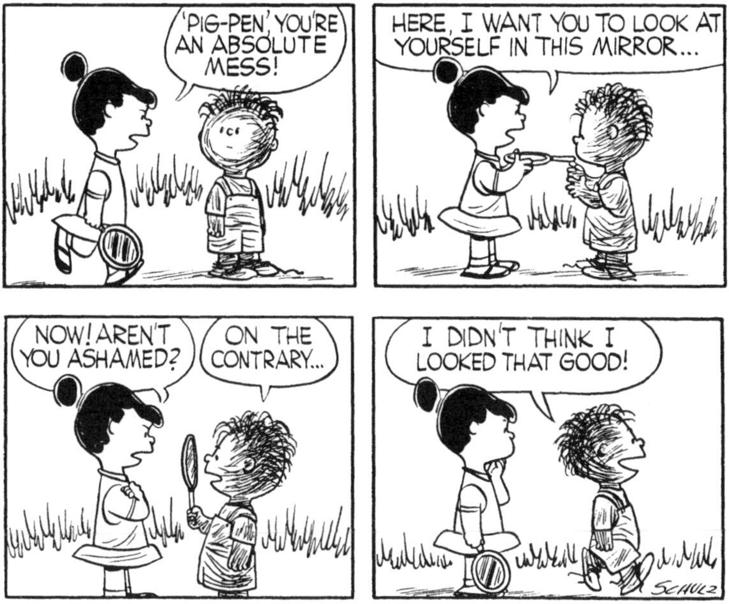
'PIG-PEN,' YOU'RE AN ABSOLUTE MESS!
HERE, I WANT YOU TO LOOK AT YOURSELF IN THIS MIRROR...
NOW! AREN'T YOU ASHAMED?
ON THE CONTRARY...
I DIDN'T THINK I LOOKED THAT GOOD!
SCHULZ

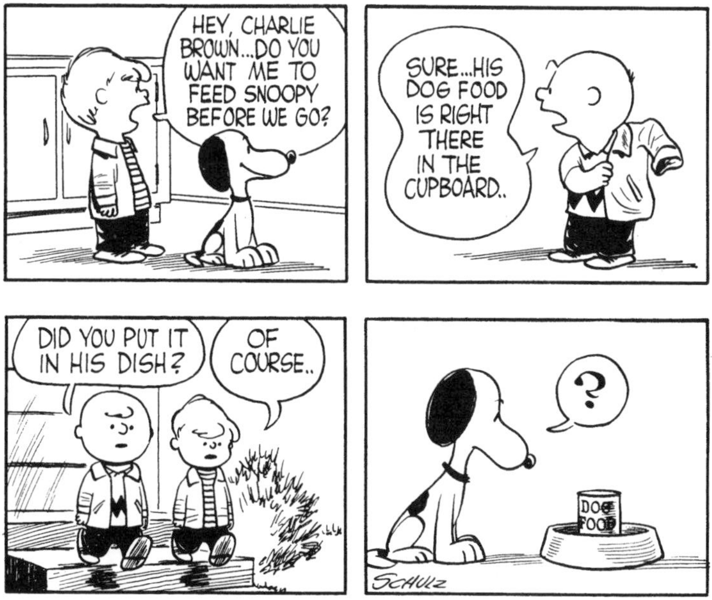
HEY, CHARLIE BROWN...DO YOU WANT ME TO FEED SNOOPY BEFORE WE GO?
SURE...HIS DOG FOOD IS RIGHT THERE IN THE CUPBOARD..
DID YOU PUT IT IN HIS DISH?
OF COURSE..
?
DOG FOOD
SCHULZ

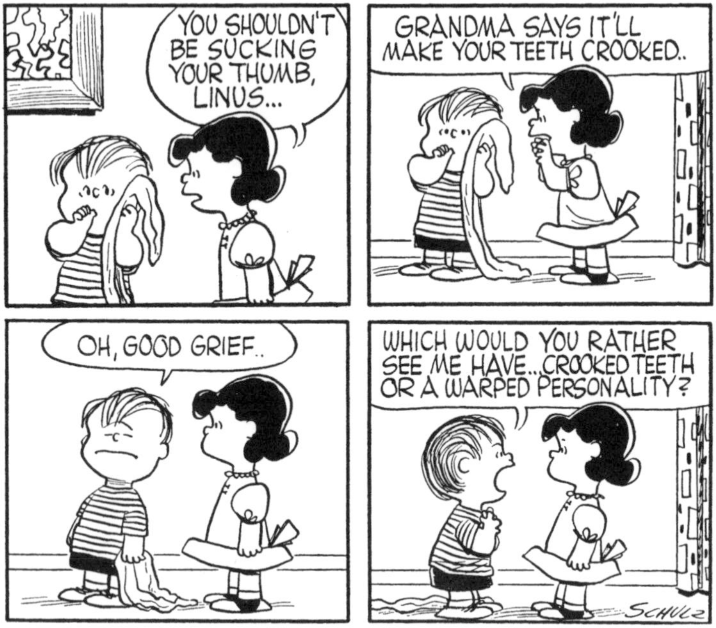
YOU SHOULDN'T BE SUCKING YOUR THUMB, LINUS...
GRANDMA SAYS IT'LL MAKE YOUR TEETH CROOKED..
OH, GOOD GRIEF..
WHICH WOULD YOU RATHER SEE ME HAVE...CROOKED TEETH OR A WARPED PERSONALITY?
SCHULZ

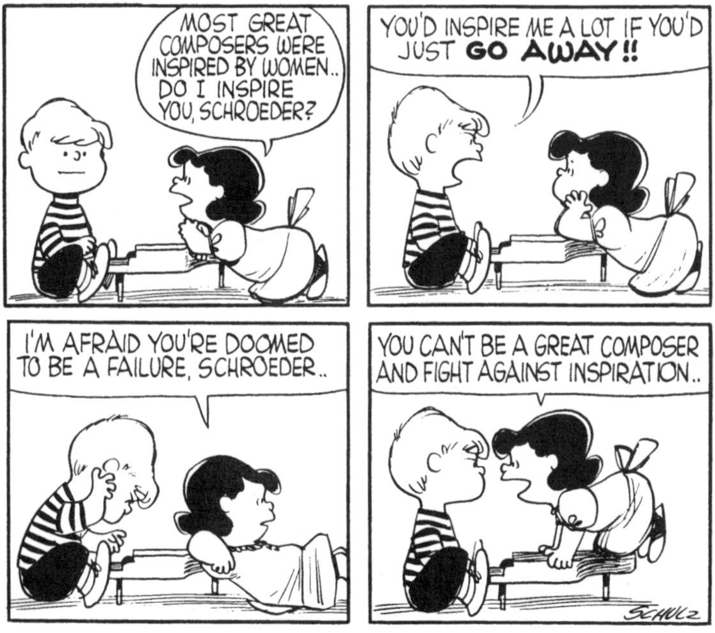
MOST GREAT COMPOSERS WERE INSPIRED BY WOMEN.. DO I INSPIRE YOU, SCHROEDER?
YOU'D INSPIRE ME A LOT IF YOU'D JUST **GO AWAY!!**
I'M AFRAID YOU'RE DOOMED TO BE A FAILURE, SCHROEDER..
YOU CAN'T BE A GREAT COMPOSER AND FIGHT AGAINST INSPIRATION..
SCHULZ

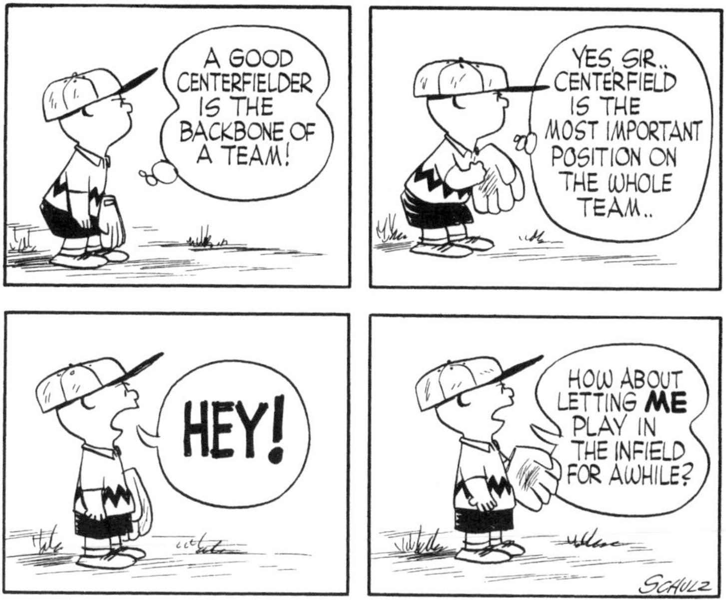
A GOOD CENTERFIELDER IS THE BACKBONE OF A TEAM!
YES, SIR.. CENTERFIELD IS THE MOST IMPORTANT POSITION ON THE WHOLE TEAM..
HEY!
HOW ABOUT LETTING ME PLAY IN THE INFIELD FOR AWHILE?
SCHULZ

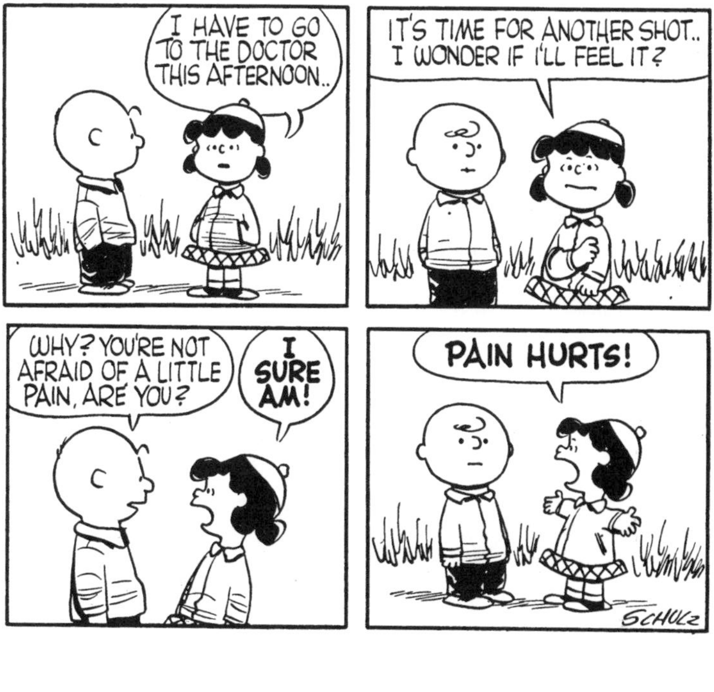
I HAVE TO GO TO THE DOCTOR THIS AFTERNOON..
IT'S TIME FOR ANOTHER SHOT.. I WONDER IF I'LL FEEL IT?
WHY? YOU'RE NOT AFRAID OF A LITTLE PAIN, ARE YOU?
I SURE AM!
PAIN HURTS!
SCHULZ

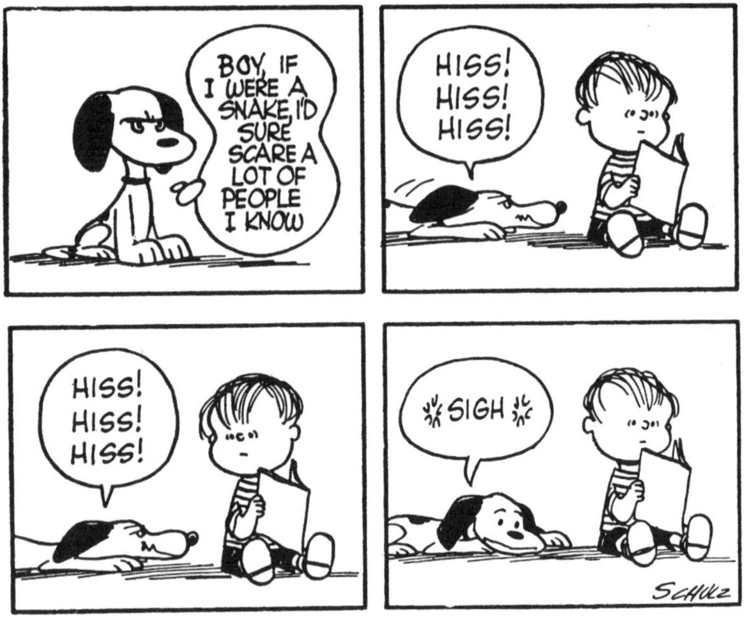
BOY, IF I WERE A SNAKE, I'D SURE SCARE A LOT OF PEOPLE I KNOW
HISS! HISS! HISS!
HISS! HISS! HISS!
SIGH
SCHULZ

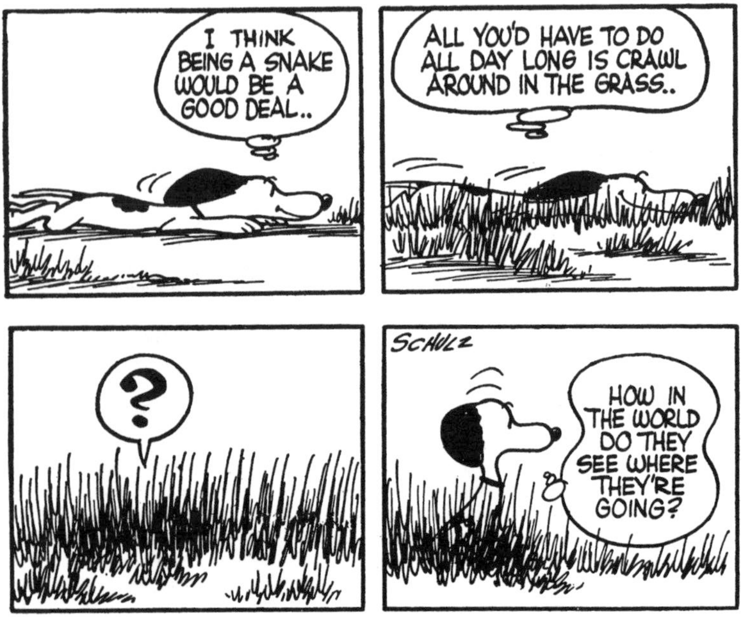
I THINK BEING A SNAKE WOULD BE A GOOD DEAL..
ALL YOU'D HAVE TO DO ALL DAY LONG IS CRAWL AROUND IN THE GRASS..
?
SCHULZ
HOW IN THE WORLD DO THEY SEE WHERE THEY'RE GOING?

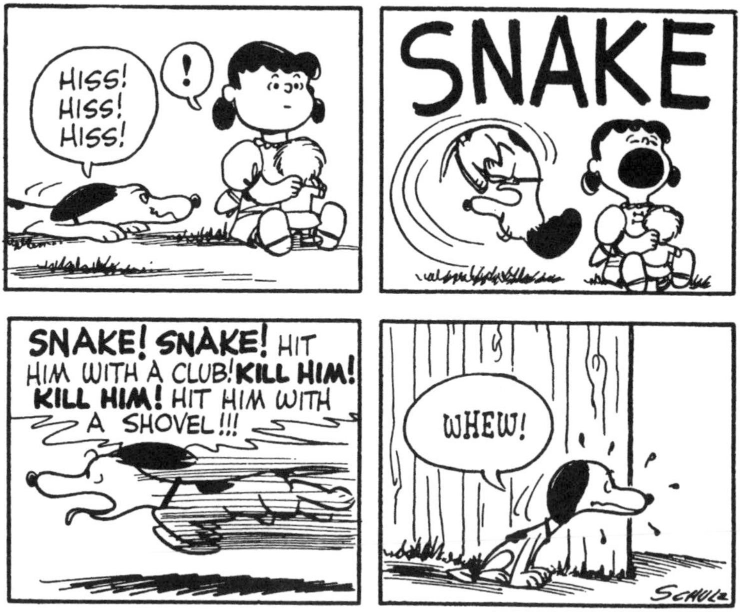
HISS! HISS! HISS!
!
SNAKE
SNAKE! SNAKE! HIT HIM WITH A CLUB! KILL HIM! KILL HIM! HIT HIM WITH A SHOVEL!!!
WHEW!
SCHULZ

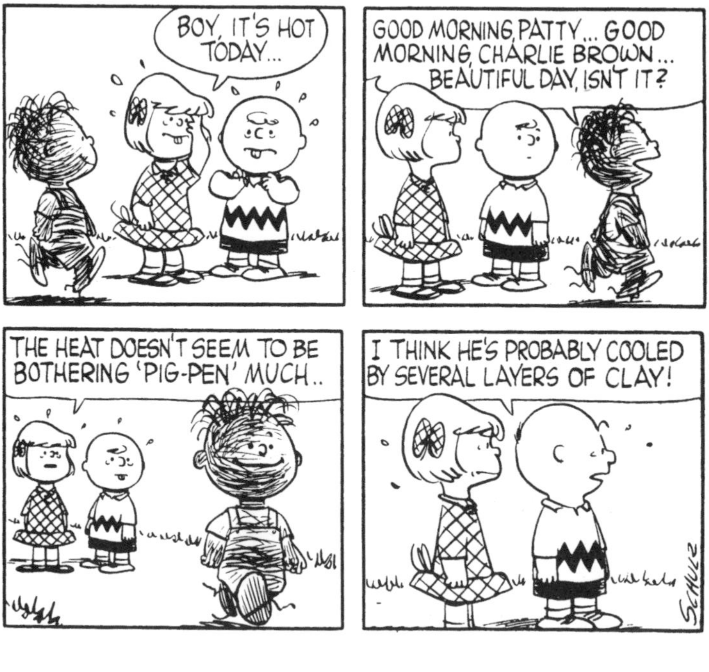
BOY, IT'S HOT TODAY...
GOOD MORNING, PATTY... GOOD MORNING, CHARLIE BROWN... BEAUTIFUL DAY, ISN'T IT?
THE HEAT DOESN'T SEEM TO BE BOTHERING 'PIG-PEN' MUCH..
I THINK HE'S PROBABLY COOLED BY SEVERAL LAYERS OF CLAY!
SCHULZ

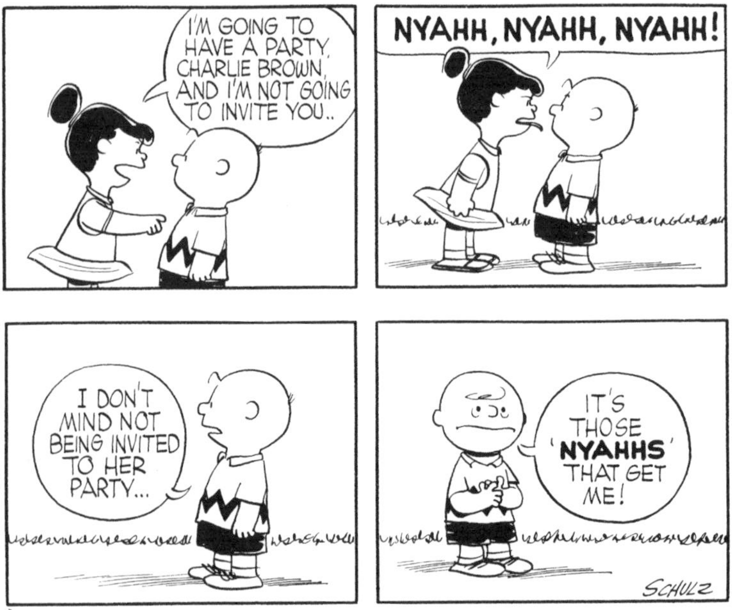

I'M GOING TO HAVE A PARTY, CHARLIE BROWN, AND I'M NOT GOING TO INVITE YOU..
NYAHH, NYAHH, NYAHH!
I DON'T MIND NOT BEING INVITED TO HER PARTY...
IT'S THOSE 'NYAHHS' THAT GET ME!
SCHULZ

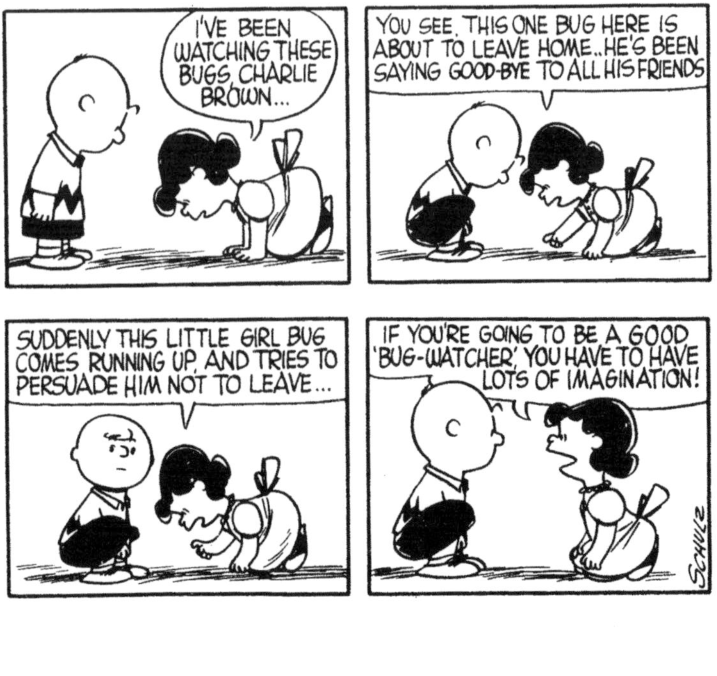

I'VE BEEN WATCHING THESE BUGS, CHARLIE BROWN...
YOU SEE, THIS ONE BUG HERE IS ABOUT TO LEAVE HOME..HE'S BEEN SAYING GOOD-BYE TO ALL HIS FRIENDS
SUDDENLY THIS LITTLE GIRL BUG COMES RUNNING UP, AND TRIES TO PERSUADE HIM NOT TO LEAVE...
IF YOU'RE GOING TO BE A GOOD 'BUG-WATCHER,' YOU HAVE TO HAVE LOTS OF IMAGINATION!
SCHULZ

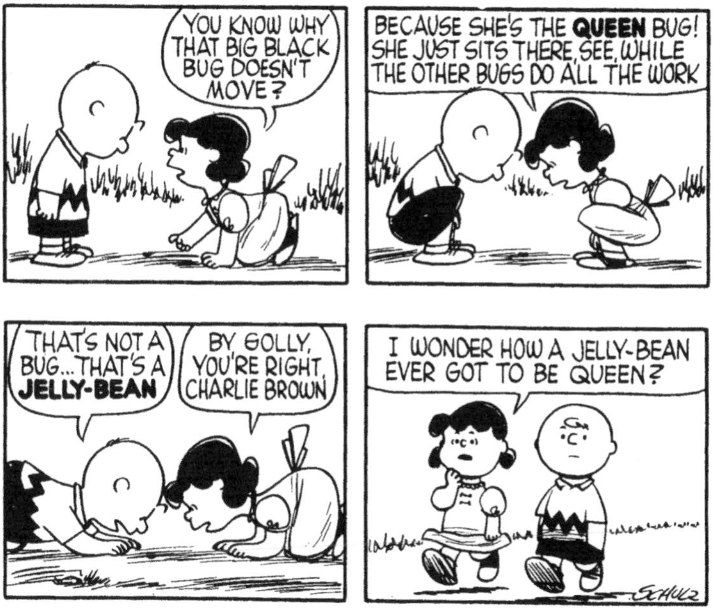
YOU KNOW WHY THAT BIG BLACK BUG DOESN'T MOVE?
BECAUSE SHE'S THE **QUEEN** BUG! SHE JUST SITS THERE, SEE, WHILE THE OTHER BUGS DO ALL THE WORK
THAT'S NOT A BUG...THAT'S A **JELLY-BEAN**
BY GOLLY, YOU'RE RIGHT, CHARLIE BROWN
I WONDER HOW A JELLY-BEAN EVER GOT TO BE QUEEN?
SCHULZ

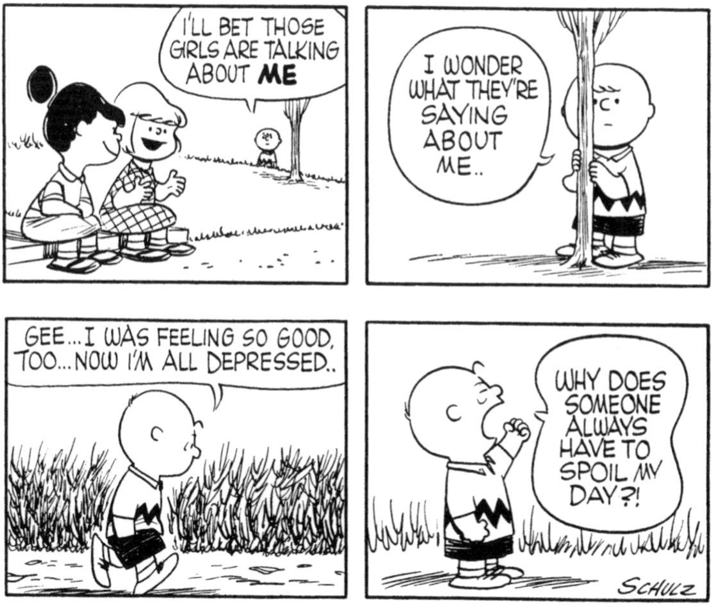
I'LL BET THOSE GIRLS ARE TALKING ABOUT **ME**
I WONDER WHAT THEY'RE SAYING ABOUT ME..
GEE...I WAS FEELING SO GOOD, TOO...NOW I'M ALL DEPRESSED..
WHY DOES SOMEONE ALWAYS HAVE TO SPOIL MY DAY?!
SCHULZ

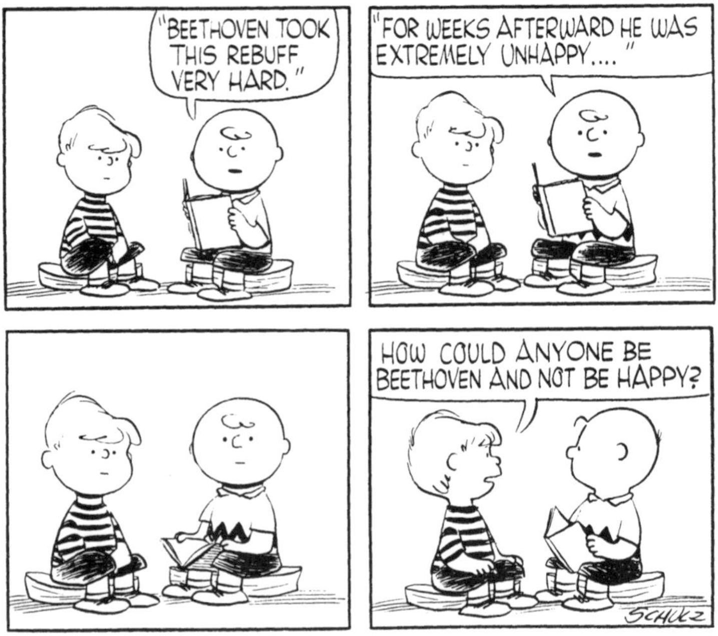
"BEETHOVEN TOOK THIS REBUFF VERY HARD."
"FOR WEEKS AFTERWARD HE WAS EXTREMELY UNHAPPY...."
HOW COULD ANYONE BE BEETHOVEN AND NOT BE HAPPY?
SCHULZ

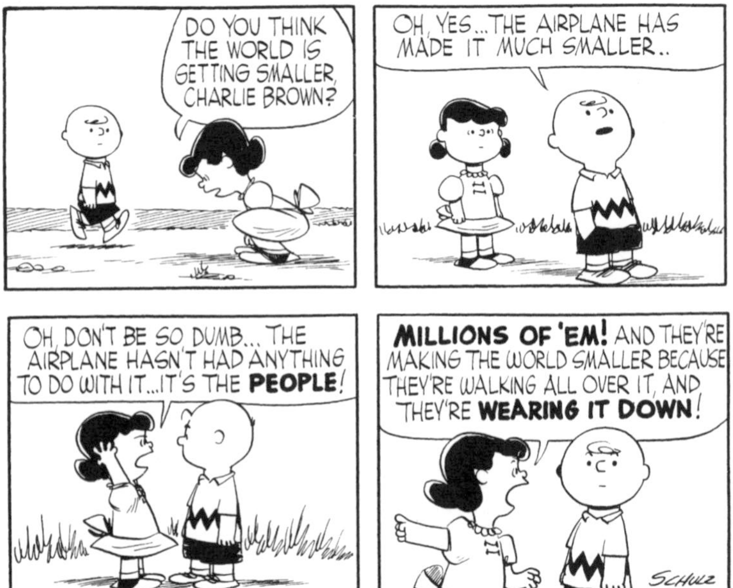
DO YOU THINK THE WORLD IS GETTING SMALLER, CHARLIE BROWN?
OH, YES...THE AIRPLANE HAS MADE IT MUCH SMALLER..
OH, DON'T BE SO DUMB... THE AIRPLANE HASN'T HAD ANYTHING TO DO WITH IT...IT'S THE PEOPLE!
MILLIONS OF 'EM! AND THEY'RE MAKING THE WORLD SMALLER BECAUSE THEY'RE WALKING ALL OVER IT, AND THEY'RE WEARING IT DOWN!
SCHULZ

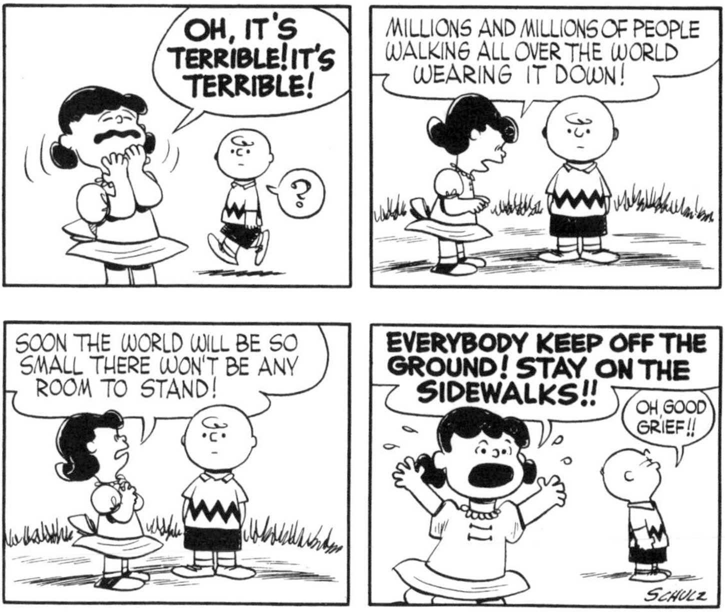

OH, IT'S TERRIBLE! IT'S TERRIBLE!
?
MILLIONS AND MILLIONS OF PEOPLE WALKING ALL OVER THE WORLD WEARING IT DOWN!
SOON THE WORLD WILL BE SO SMALL THERE WON'T BE ANY ROOM TO STAND!
EVERYBODY KEEP OFF THE GROUND! STAY ON THE SIDEWALKS!!
OH GOOD GRIEF!!
SCHULZ

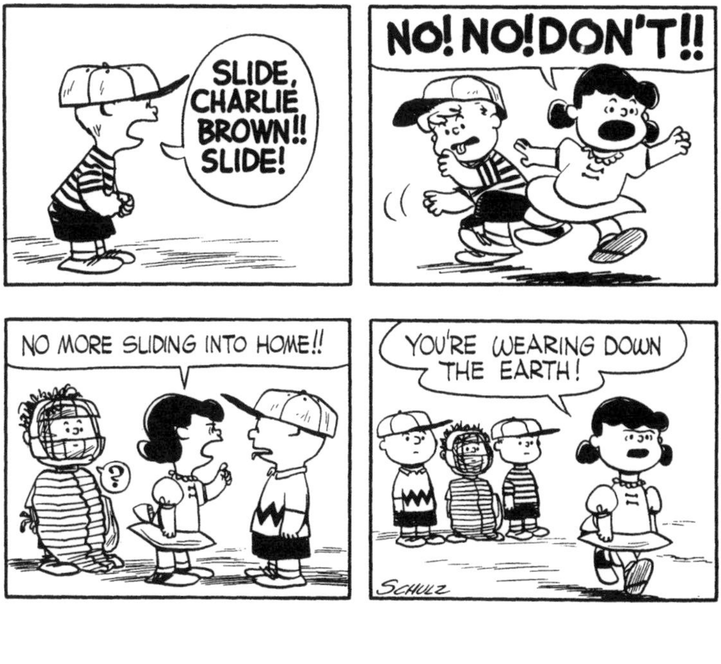

SLIDE, CHARLIE BROWN!! SLIDE!
NO! NO! DON'T!!
NO MORE SLIDING INTO HOME!!
?
YOU'RE WEARING DOWN THE EARTH!
SCHULZ

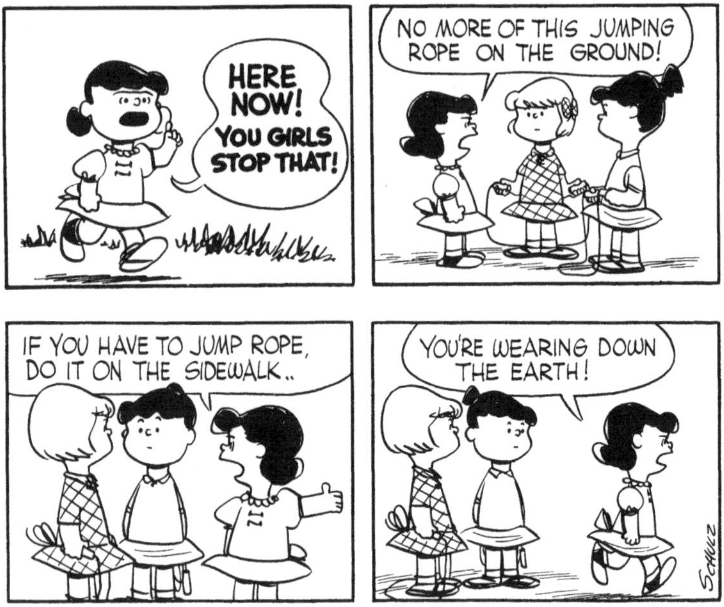
HERE NOW! YOU GIRLS STOP THAT!
NO MORE OF THIS JUMPING ROPE ON THE GROUND!
IF YOU HAVE TO JUMP ROPE, DO IT ON THE SIDEWALK..
YOU'RE WEARING DOWN THE EARTH!
SCHULZ

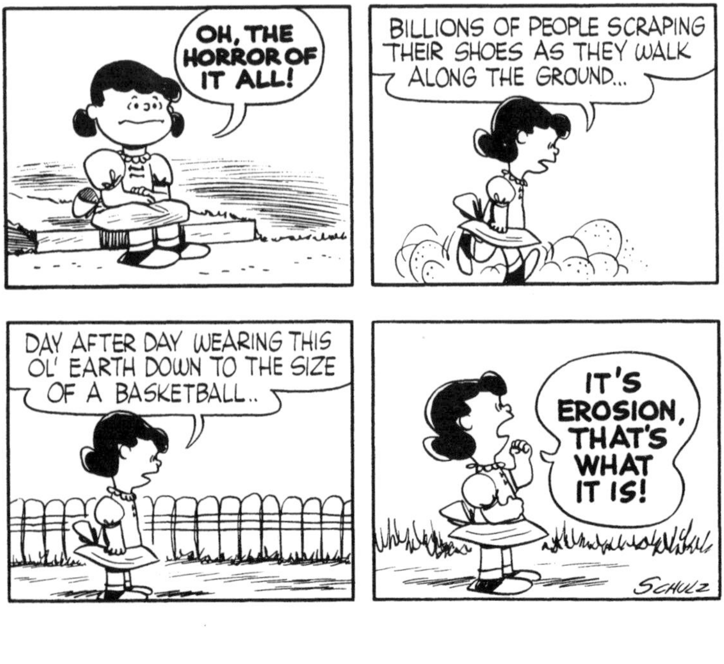
OH, THE HORROR OF IT ALL!
BILLIONS OF PEOPLE SCRAPING THEIR SHOES AS THEY WALK ALONG THE GROUND...
DAY AFTER DAY WEARING THIS OL' EARTH DOWN TO THE SIZE OF A BASKETBALL..
IT'S EROSION, THAT'S WHAT IT IS!
SCHULZ

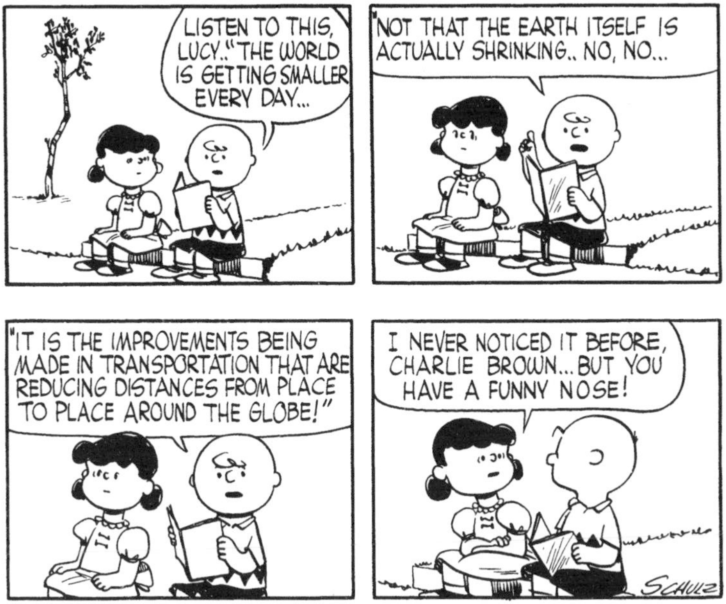
LISTEN TO THIS, LUCY.."THE WORLD IS GETTING SMALLER EVERY DAY...
"NOT THAT THE EARTH ITSELF IS ACTUALLY SHRINKING.. NO, NO...
"IT IS THE IMPROVEMENTS BEING MADE IN TRANSPORTATION THAT ARE REDUCING DISTANCES FROM PLACE TO PLACE AROUND THE GLOBE!"
I NEVER NOTICED IT BEFORE, CHARLIE BROWN... BUT YOU HAVE A FUNNY NOSE!
SCHULZ

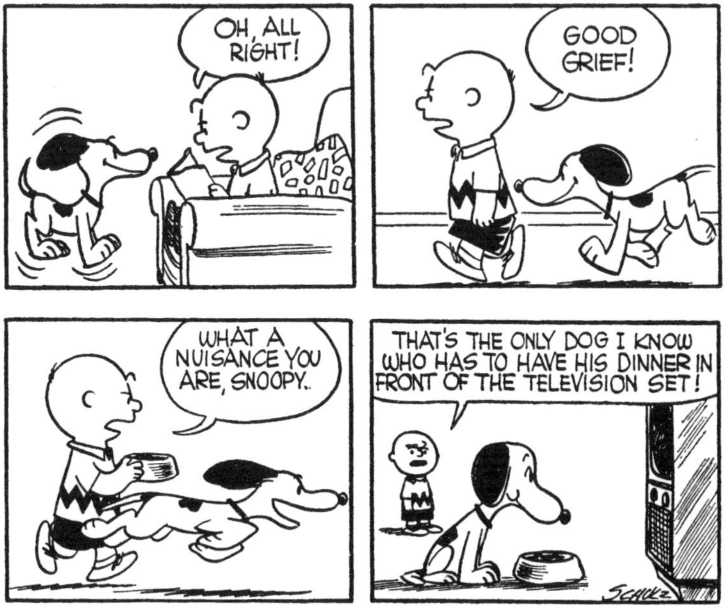
OH, ALL RIGHT!
GOOD GRIEF!
WHAT A NUISANCE YOU ARE, SNOOPY..
THAT'S THE ONLY DOG I KNOW WHO HAS TO HAVE HIS DINNER IN FRONT OF THE TELEVISION SET!
SCHULZ

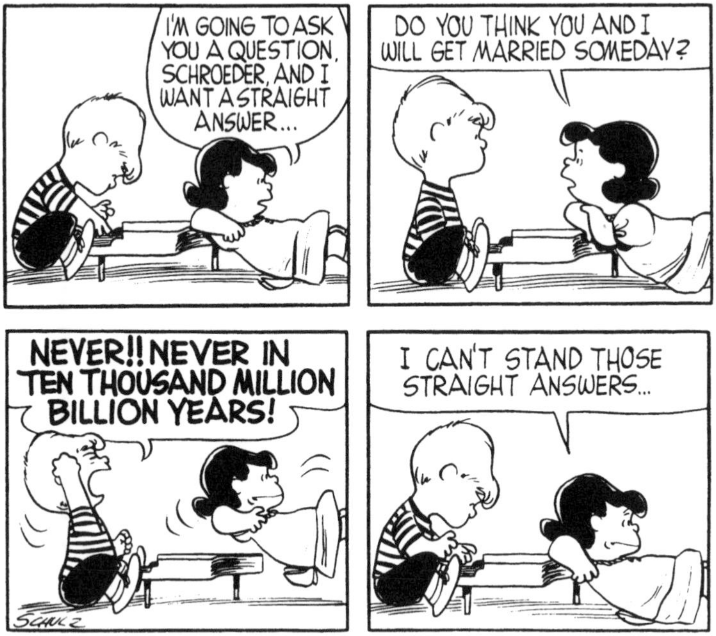
I'M GOING TO ASK YOU A QUESTION, SCHROEDER, AND I WANT A STRAIGHT ANSWER...
DO YOU THINK YOU AND I WILL GET MARRIED SOMEDAY?
NEVER!! NEVER IN TEN THOUSAND MILLION BILLION YEARS!
I CAN'T STAND THOSE STRAIGHT ANSWERS...
SCHULZ

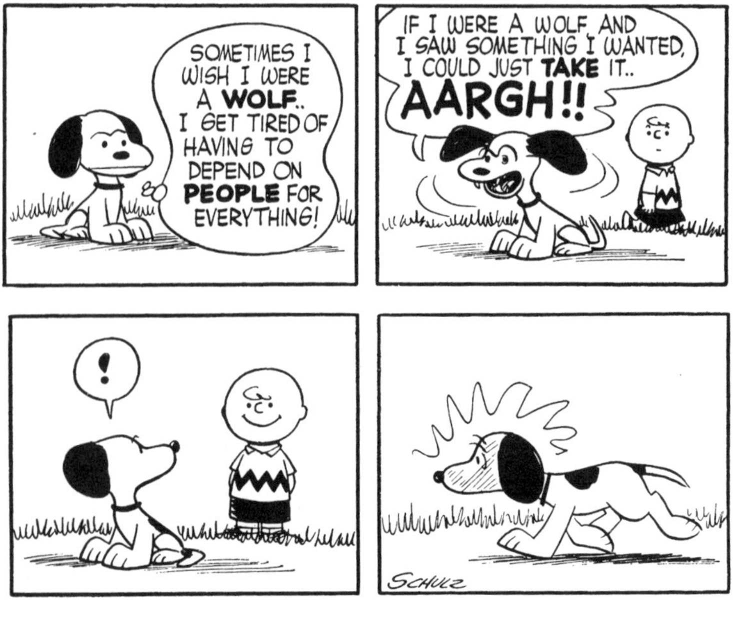
SOMETIMES I WISH I WERE A WOLF.. I GET TIRED OF HAVING TO DEPEND ON PEOPLE FOR EVERYTHING!
IF I WERE A WOLF AND I SAW SOMETHING I WANTED, I COULD JUST TAKE IT..
AARGH!!
!
SCHULZ

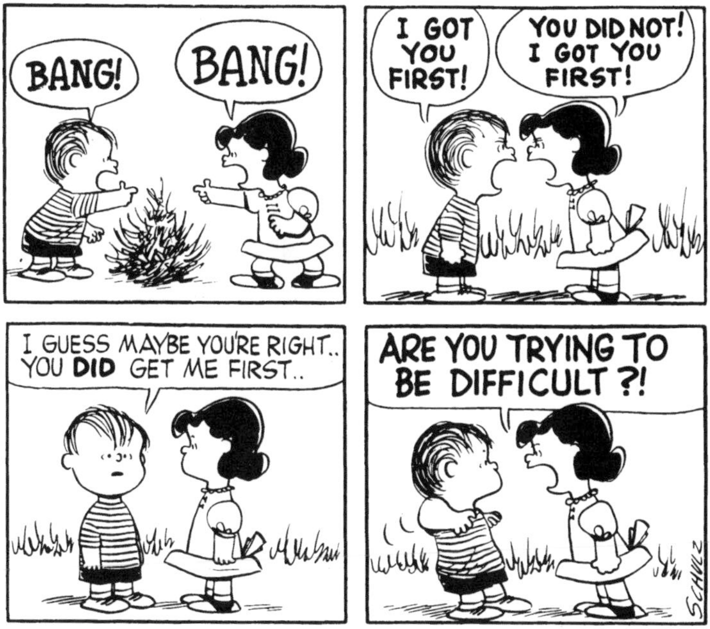
BANG!
BANG!
I GOT YOU FIRST!
YOU DID NOT! I GOT YOU FIRST!
I GUESS MAYBE YOU'RE RIGHT.. YOU **DID** GET ME FIRST..
ARE YOU TRYING TO BE DIFFICULT ?!
SCHULZ

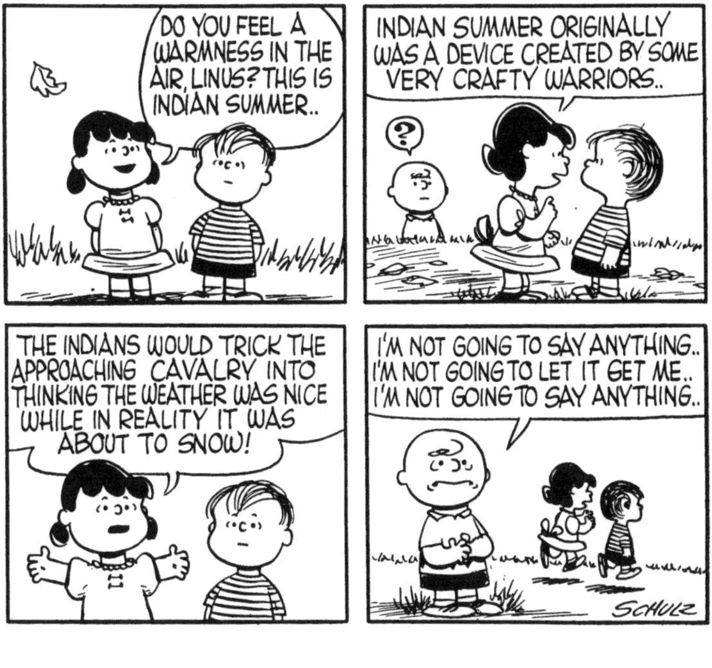
DO YOU FEEL A WARMNESS IN THE AIR, LINUS? THIS IS INDIAN SUMMER..
INDIAN SUMMER ORIGINALLY WAS A DEVICE CREATED BY SOME VERY CRAFTY WARRIORS..
?
THE INDIANS WOULD TRICK THE APPROACHING CAVALRY INTO THINKING THE WEATHER WAS NICE WHILE IN REALITY IT WAS ABOUT TO SNOW!
I'M NOT GOING TO SAY ANYTHING.. I'M NOT GOING TO LET IT GET ME.. I'M NOT GOING TO SAY ANYTHING..
SCHULZ

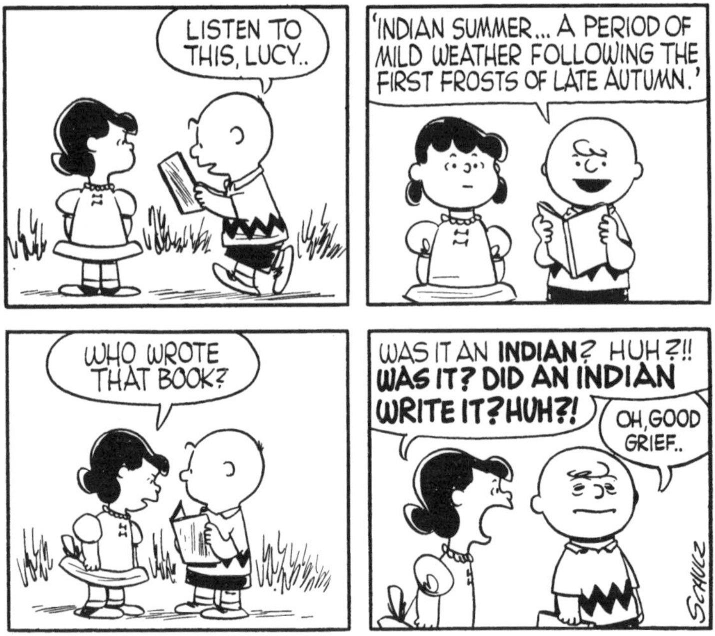
LISTEN TO THIS, LUCY..
'INDIAN SUMMER... A PERIOD OF MILD WEATHER FOLLOWING THE FIRST FROSTS OF LATE AUTUMN.'
WHO WROTE THAT BOOK?
WAS IT AN **INDIAN**? HUH?!! **WAS IT? DID AN INDIAN WRITE IT? HUH?!**
OH, GOOD GRIEF..
SCHULZ

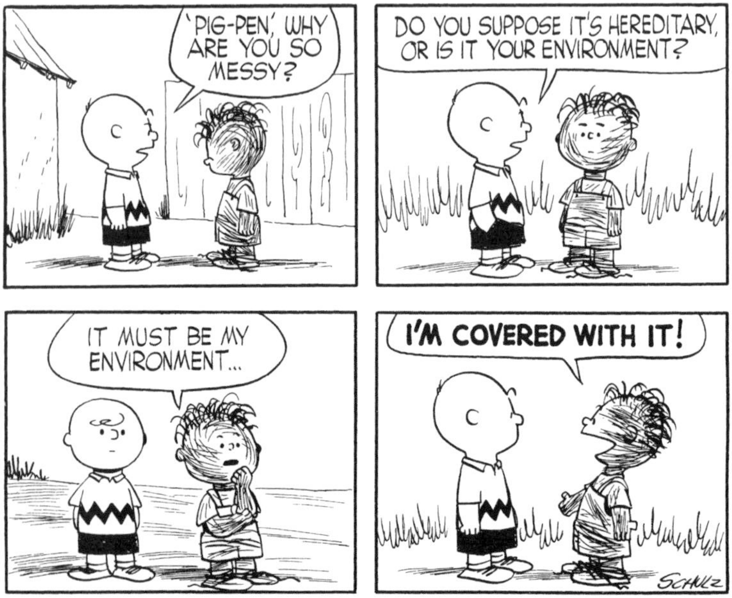
'PIG-PEN,' WHY ARE YOU SO MESSY?
DO YOU SUPPOSE IT'S HEREDITARY, OR IS IT YOUR ENVIRONMENT?
IT MUST BE MY ENVIRONMENT...
I'M COVERED WITH IT!
SCHULZ

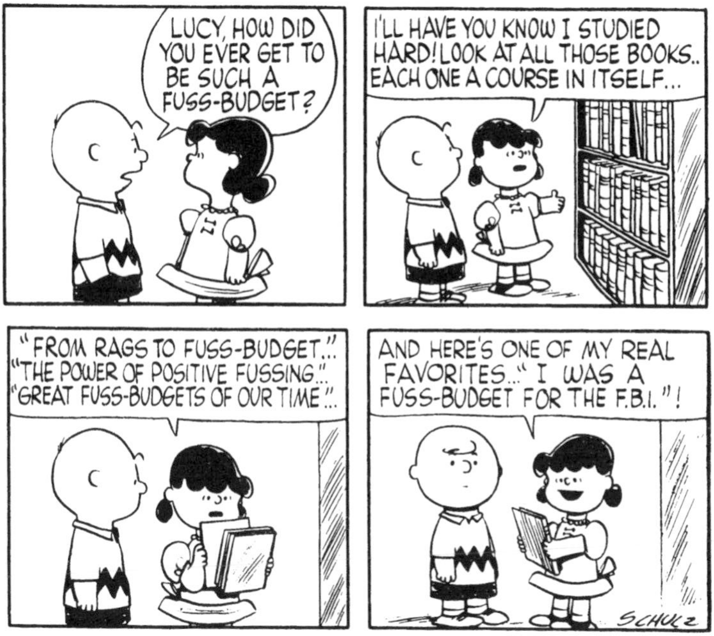
LUCY, HOW DID YOU EVER GET TO BE SUCH A FUSS-BUDGET?
I'LL HAVE YOU KNOW I STUDIED HARD! LOOK AT ALL THOSE BOOKS.. EACH ONE A COURSE IN ITSELF...
"FROM RAGS TO FUSS-BUDGET.." "THE POWER OF POSITIVE FUSSING.." "GREAT FUSS-BUDGETS OF OUR TIME"..
AND HERE'S ONE OF MY REAL FAVORITES.."I WAS A FUSS-BUDGET FOR THE F.B.I."!
SCHULZ

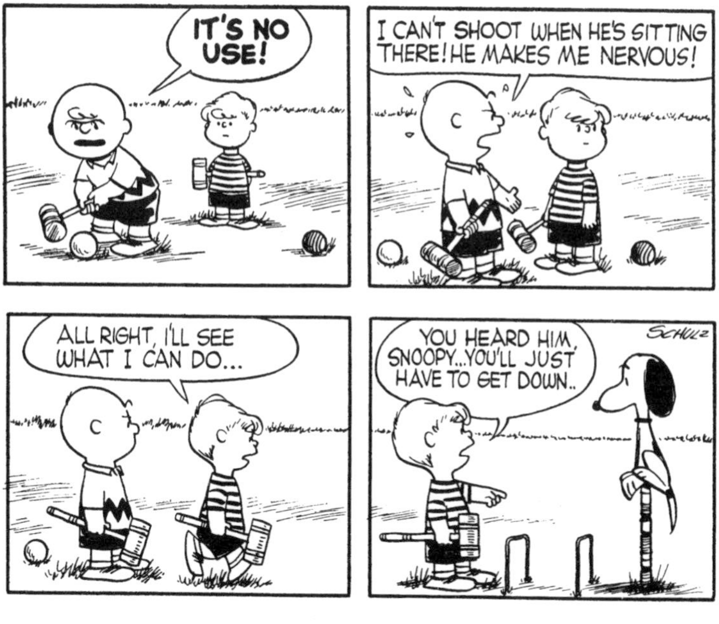
IT'S NO USE!
I CAN'T SHOOT WHEN HE'S SITTING THERE! HE MAKES ME NERVOUS!
ALL RIGHT, I'LL SEE WHAT I CAN DO...
SCHULZ
YOU HEARD HIM, SNOOPY...YOU'LL JUST HAVE TO GET DOWN..

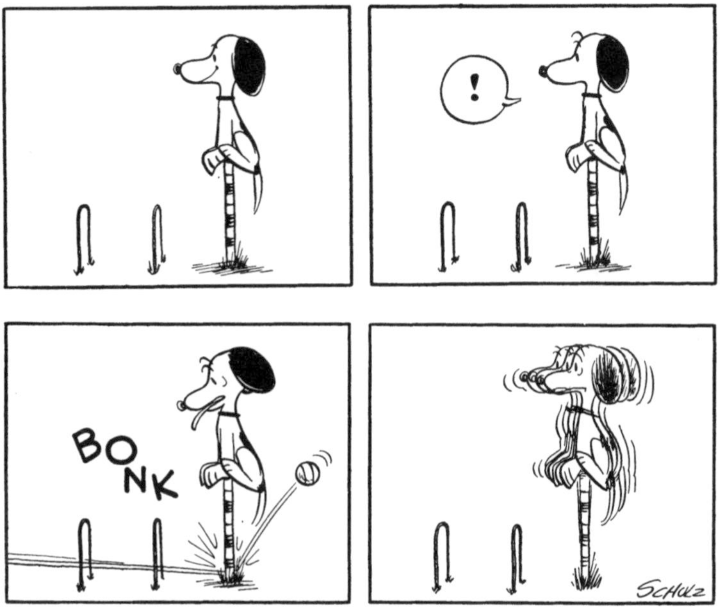
!
BONK
SCHULZ

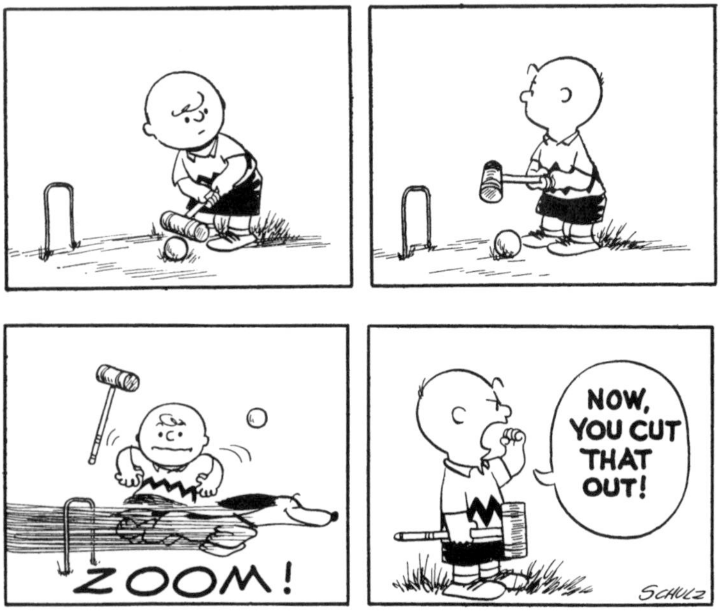
ZOOM!
NOW, YOU CUT THAT OUT!
SCHULZ

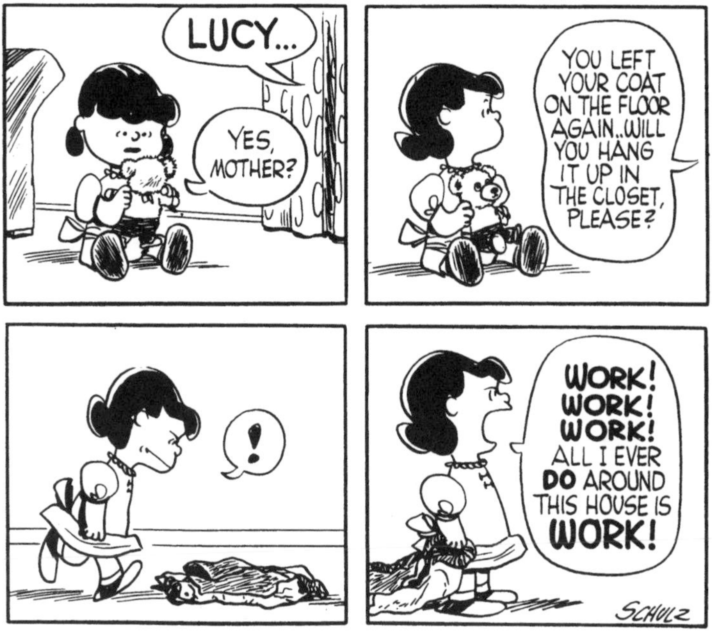
LUCY...
YES, MOTHER?
YOU LEFT YOUR COAT ON THE FLOOR AGAIN..WILL YOU HANG IT UP IN THE CLOSET, PLEASE?
!
WORK! WORK! WORK! ALL I EVER DO AROUND THIS HOUSE IS WORK!
SCHULZ

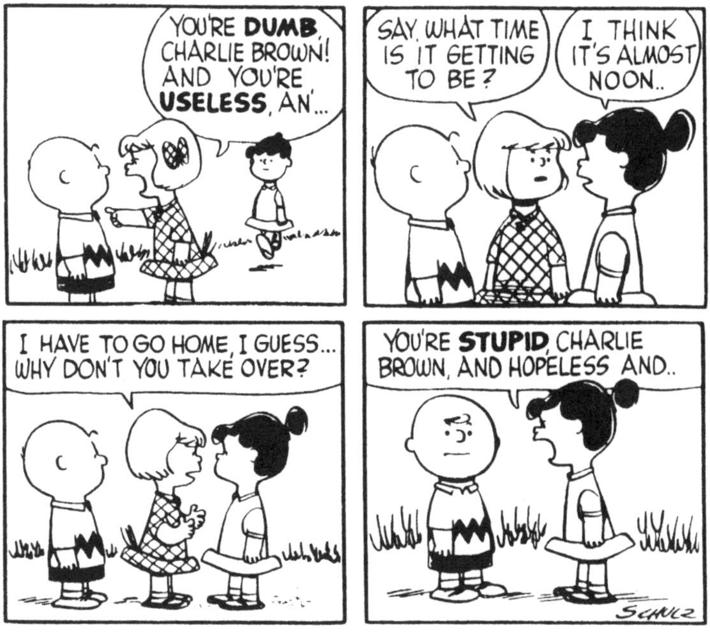
YOU'RE DUMB, CHARLIE BROWN! AND YOU'RE USELESS, AN'...
SAY, WHAT TIME IS IT GETTING TO BE?
I THINK IT'S ALMOST NOON..
I HAVE TO GO HOME, I GUESS... WHY DON'T YOU TAKE OVER?
YOU'RE STUPID, CHARLIE BROWN, AND HOPELESS AND..
SCHULZ

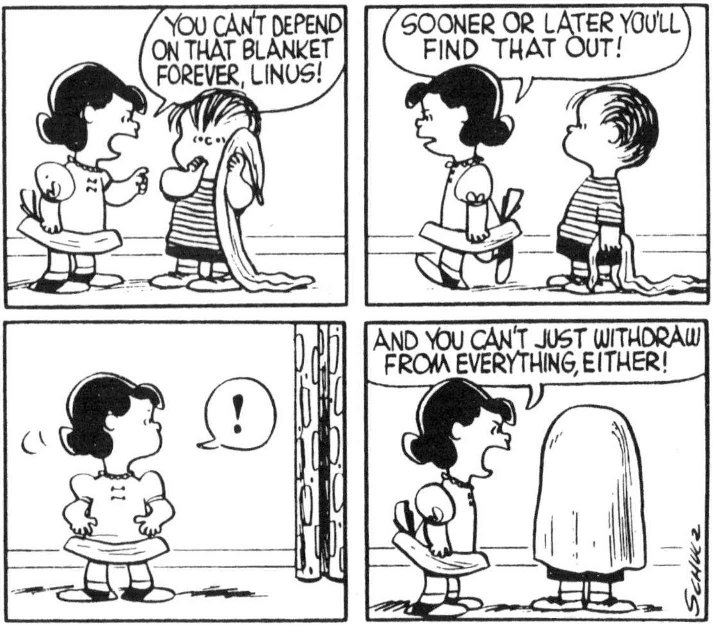
YOU CAN'T DEPEND ON THAT BLANKET FOREVER, LINUS!
SOONER OR LATER YOU'LL FIND THAT OUT!
!
AND YOU CAN'T JUST WITHDRAW FROM EVERYTHING, EITHER!
SCHULZ

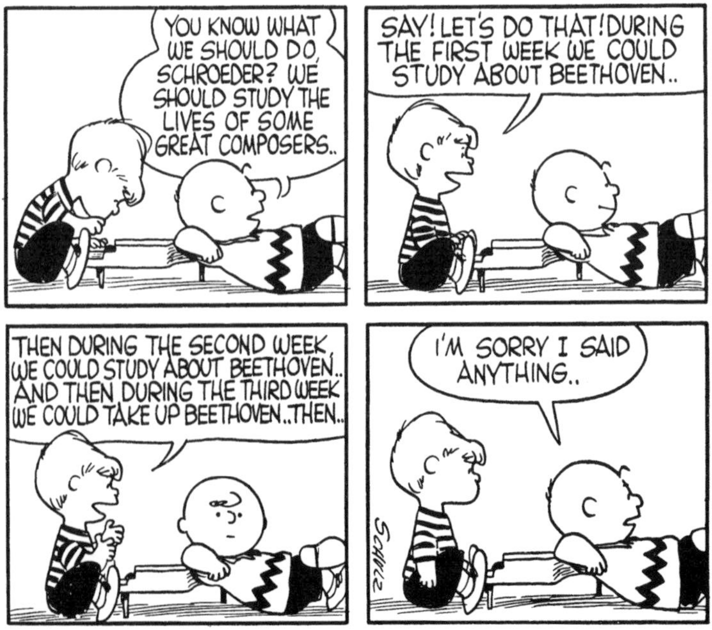
YOU KNOW WHAT WE SHOULD DO, SCHROEDER? WE SHOULD STUDY THE LIVES OF SOME GREAT COMPOSERS..
SAY! LET'S DO THAT! DURING THE FIRST WEEK WE COULD STUDY ABOUT BEETHOVEN..
THEN DURING THE SECOND WEEK, WE COULD STUDY ABOUT BEETHOVEN.. AND THEN DURING THE THIRD WEEK WE COULD TAKE UP BEETHOVEN..THEN..
I'M SORRY I SAID ANYTHING..
SCHULZ

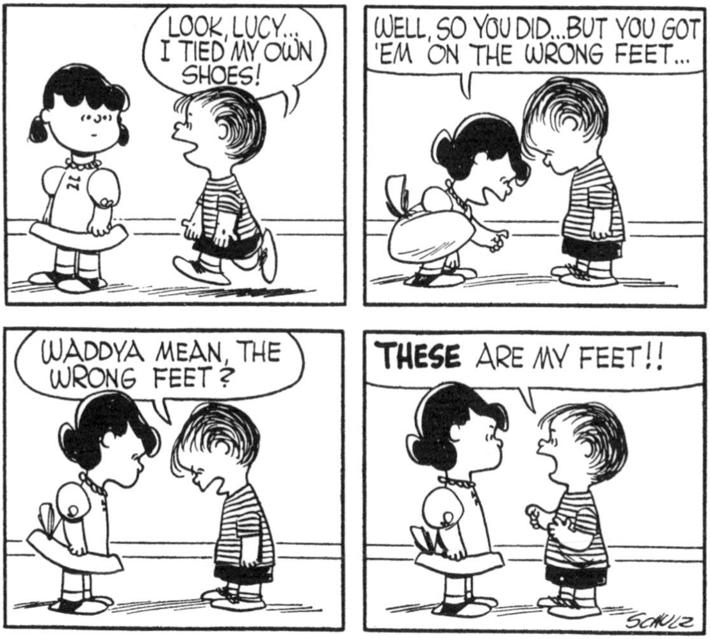
LOOK, LUCY... I TIED MY OWN SHOES!
WELL, SO YOU DID...BUT YOU GOT 'EM ON THE WRONG FEET...
WADDYA MEAN, THE WRONG FEET?
THESE ARE MY FEET!!
SCHULZ

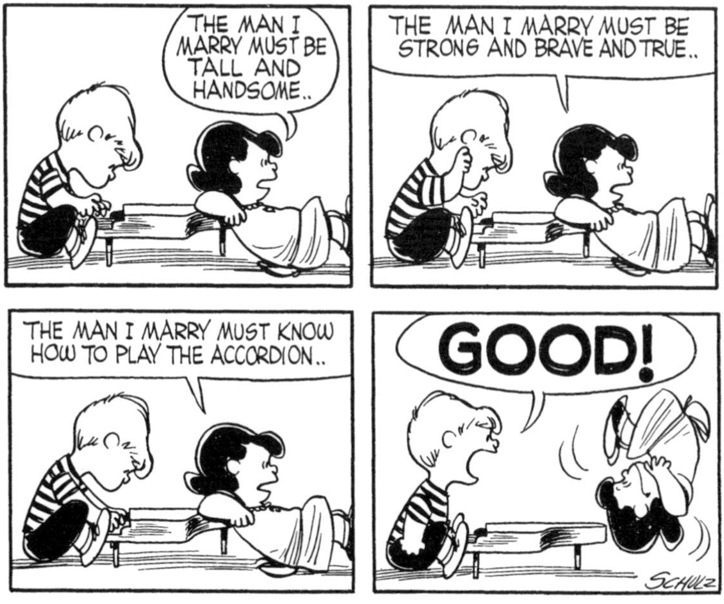
THE MAN I MARRY MUST BE TALL AND HANDSOME..
THE MAN I MARRY MUST BE STRONG AND BRAVE AND TRUE..
THE MAN I MARRY MUST KNOW HOW TO PLAY THE ACCORDION..
GOOD!
SCHULZ

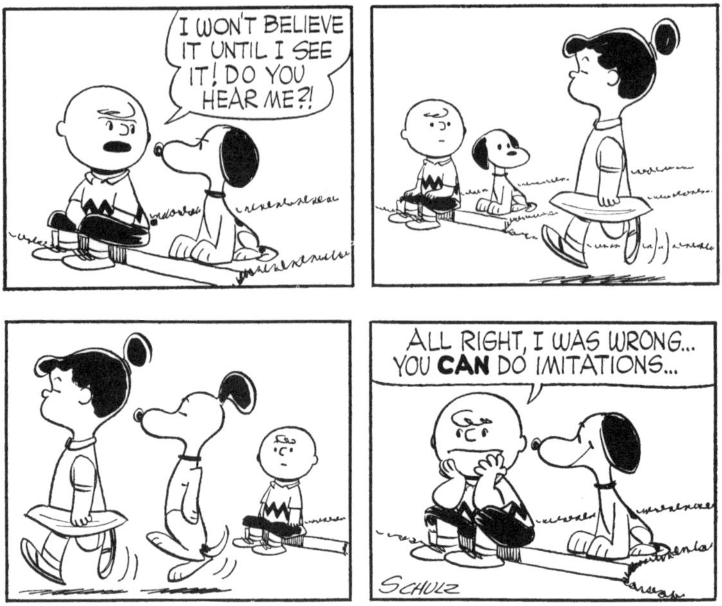
I WON'T BELIEVE IT UNTIL I SEE IT! DO YOU HEAR ME?!
ALL RIGHT, I WAS WRONG... YOU **CAN** DO IMITATIONS...
SCHULZ

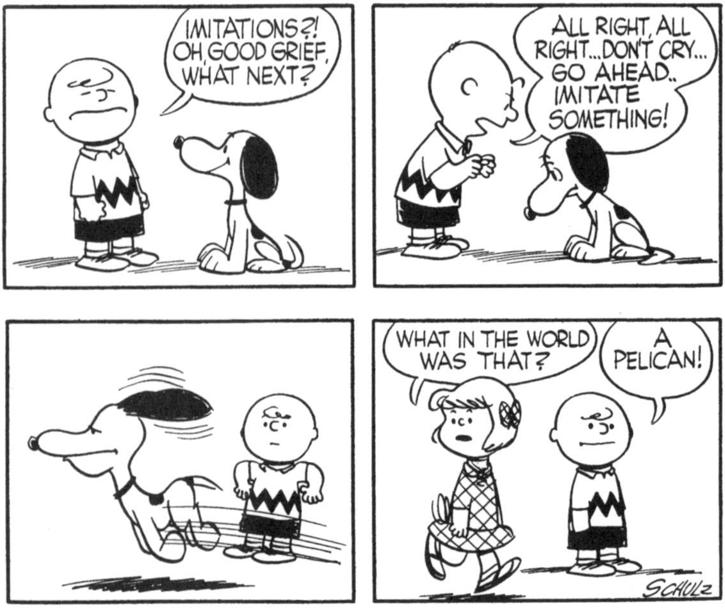
IMITATIONS?! OH, GOOD GRIEF, WHAT NEXT?
ALL RIGHT, ALL RIGHT...DON'T CRY... GO AHEAD.. IMITATE SOMETHING!
WHAT IN THE WORLD WAS THAT?
A PELICAN!
SCHULZ

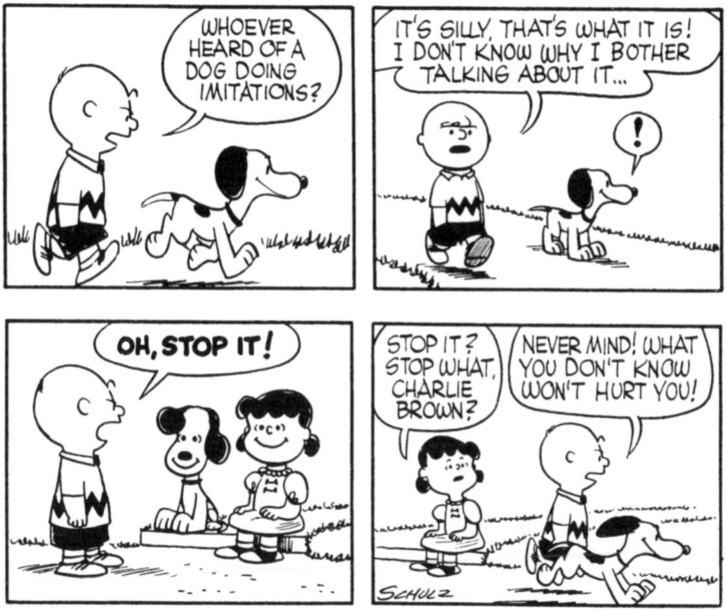
WHOEVER HEARD OF A DOG DOING IMITATIONS?
IT'S SILLY, THAT'S WHAT IT IS! I DON'T KNOW WHY I BOTHER TALKING ABOUT IT...
!
OH, STOP IT!
STOP IT? STOP WHAT, CHARLIE BROWN?
NEVER MIND! WHAT YOU DON'T KNOW WON'T HURT YOU!
SCHULZ

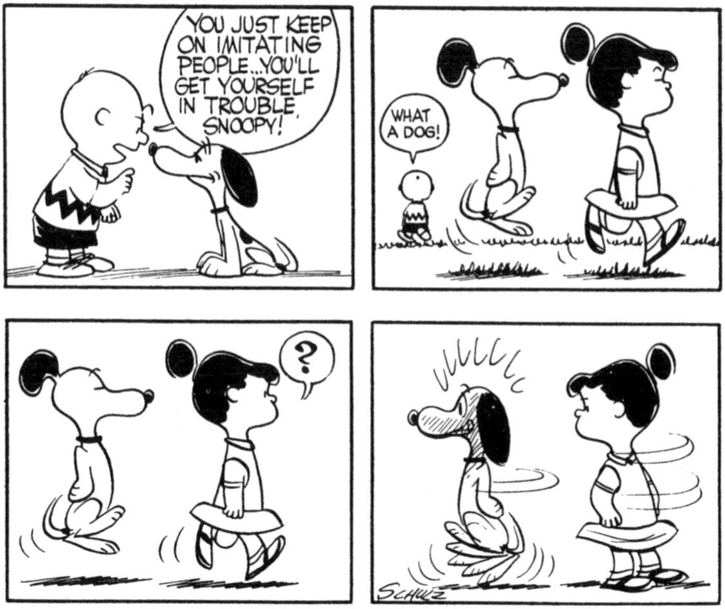
YOU JUST KEEP ON IMITATING PEOPLE...YOU'LL GET YOURSELF IN TROUBLE, SNOOPY!
WHAT A DOG!
?
SCHULZ

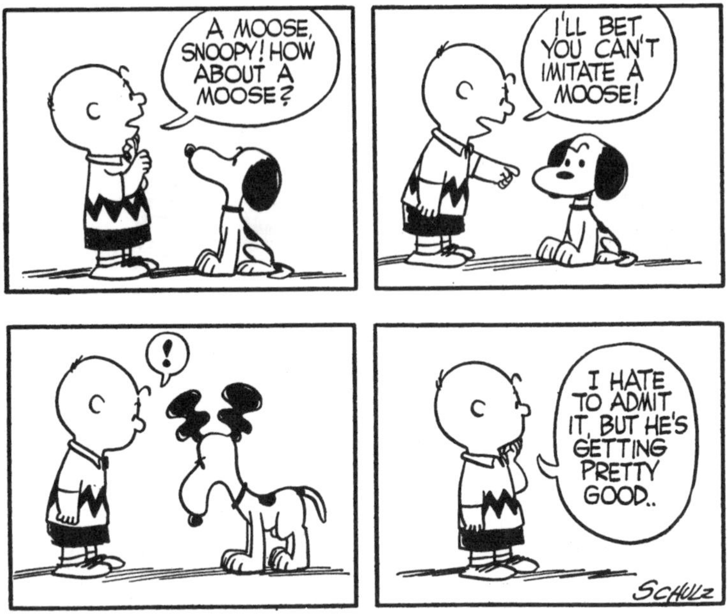
A MOOSE, SNOOPY! HOW ABOUT A MOOSE?
I'LL BET YOU CAN'T IMITATE A MOOSE!
!
I HATE TO ADMIT IT, BUT HE'S GETTING PRETTY GOOD..
SCHULZ

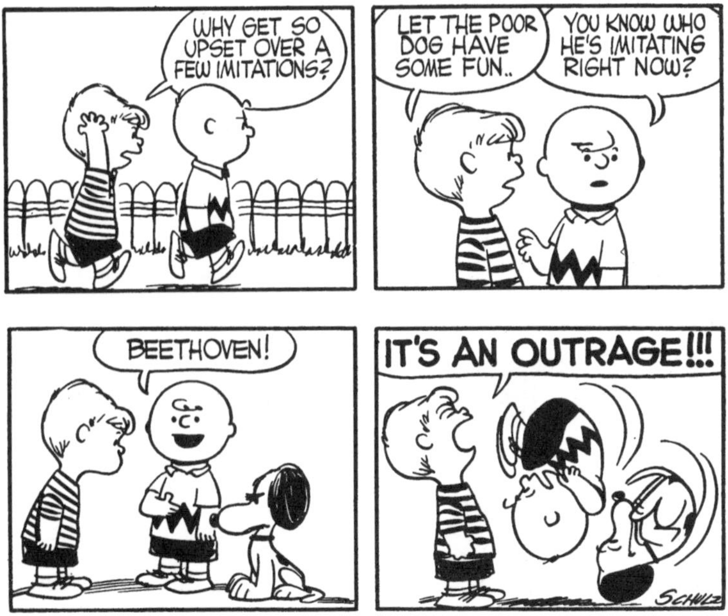
WHY GET SO UPSET OVER A FEW IMITATIONS?
LET THE POOR DOG HAVE SOME FUN..
YOU KNOW WHO HE'S IMITATING RIGHT NOW?
BEETHOVEN!
IT'S AN OUTRAGE!!!
SCHULZ

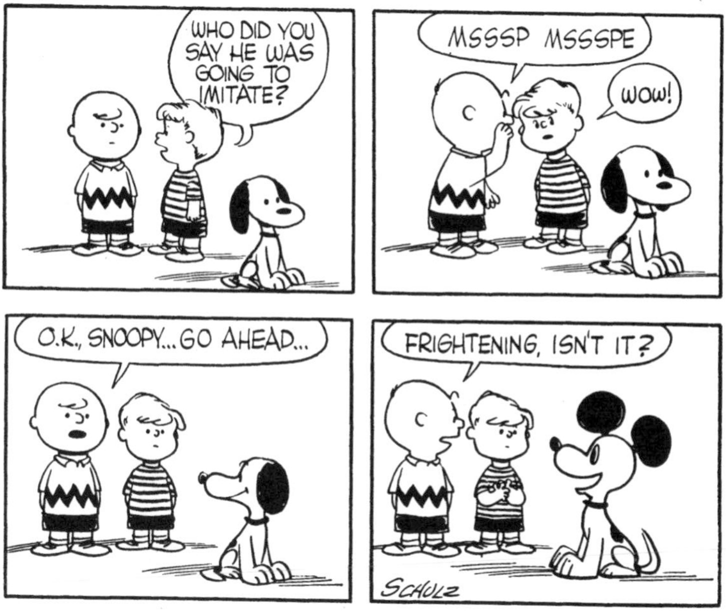
WHO DID YOU SAY HE WAS GOING TO IMITATE?
MSSSP MSSSPE
WOW!
O.K., SNOOPY...GO AHEAD...
FRIGHTENING, ISN'T IT?
SCHULZ

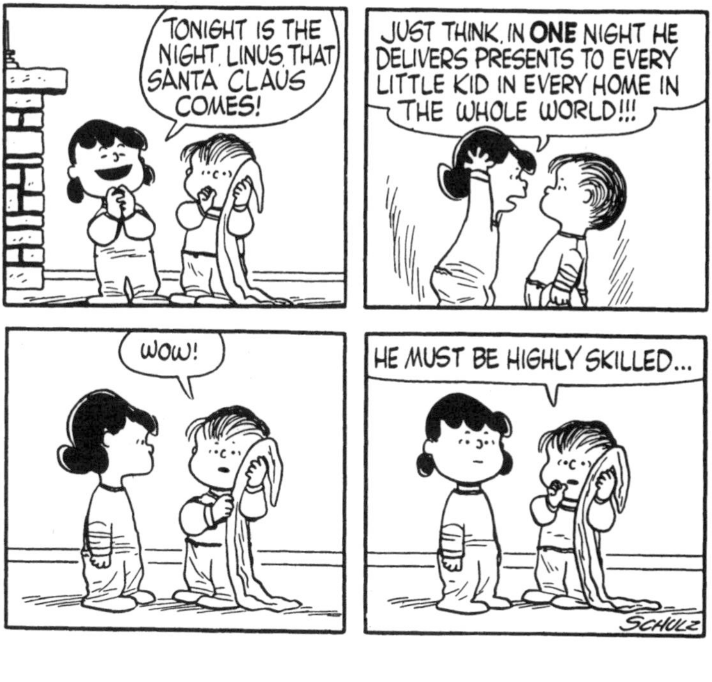
TONIGHT IS THE NIGHT, LINUS, THAT SANTA CLAUS COMES!
JUST THINK, IN ONE NIGHT HE DELIVERS PRESENTS TO EVERY LITTLE KID IN EVERY HOME IN THE WHOLE WORLD!!!
WOW!
HE MUST BE HIGHLY SKILLED...
SCHULZ

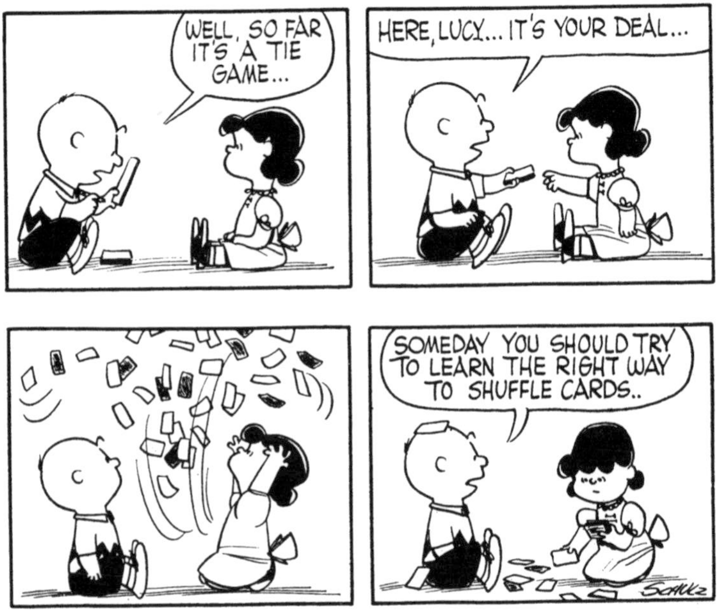

WELL, SO FAR IT'S A TIE GAME...
HERE, LUCY... IT'S YOUR DEAL...
SOMEDAY YOU SHOULD TRY TO LEARN THE RIGHT WAY TO SHUFFLE CARDS..
SCHULZ

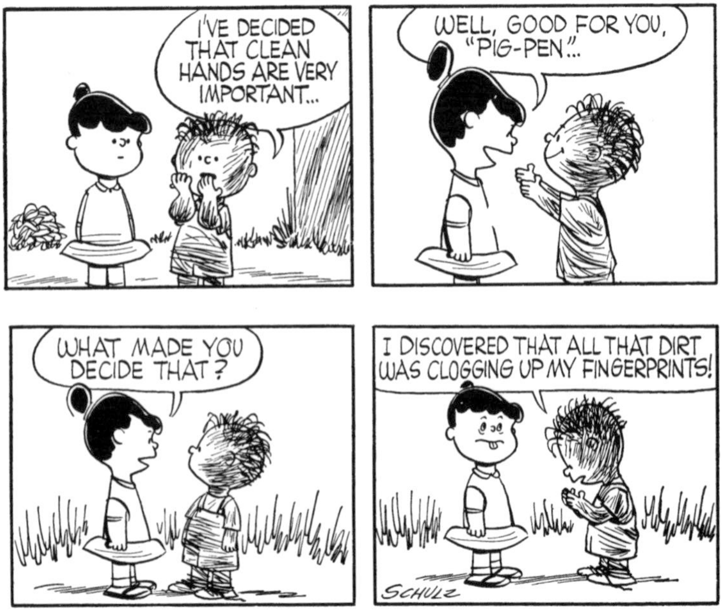

I'VE DECIDED THAT CLEAN HANDS ARE VERY IMPORTANT...
WELL, GOOD FOR YOU, "PIG-PEN"...
WHAT MADE YOU DECIDE THAT?
I DISCOVERED THAT ALL THAT DIRT WAS CLOGGING UP MY FINGERPRINTS!
SCHULZ

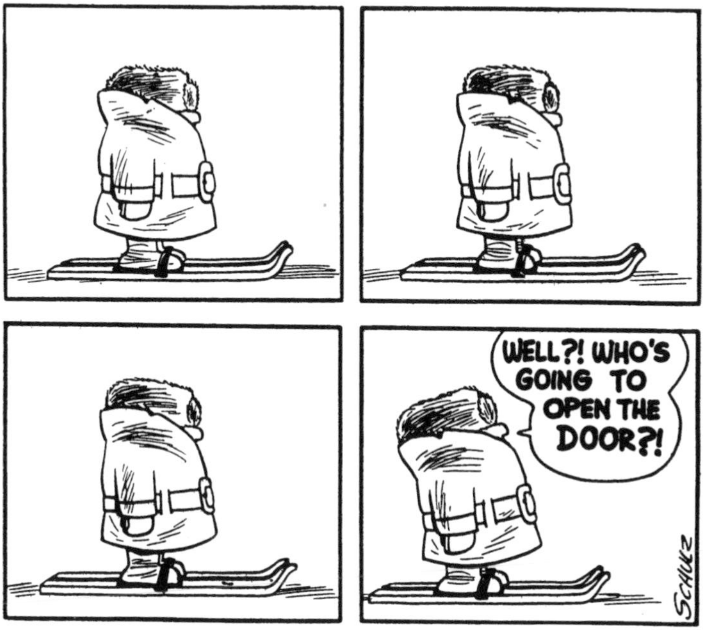
WELL?! WHO'S GOING TO OPEN THE DOOR?!
SCHULZ

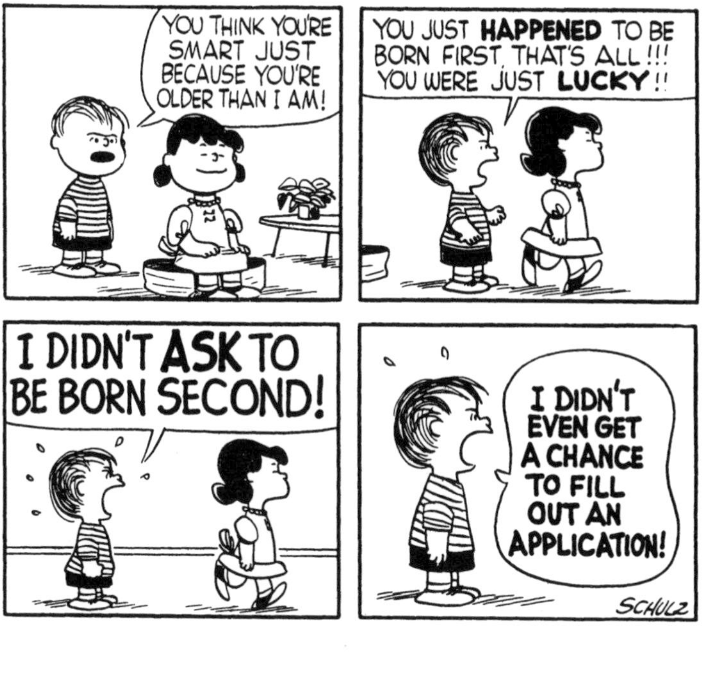
YOU THINK YOU'RE SMART JUST BECAUSE YOU'RE OLDER THAN I AM!
YOU JUST HAPPENED TO BE BORN FIRST, THAT'S ALL!!! YOU WERE JUST LUCKY!!
I DIDN'T ASK TO BE BORN SECOND!
I DIDN'T EVEN GET A CHANCE TO FILL OUT AN APPLICATION!
SCHULZ

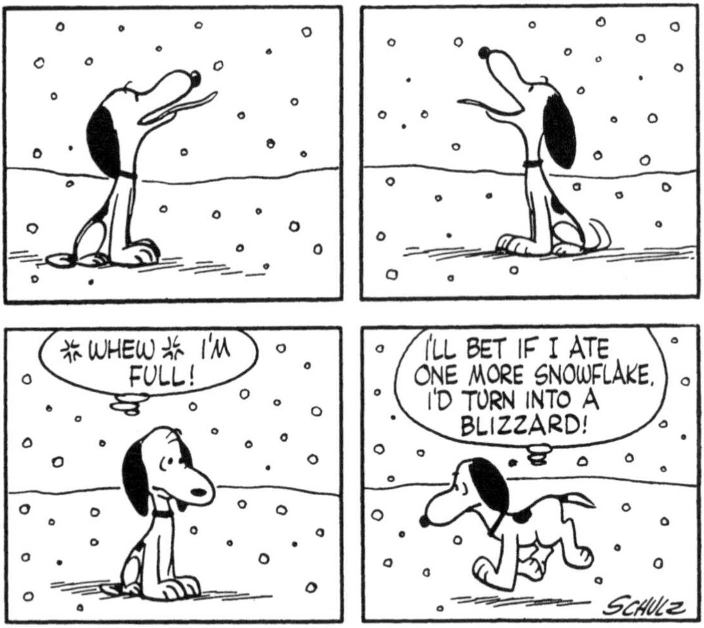
WHEW I'M FULL!
I'LL BET IF I ATE ONE MORE SNOWFLAKE, I'D TURN INTO A BLIZZARD!
SCHULZ

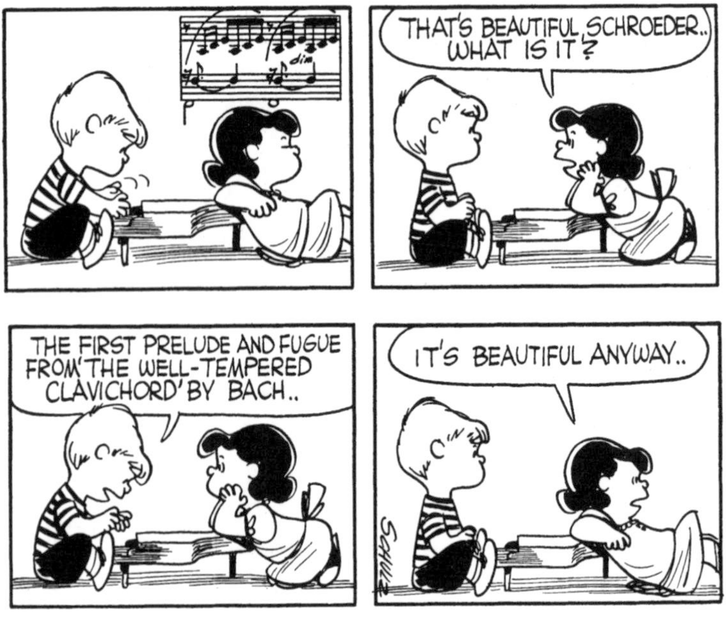
THAT'S BEAUTIFUL, SCHROEDER.. WHAT IS IT?
THE FIRST PRELUDE AND FUGUE FROM 'THE WELL-TEMPERED CLAVICHORD' BY BACH..
IT'S BEAUTIFUL ANYWAY..
SCHULZ

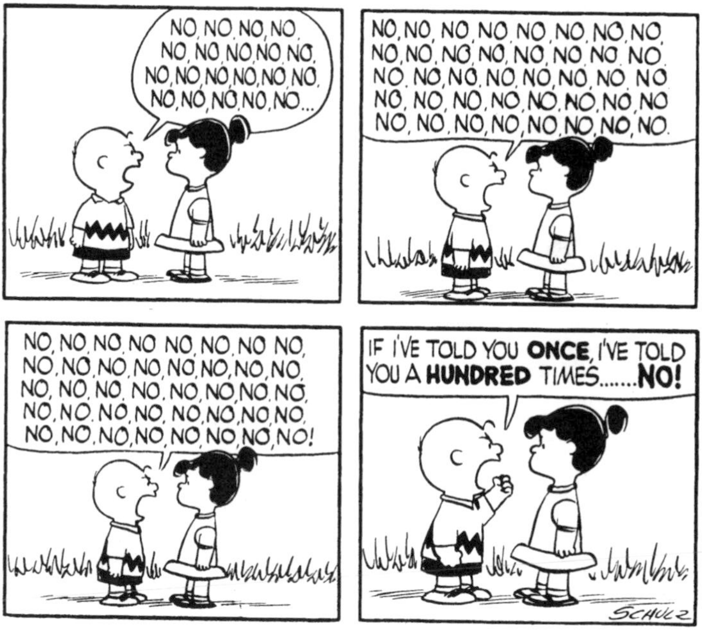
NO, NO, NO, NO, NO, NO, NO, NO, NO, NO, NO, NO, NO, NO, NO, NO, NO, NO, NO, NO...
NO, NO, NO, NO, NO, NO, NO, NO, NO, NO, NO, NO, NO, NO, NO, NO, NO, NO, NO, NO, NO, NO, NO, NO, NO, NO, NO, NO, NO, NO, NO, NO, NO, NO, NO, NO, NO, NO, NO, NO.
NO, NO, NO, NO, NO, NO, NO, NO, NO, NO, NO, NO, NO, NO, NO, NO, NO, NO, NO, NO, NO, NO, NO, NO, NO, NO, NO, NO, NO, NO, NO, NO, NO, NO, NO, NO, NO, NO, NO, NO!
IF I'VE TOLD YOU **ONCE**, I'VE TOLD YOU A **HUNDRED** TIMES.......**NO!**
SCHULZ

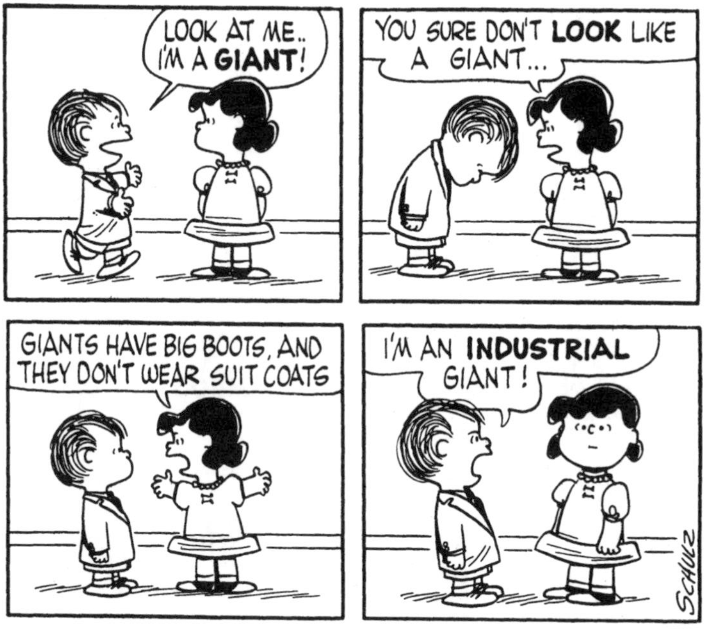
LOOK AT ME.. I'M A **GIANT**!
YOU SURE DON'T **LOOK** LIKE A GIANT...
GIANTS HAVE BIG BOOTS, AND THEY DON'T WEAR SUIT COATS
I'M AN **INDUSTRIAL** GIANT!
SCHULZ

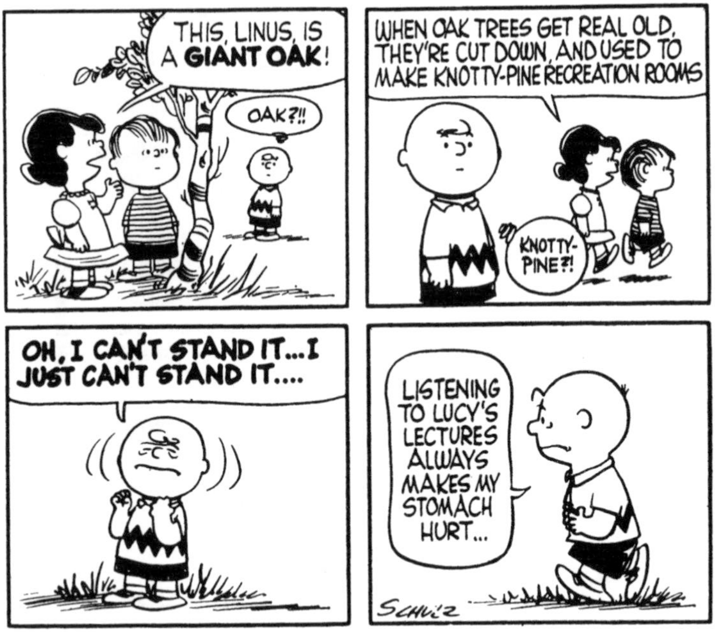
THIS, LINUS, IS A **GIANT OAK**!
OAK?!!
WHEN OAK TREES GET REAL OLD, THEY'RE CUT DOWN, AND USED TO MAKE KNOTTY-PINE RECREATION ROOMS
KNOTTY-PINE?!
OH, I CAN'T STAND IT...I JUST CAN'T STAND IT....
LISTENING TO LUCY'S LECTURES ALWAYS MAKES MY STOMACH HURT...
SCHULZ

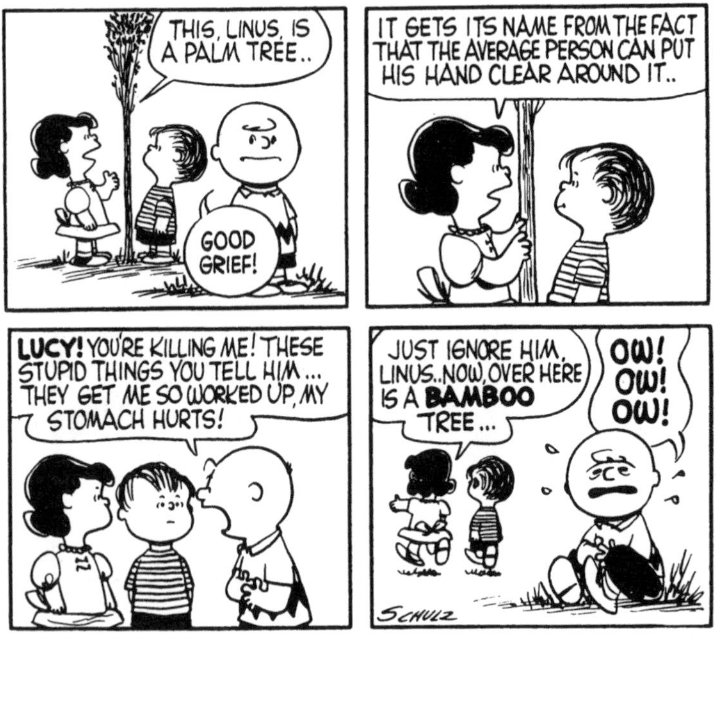
THIS, LINUS, IS A PALM TREE..
GOOD GRIEF!
IT GETS ITS NAME FROM THE FACT THAT THE AVERAGE PERSON CAN PUT HIS HAND CLEAR AROUND IT..
LUCY! YOU'RE KILLING ME! THESE STUPID THINGS YOU TELL HIM... THEY GET ME SO WORKED UP, MY STOMACH HURTS!
JUST IGNORE HIM, LINUS..NOW, OVER HERE IS A **BAMBOO** TREE...
OW! OW! OW!
SCHULZ

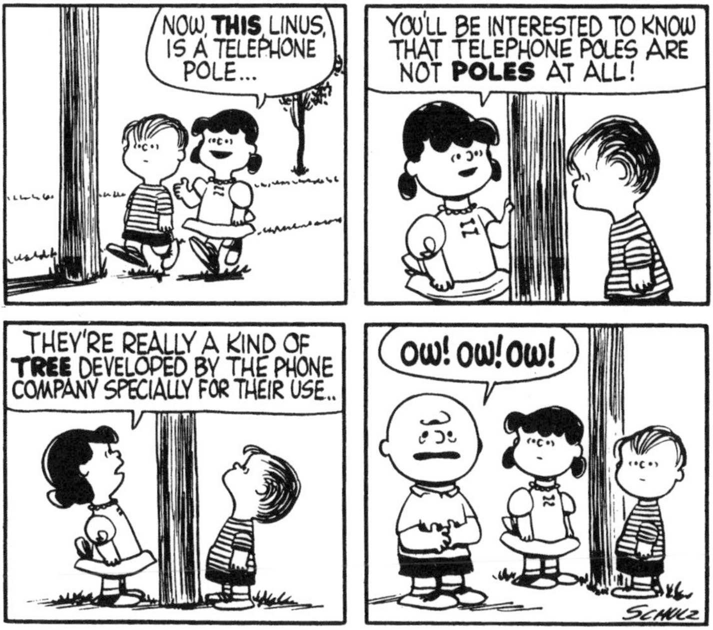
NOW, **THIS** LINUS, IS A TELEPHONE POLE...
YOU'LL BE INTERESTED TO KNOW THAT TELEPHONE POLES ARE NOT **POLES** AT ALL!
THEY'RE REALLY A KIND OF **TREE** DEVELOPED BY THE PHONE COMPANY SPECIALLY FOR THEIR USE..
OW! OW! OW!
SCHULZ

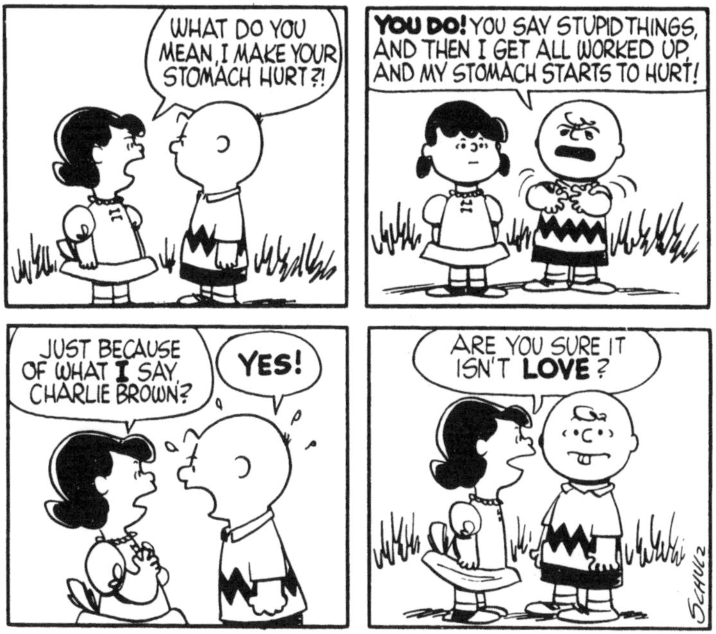
WHAT DO YOU MEAN, I MAKE YOUR STOMACH HURT?!
YOU DO! YOU SAY STUPID THINGS, AND THEN I GET ALL WORKED UP, AND MY STOMACH STARTS TO HURT!
JUST BECAUSE OF WHAT **I** SAY, CHARLIE BROWN?
YES!
ARE YOU SURE IT ISN'T **LOVE**?
SCHULZ

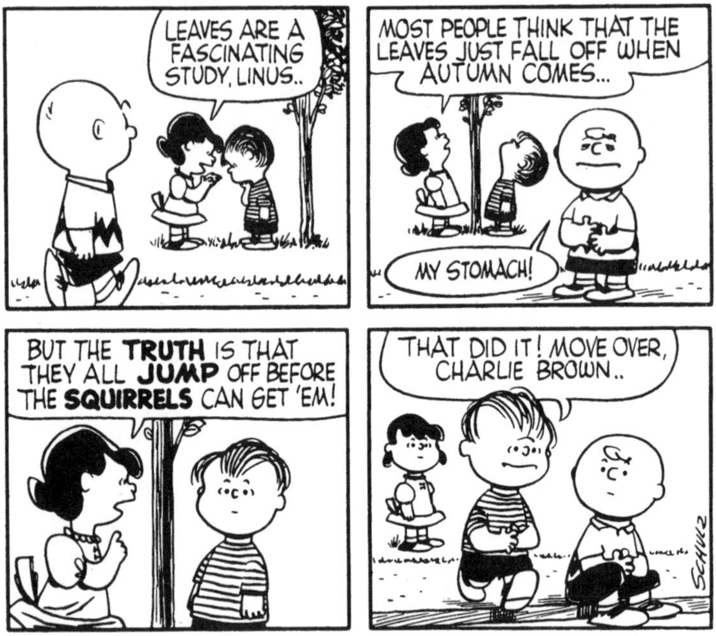
LEAVES ARE A FASCINATING STUDY, LINUS..
MOST PEOPLE THINK THAT THE LEAVES JUST FALL OFF WHEN AUTUMN COMES...
MY STOMACH!
BUT THE **TRUTH** IS THAT THEY ALL **JUMP** OFF BEFORE THE **SQUIRRELS** CAN GET 'EM!
THAT DID IT! MOVE OVER, CHARLIE BROWN..
SCHULZ

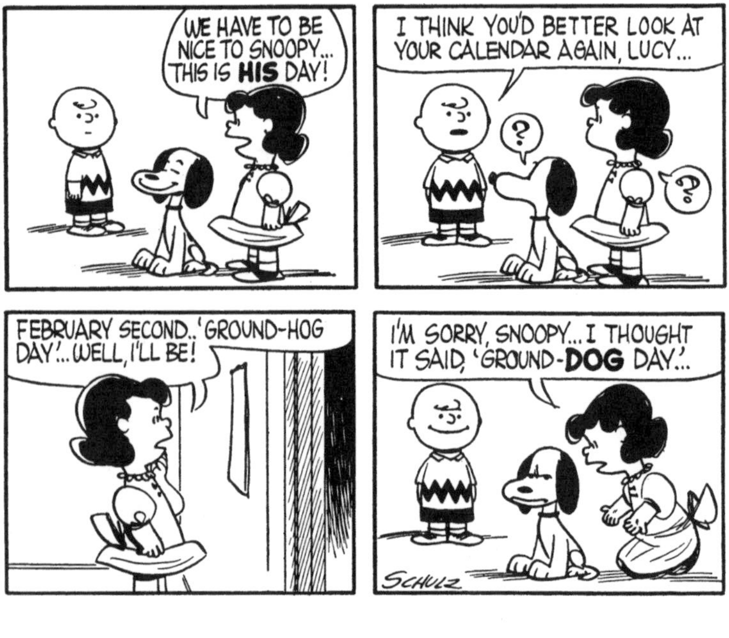
WE HAVE TO BE NICE TO SNOOPY... THIS IS **HIS** DAY!
I THINK YOU'D BETTER LOOK AT YOUR CALENDAR AGAIN, LUCY...
?
?
FEBRUARY SECOND..'GROUND-HOG DAY'...WELL, I'LL BE!
I'M SORRY, SNOOPY...I THOUGHT IT SAID, 'GROUND-**DOG** DAY'..
SCHULZ

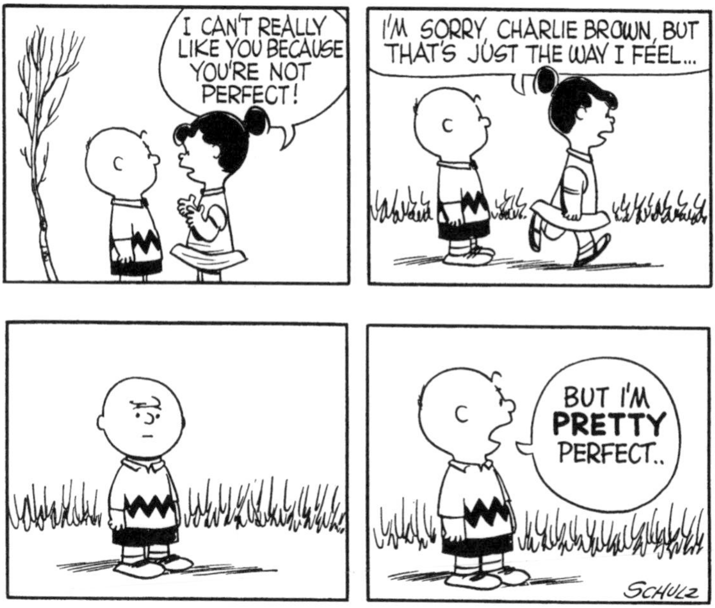
I CAN'T REALLY LIKE YOU BECAUSE YOU'RE NOT PERFECT!
I'M SORRY, CHARLIE BROWN, BUT THAT'S JUST THE WAY I FEEL...
BUT I'M **PRETTY** PERFECT..
SCHULZ

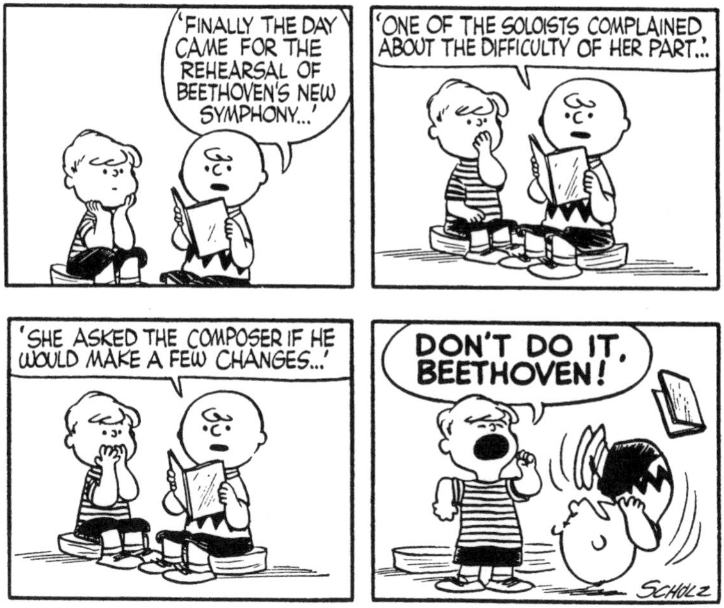
'FINALLY THE DAY CAME FOR THE REHEARSAL OF BEETHOVEN'S NEW SYMPHONY...'
'ONE OF THE SOLOISTS COMPLAINED ABOUT THE DIFFICULTY OF HER PART...'
'SHE ASKED THE COMPOSER IF HE WOULD MAKE A FEW CHANGES...'
DON'T DO IT, BEETHOVEN!
SCHULZ

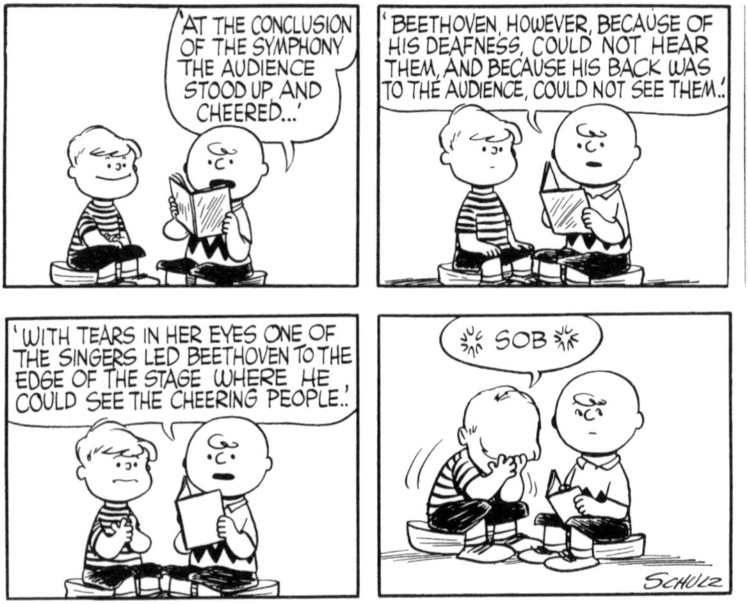
'AT THE CONCLUSION OF THE SYMPHONY THE AUDIENCE STOOD UP AND CHEERED...'
'BEETHOVEN, HOWEVER, BECAUSE OF HIS DEAFNESS, COULD NOT HEAR THEM, AND BECAUSE HIS BACK WAS TO THE AUDIENCE, COULD NOT SEE THEM.'
'WITH TEARS IN HER EYES ONE OF THE SINGERS LED BEETHOVEN TO THE EDGE OF THE STAGE WHERE HE COULD SEE THE CHEERING PEOPLE.'
SOB
SCHULZ

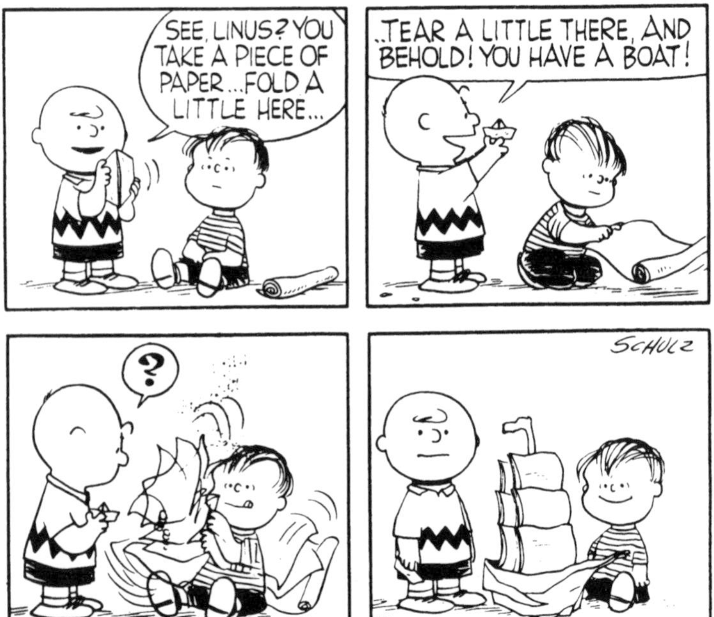
SEE, LINUS? YOU TAKE A PIECE OF PAPER...FOLD A LITTLE HERE...
..TEAR A LITTLE THERE, AND BEHOLD! YOU HAVE A BOAT!
?
SCHULZ

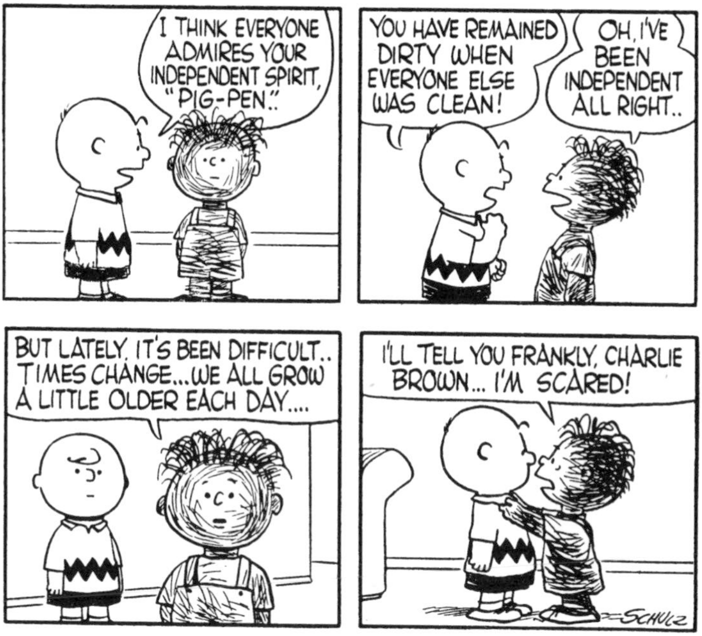
I THINK EVERYONE ADMIRES YOUR INDEPENDENT SPIRIT, "PIG-PEN."
YOU HAVE REMAINED DIRTY WHEN EVERYONE ELSE WAS CLEAN!
OH, I'VE BEEN INDEPENDENT ALL RIGHT..
BUT LATELY, IT'S BEEN DIFFICULT.. TIMES CHANGE...WE ALL GROW A LITTLE OLDER EACH DAY....
I'LL TELL YOU FRANKLY, CHARLIE BROWN... I'M SCARED!
SCHULZ

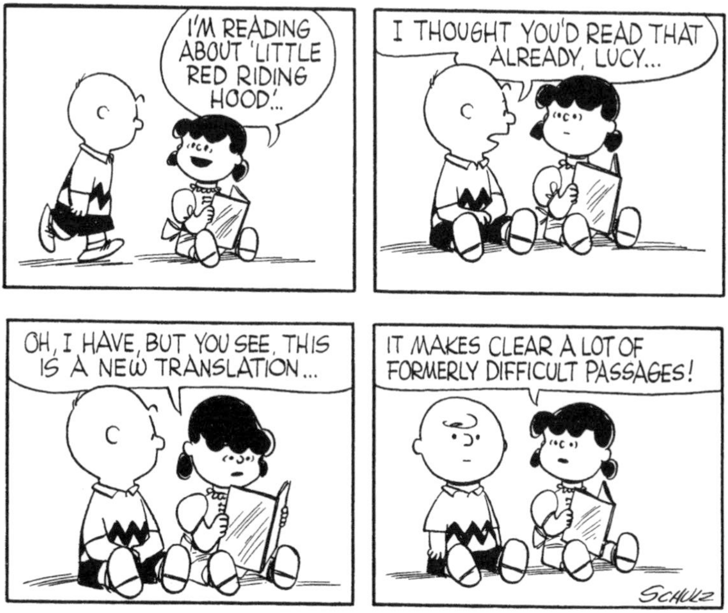
I'M READING ABOUT 'LITTLE RED RIDING HOOD'..
I THOUGHT YOU'D READ THAT ALREADY, LUCY...
OH, I HAVE, BUT YOU SEE, THIS IS A NEW TRANSLATION...
IT MAKES CLEAR A LOT OF FORMERLY DIFFICULT PASSAGES!
SCHULZ

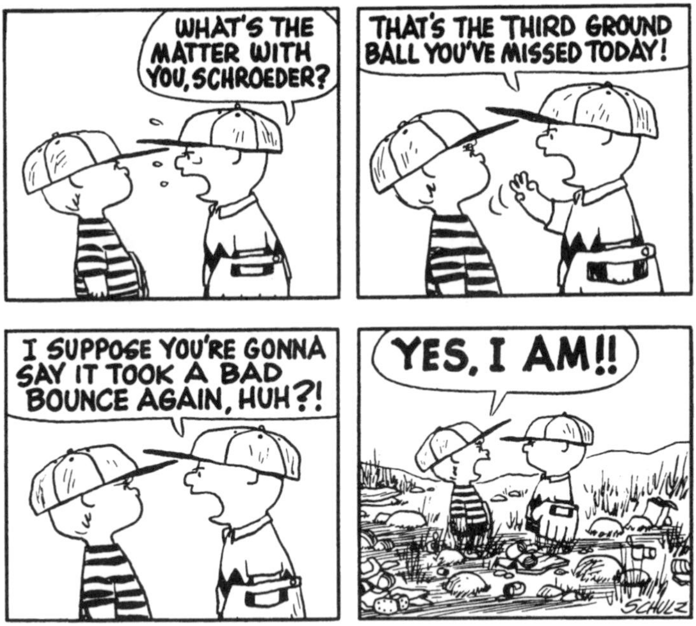
WHAT'S THE MATTER WITH YOU, SCHROEDER?
THAT'S THE THIRD GROUND BALL YOU'VE MISSED TODAY!
I SUPPOSE YOU'RE GONNA SAY IT TOOK A BAD BOUNCE AGAIN, HUH?!
YES, I AM!!
SCHULZ

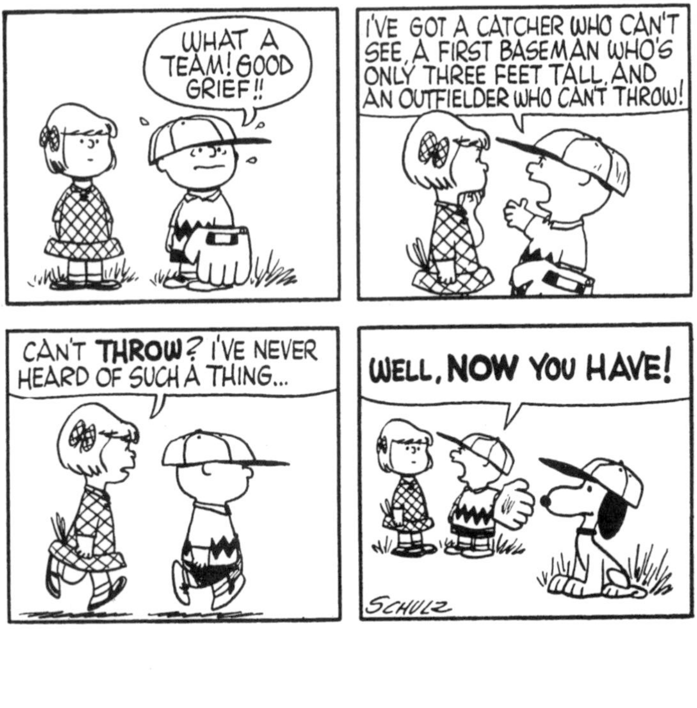
WHAT A TEAM! GOOD GRIEF!!
I'VE GOT A CATCHER WHO CAN'T SEE, A FIRST BASEMAN WHO'S ONLY THREE FEET TALL, AND AN OUTFIELDER WHO CAN'T THROW!
CAN'T **THROW**? I'VE NEVER HEARD OF SUCH A THING...
WELL, **NOW** YOU HAVE!
SCHULZ

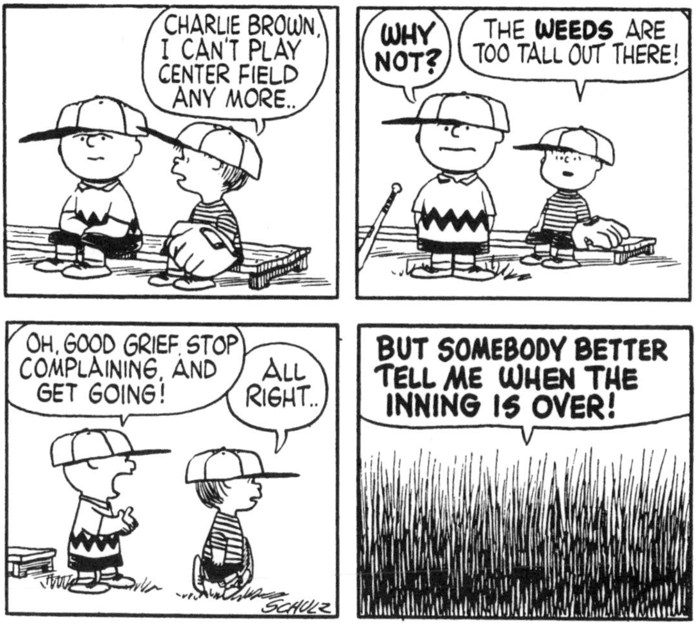
CHARLIE BROWN, I CAN'T PLAY CENTER FIELD ANY MORE..
WHY NOT?
THE WEEDS ARE TOO TALL OUT THERE!
OH, GOOD GRIEF, STOP COMPLAINING, AND GET GOING!
ALL RIGHT..
BUT SOMEBODY BETTER TELL ME WHEN THE INNING IS OVER!
SCHULZ

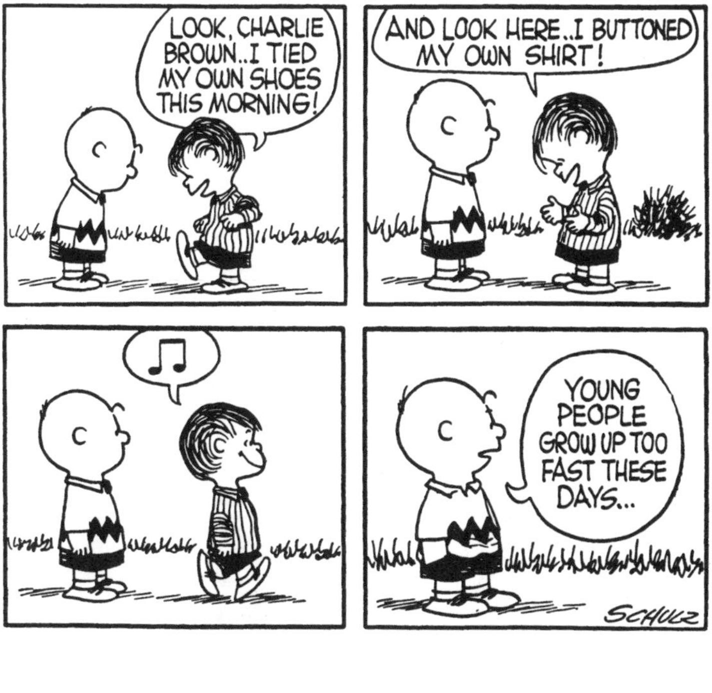
LOOK, CHARLIE BROWN..I TIED MY OWN SHOES THIS MORNING!
AND LOOK HERE..I BUTTONED MY OWN SHIRT!
YOUNG PEOPLE GROW UP TOO FAST THESE DAYS...
SCHULZ

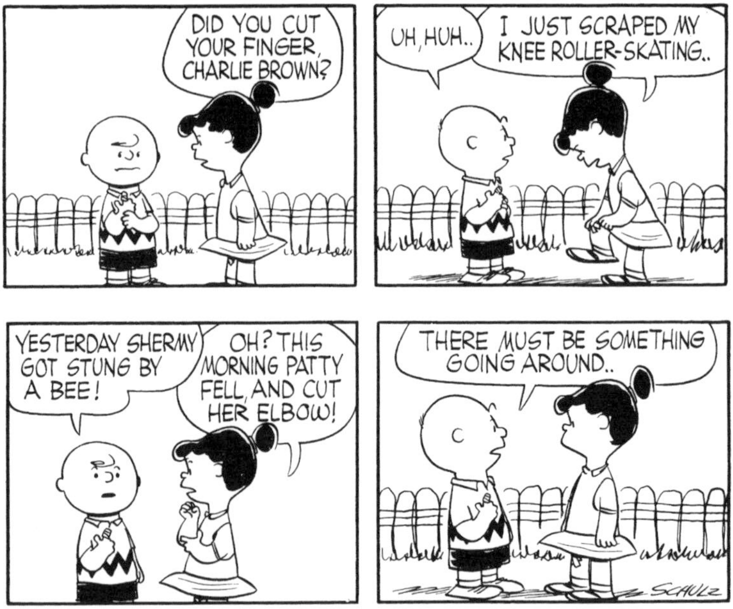
DID YOU CUT YOUR FINGER, CHARLIE BROWN?
UH, HUH..
I JUST SCRAPED MY KNEE ROLLER-SKATING..
YESTERDAY SHERMY GOT STUNG BY A BEE!
OH? THIS MORNING PATTY FELL, AND CUT HER ELBOW!
THERE MUST BE SOMETHING GOING AROUND..
SCHULZ

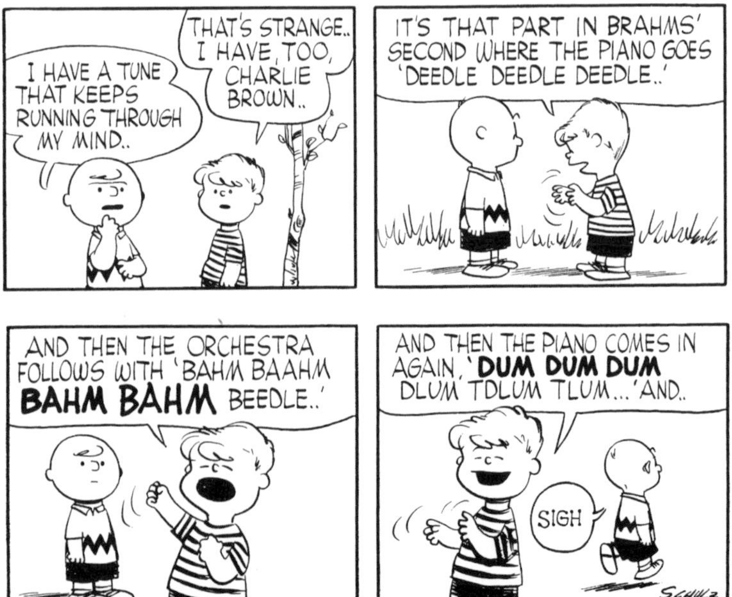
I HAVE A TUNE THAT KEEPS RUNNING THROUGH MY MIND..
THAT'S STRANGE.. I HAVE, TOO, CHARLIE BROWN..
IT'S THAT PART IN BRAHMS' SECOND WHERE THE PIANO GOES 'DEEDLE DEEDLE DEEDLE..'
AND THEN THE ORCHESTRA FOLLOWS WITH 'BAHM BAAHM **BAHM BAHM** BEEDLE..'
AND THEN THE PIANO COMES IN AGAIN, '**DUM DUM DUM** DLUM TDLUM TLUM...' AND..
SIGH
SCHULZ

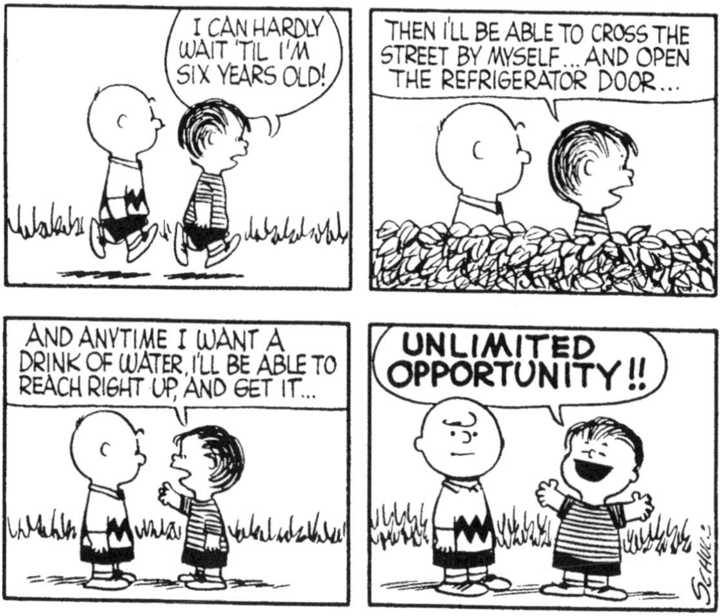
I CAN HARDLY WAIT 'TIL I'M SIX YEARS OLD!
THEN I'LL BE ABLE TO CROSS THE STREET BY MYSELF... AND OPEN THE REFRIGERATOR DOOR...
AND ANYTIME I WANT A DRINK OF WATER, I'LL BE ABLE TO REACH RIGHT UP, AND GET IT...
UNLIMITED OPPORTUNITY!!
SCHULZ

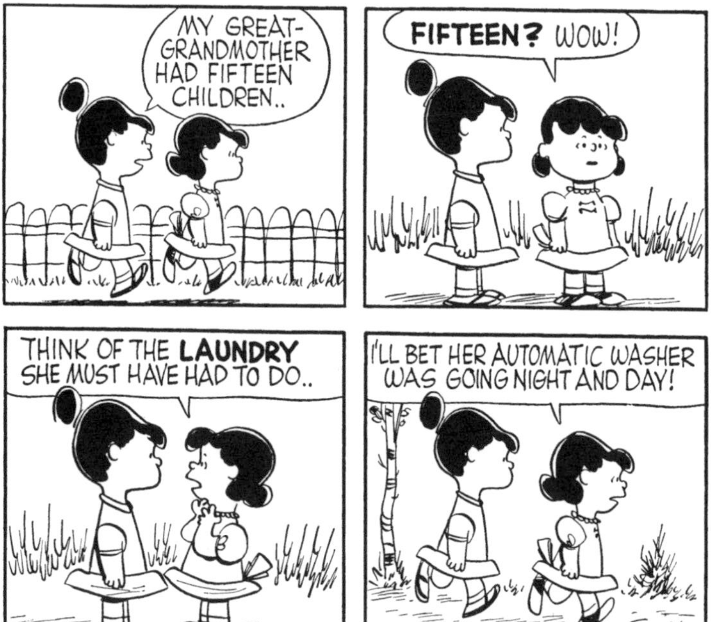
MY GREAT-GRANDMOTHER HAD FIFTEEN CHILDREN..
FIFTEEN? WOW!
THINK OF THE LAUNDRY SHE MUST HAVE HAD TO DO..
I'LL BET HER AUTOMATIC WASHER WAS GOING NIGHT AND DAY!
SCHULZ

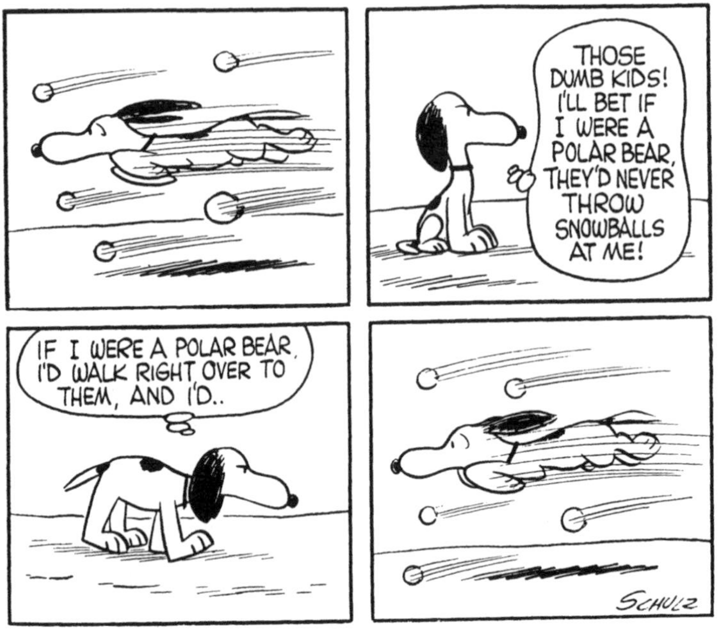
THOSE DUMB KIDS! I'LL BET IF I WERE A POLAR BEAR, THEY'D NEVER THROW SNOWBALLS AT ME!
IF I WERE A POLAR BEAR, I'D WALK RIGHT OVER TO THEM, AND I'D..
SCHULZ

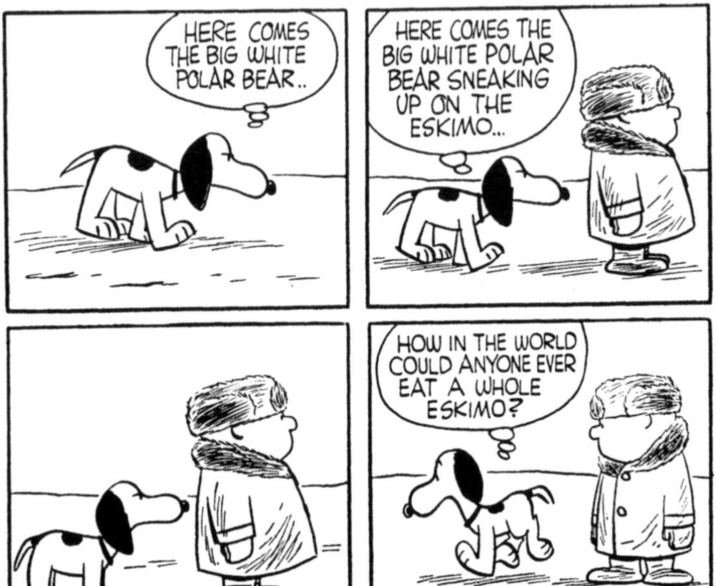
HERE COMES THE BIG WHITE POLAR BEAR..
HERE COMES THE BIG WHITE POLAR BEAR SNEAKING UP ON THE ESKIMO...
HOW IN THE WORLD COULD ANYONE EVER EAT A WHOLE ESKIMO?
SCHULZ

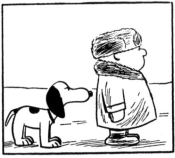

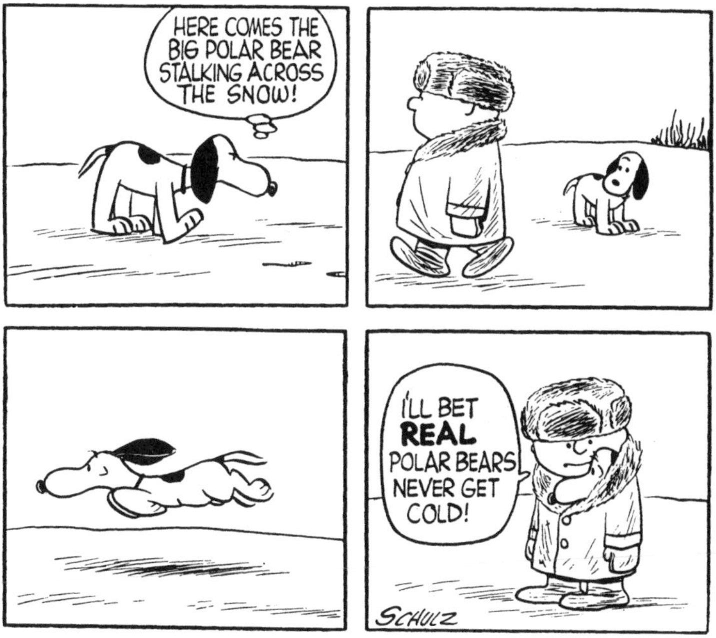
HERE COMES THE BIG POLAR BEAR STALKING ACROSS THE SNOW!
I'LL BET REAL POLAR BEARS NEVER GET COLD!
SCHULZ

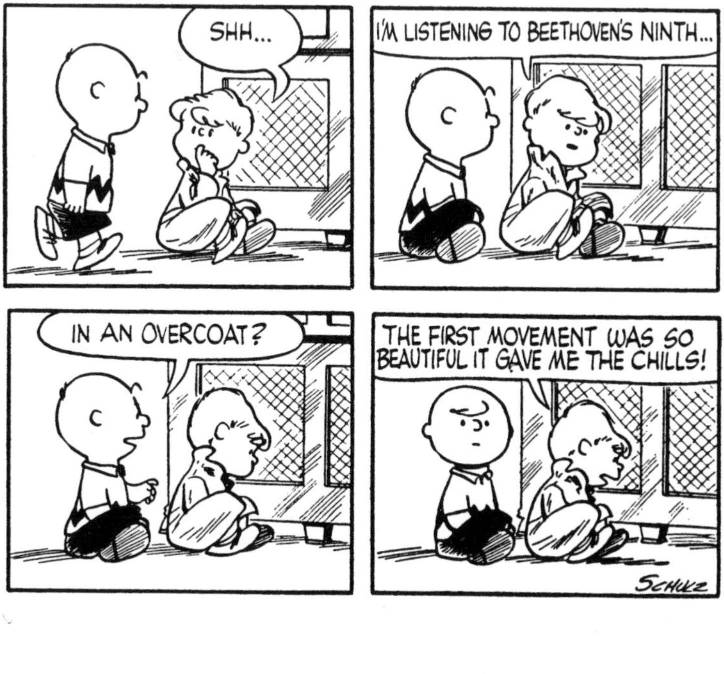
SHH...
I'M LISTENING TO BEETHOVEN'S NINTH...
IN AN OVERCOAT?
THE FIRST MOVEMENT WAS SO BEAUTIFUL IT GAVE ME THE CHILLS!
SCHULZ

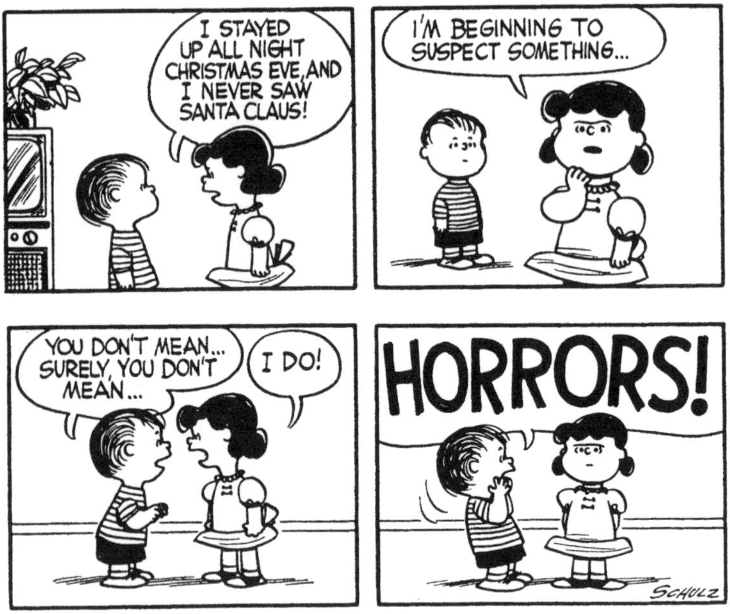
I STAYED UP ALL NIGHT CHRISTMAS EVE, AND I NEVER SAW SANTA CLAUS!
I'M BEGINNING TO SUSPECT SOMETHING...
YOU DON'T MEAN... SURELY, YOU DON'T MEAN...
I DO!
HORRORS!
SCHULZ

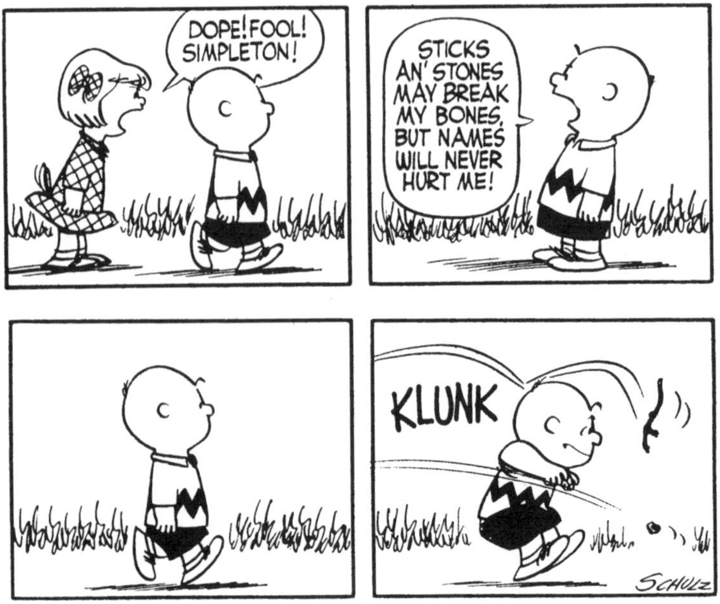
DOPE! FOOL! SIMPLETON!
STICKS AN' STONES MAY BREAK MY BONES, BUT NAMES WILL NEVER HURT ME!
KLUNK
SCHULZ

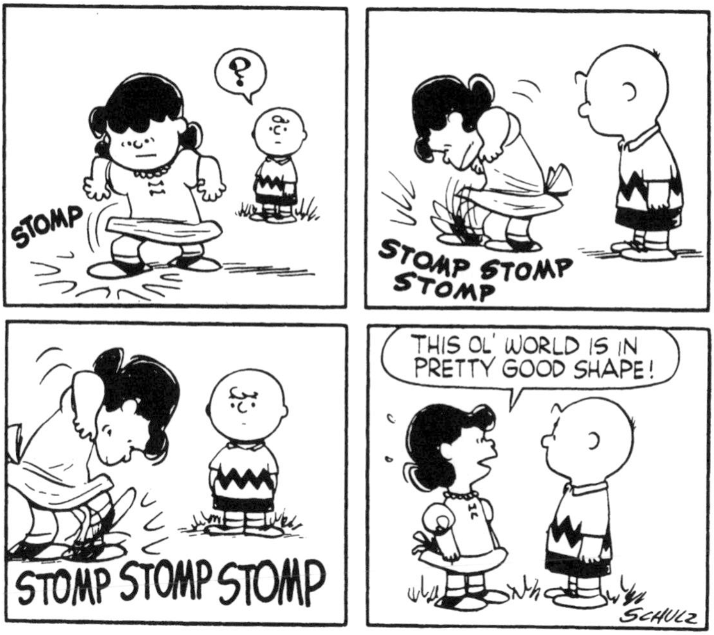
?
STOMP
STOMP STOMP
STOMP
STOMP STOMP STOMP
THIS OL' WORLD IS IN PRETTY GOOD SHAPE!
SCHULZ

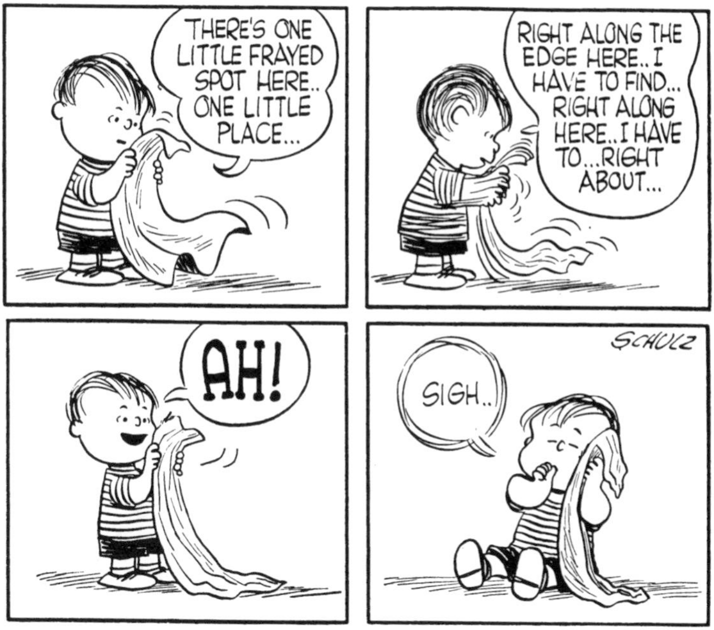
THERE'S ONE LITTLE FRAYED SPOT HERE.. ONE LITTLE PLACE...
RIGHT ALONG THE EDGE HERE..I HAVE TO FIND... RIGHT ALONG HERE..I HAVE TO...RIGHT ABOUT...
AH!
SCHULZ
SIGH..

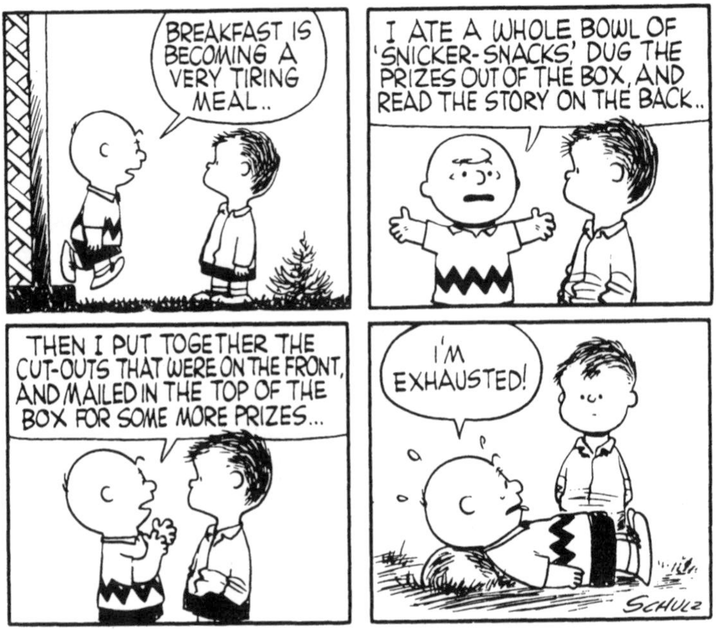
BREAKFAST IS BECOMING A VERY TIRING MEAL..
I ATE A WHOLE BOWL OF 'SNICKER-SNACKS,' DUG THE PRIZES OUT OF THE BOX, AND READ THE STORY ON THE BACK..
THEN I PUT TOGETHER THE CUT-OUTS THAT WERE ON THE FRONT, AND MAILED IN THE TOP OF THE BOX FOR SOME MORE PRIZES...
I'M EXHAUSTED!
SCHULZ

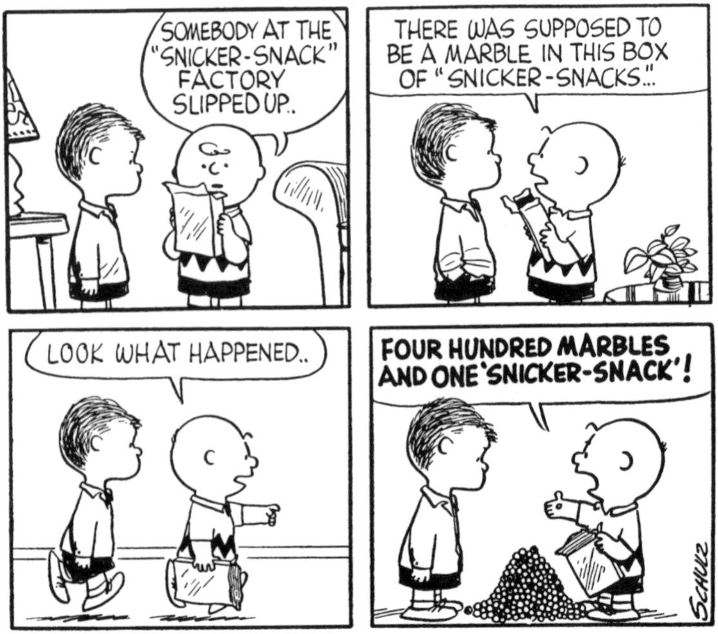
SOMEBODY AT THE "SNICKER-SNACK" FACTORY SLIPPED UP..
THERE WAS SUPPOSED TO BE A MARBLE IN THIS BOX OF "SNICKER-SNACKS."..
LOOK WHAT HAPPENED..
FOUR HUNDRED MARBLES AND ONE 'SNICKER-SNACK'!
SCHULZ

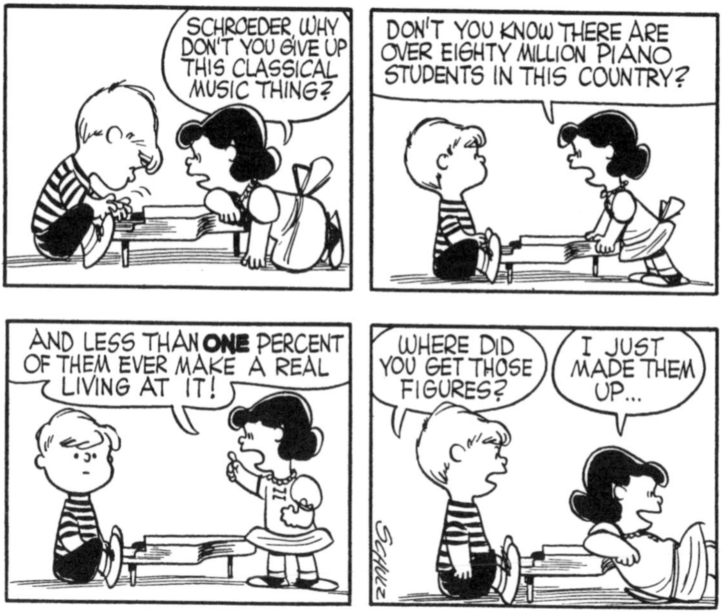
SCHROEDER, WHY DON'T YOU GIVE UP THIS CLASSICAL MUSIC THING?
DON'T YOU KNOW THERE ARE OVER EIGHTY MILLION PIANO STUDENTS IN THIS COUNTRY?
AND LESS THAN ONE PERCENT OF THEM EVER MAKE A REAL LIVING AT IT!
WHERE DID YOU GET THOSE FIGURES?
I JUST MADE THEM UP...
SCHULZ

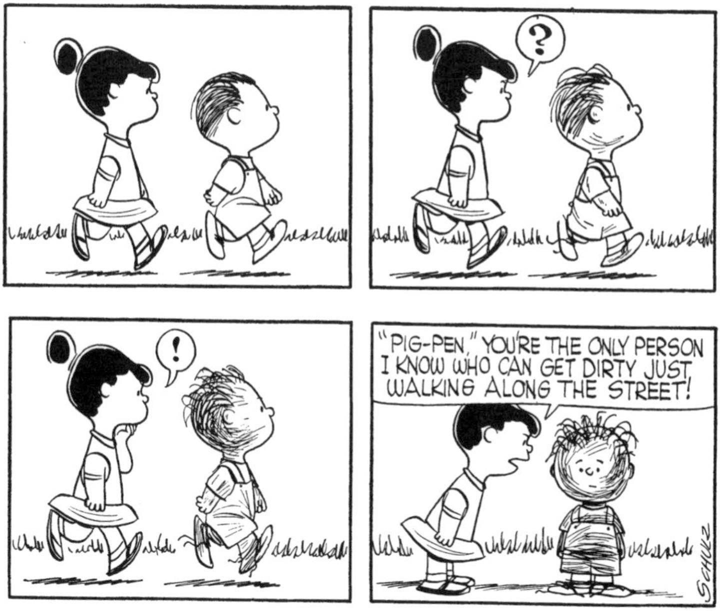
?
!
"PIG-PEN," YOU'RE THE ONLY PERSON I KNOW WHO CAN GET DIRTY JUST WALKING ALONG THE STREET!
SCHULZ

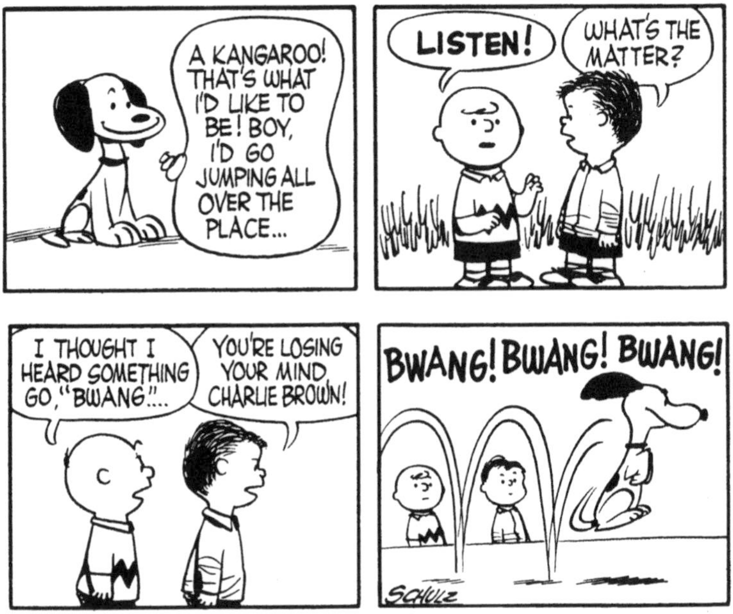
A KANGAROO! THAT'S WHAT I'D LIKE TO BE! BOY, I'D GO JUMPING ALL OVER THE PLACE...
LISTEN!
WHAT'S THE MATTER?
I THOUGHT I HEARD SOMETHING GO, "BWANG"...
YOU'RE LOSING YOUR MIND CHARLIE BROWN!
BWANG! BWANG! BWANG!
SCHULZ

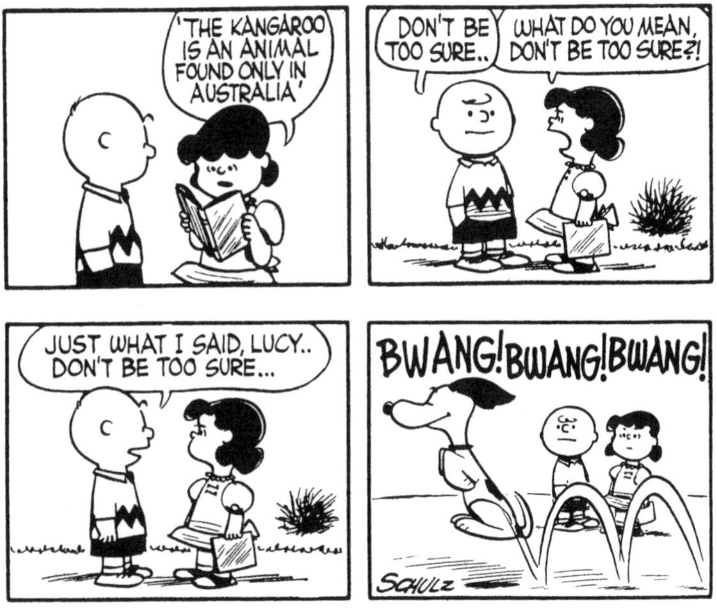
'THE KANGAROO IS AN ANIMAL FOUND ONLY IN AUSTRALIA'
DON'T BE TOO SURE..
WHAT DO YOU MEAN, DON'T BE TOO SURE?!
JUST WHAT I SAID, LUCY.. DON'T BE TOO SURE...
BWANG! BWANG! BWANG!
SCHULZ

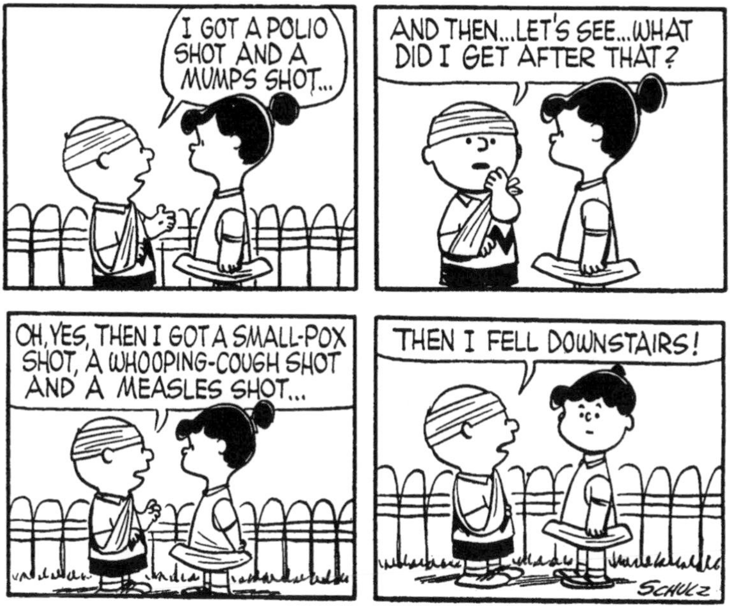
I GOT A POLIO SHOT AND A MUMPS SHOT...
AND THEN...LET'S SEE...WHAT DID I GET AFTER THAT?
OH, YES, THEN I GOT A SMALL-POX SHOT, A WHOOPING-COUGH SHOT AND A MEASLES SHOT...
THEN I FELL DOWNSTAIRS!
SCHULZ

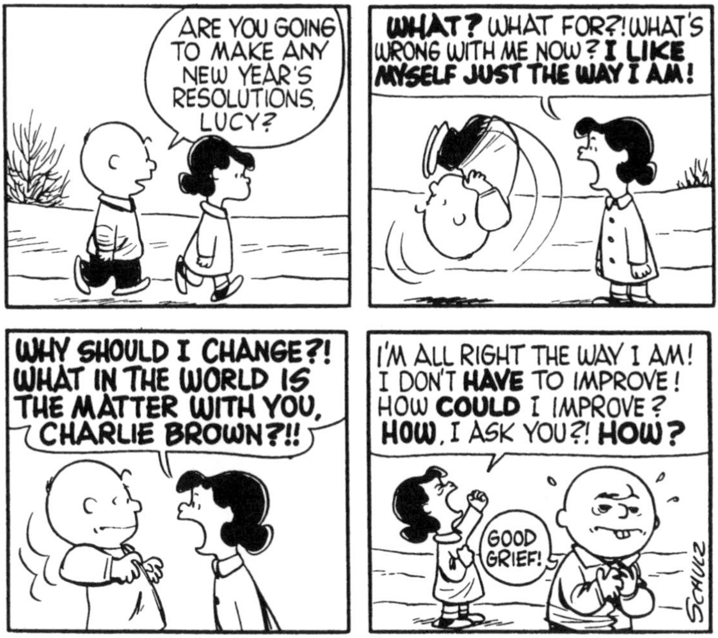
ARE YOU GOING TO MAKE ANY NEW YEAR'S RESOLUTIONS, LUCY?
WHAT? WHAT FOR?! WHAT'S WRONG WITH ME NOW? I LIKE MYSELF JUST THE WAY I AM!
WHY SHOULD I CHANGE?! WHAT IN THE WORLD IS THE MATTER WITH YOU, CHARLIE BROWN?!!
I'M ALL RIGHT THE WAY I AM! I DON'T HAVE TO IMPROVE! HOW COULD I IMPROVE? HOW, I ASK YOU?! HOW?
GOOD GRIEF!
SCHULZ

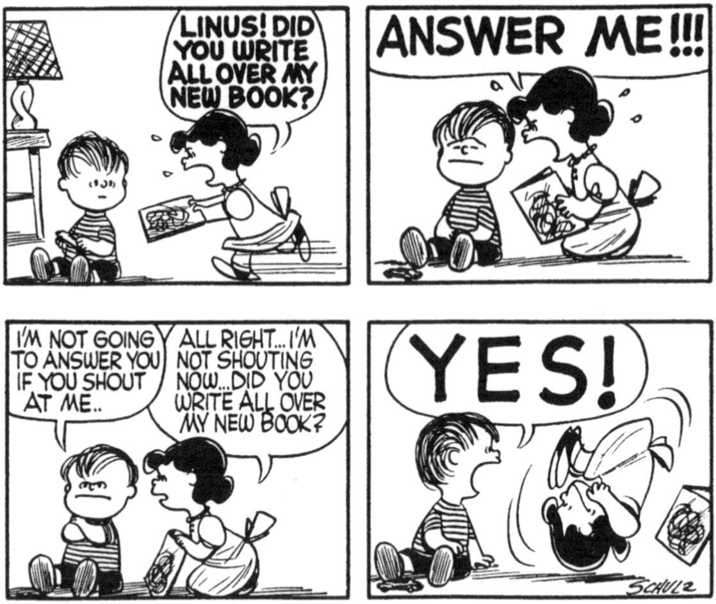
LINUS! DID YOU WRITE ALL OVER MY NEW BOOK?
ANSWER ME!!!
I'M NOT GOING TO ANSWER YOU IF YOU SHOUT AT ME..
ALL RIGHT... I'M NOT SHOUTING NOW...DID YOU WRITE ALL OVER MY NEW BOOK?
YES!
SCHULZ

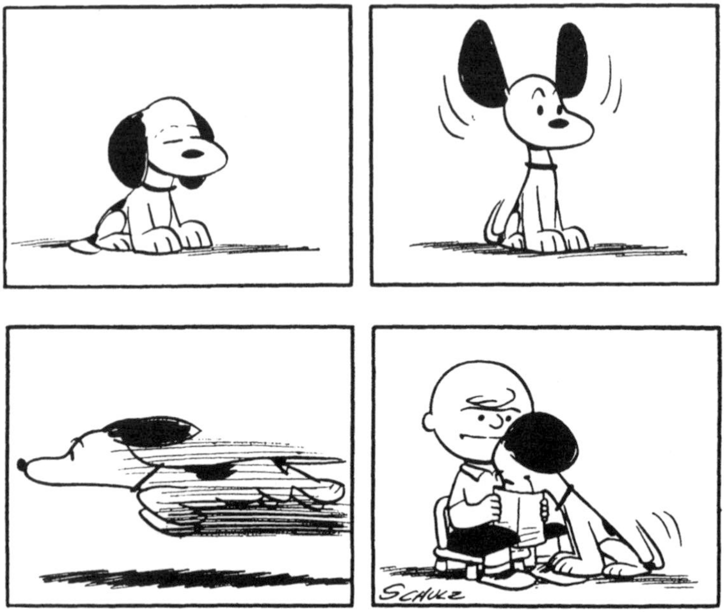
SCHULZ

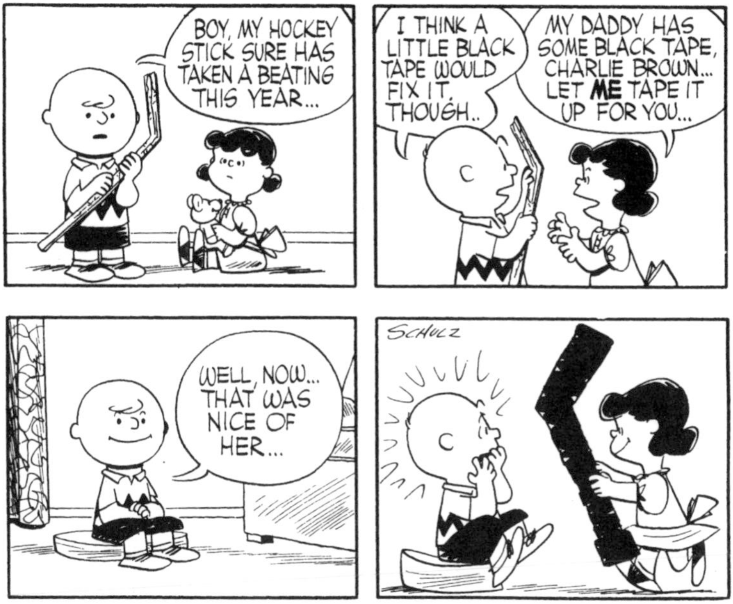
BOY, MY HOCKEY STICK SURE HAS TAKEN A BEATING THIS YEAR...
I THINK A LITTLE BLACK TAPE WOULD FIX IT, THOUGH..
MY DADDY HAS SOME BLACK TAPE, CHARLIE BROWN... LET ME TAPE IT UP FOR YOU...
WELL, NOW... THAT WAS NICE OF HER...
SCHULZ

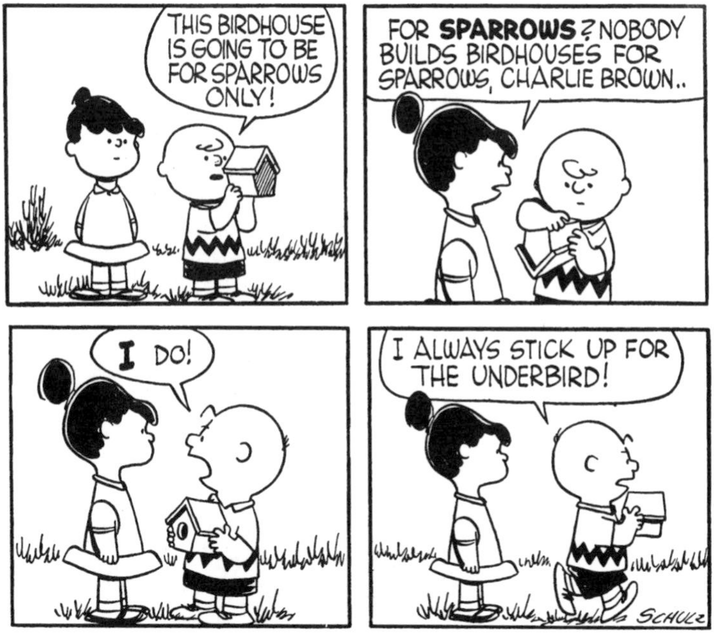
THIS BIRDHOUSE IS GOING TO BE FOR SPARROWS ONLY!
FOR SPARROWS? NOBODY BUILDS BIRDHOUSES FOR SPARROWS, CHARLIE BROWN..
I DO!
I ALWAYS STICK UP FOR THE UNDERBIRD!
SCHULZ

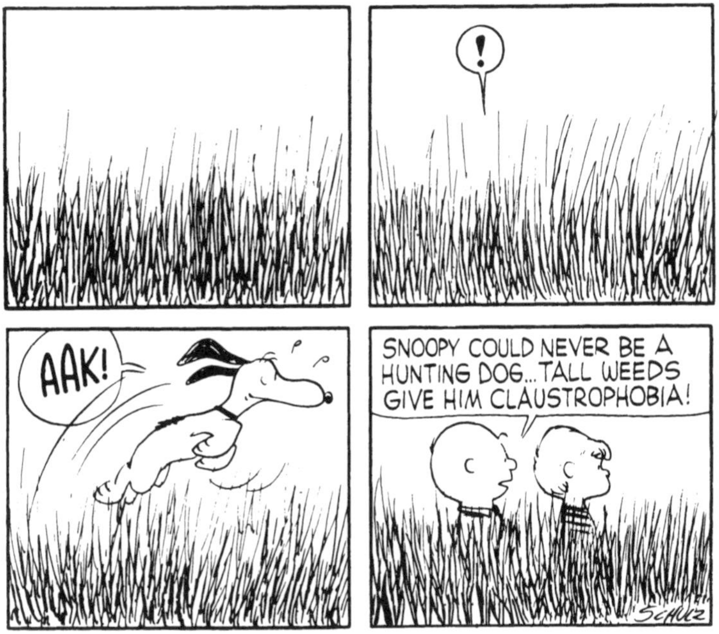
!
AAK!
SNOOPY COULD NEVER BE A HUNTING DOG...TALL WEEDS GIVE HIM CLAUSTROPHOBIA!
SCHULZ

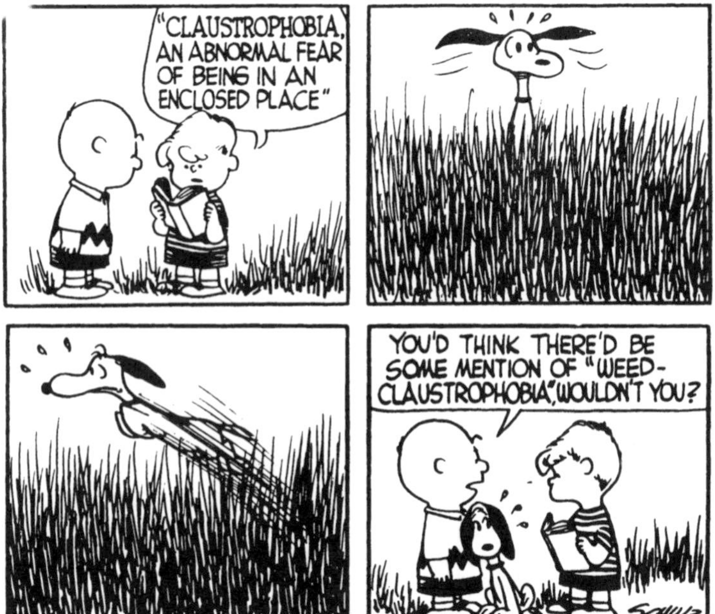
"CLAUSTROPHOBIA, AN ABNORMAL FEAR OF BEING IN AN ENCLOSED PLACE"
YOU'D THINK THERE'D BE SOME MENTION OF "WEED-CLAUSTROPHOBIA," WOULDN'T YOU?
SCHULZ

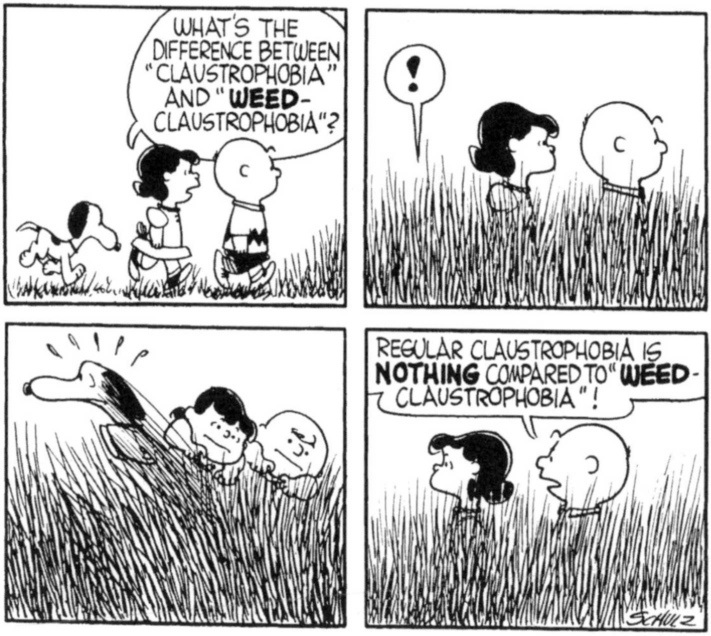
WHAT'S THE DIFFERENCE BETWEEN "CLAUSTROPHOBIA" AND "WEED-CLAUSTROPHOBIA"?
!
REGULAR CLAUSTROPHOBIA IS NOTHING COMPARED TO "WEED-CLAUSTROPHOBIA"!
SCHULZ

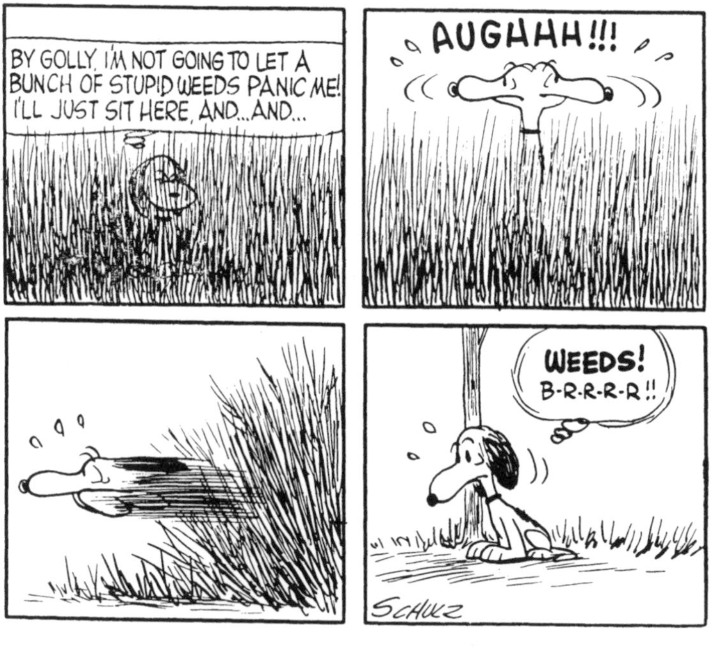
BY GOLLY, I'M NOT GOING TO LET A BUNCH OF STUPID WEEDS PANIC ME! I'LL JUST SIT HERE, AND...AND...
AUGHHH!!!
WEEDS! B-R-R-R-R!!
SCHULZ

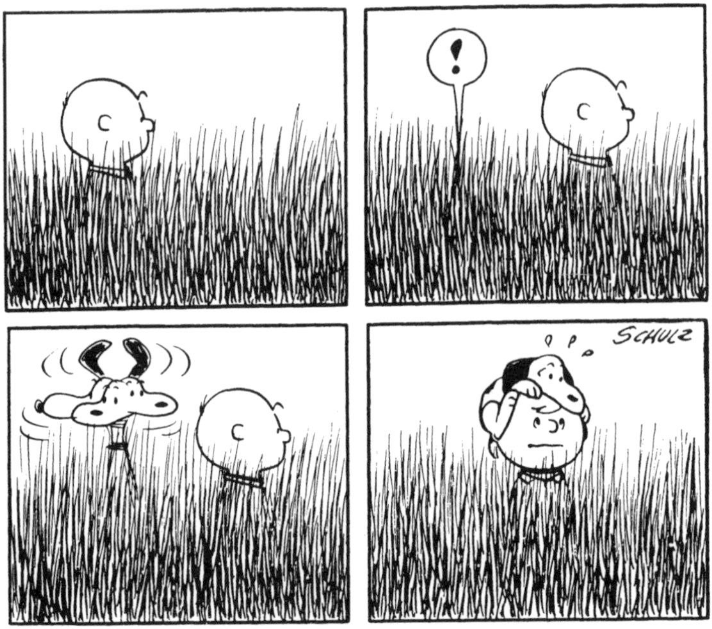
!
SCHULZ

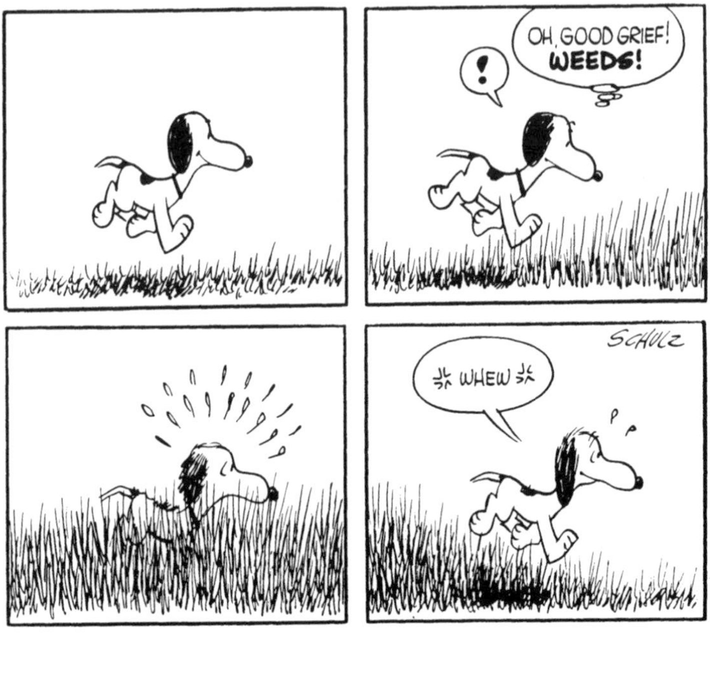
!
OH, GOOD GRIEF! WEEDS!
WHEW
SCHULZ

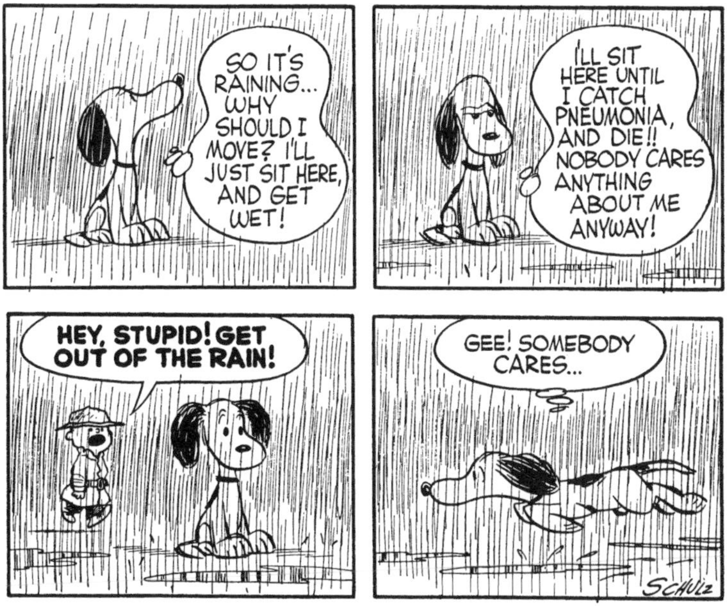
SO IT'S RAINING... WHY SHOULD I MOVE? I'LL JUST SIT HERE, AND GET WET!
I'LL SIT HERE UNTIL I CATCH PNEUMONIA, AND DIE!! NOBODY CARES ANYTHING ABOUT ME ANYWAY!
HEY, STUPID! GET OUT OF THE RAIN!
GEE! SOMEBODY CARES...
SCHULZ

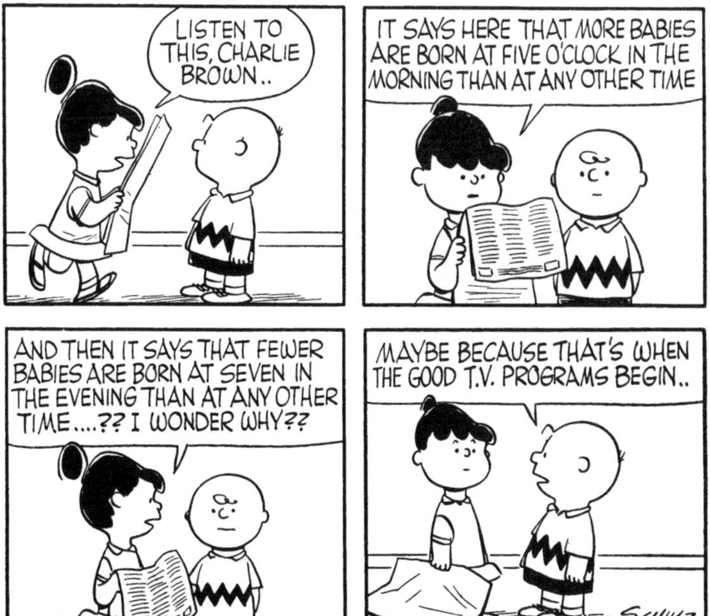
LISTEN TO THIS, CHARLIE BROWN..
IT SAYS HERE THAT MORE BABIES ARE BORN AT FIVE O'CLOCK IN THE MORNING THAN AT ANY OTHER TIME
AND THEN IT SAYS THAT FEWER BABIES ARE BORN AT SEVEN IN THE EVENING THAN AT ANY OTHER TIME....?? I WONDER WHY??
MAYBE BECAUSE THAT'S WHEN THE GOOD T.V. PROGRAMS BEGIN..
SCHULZ

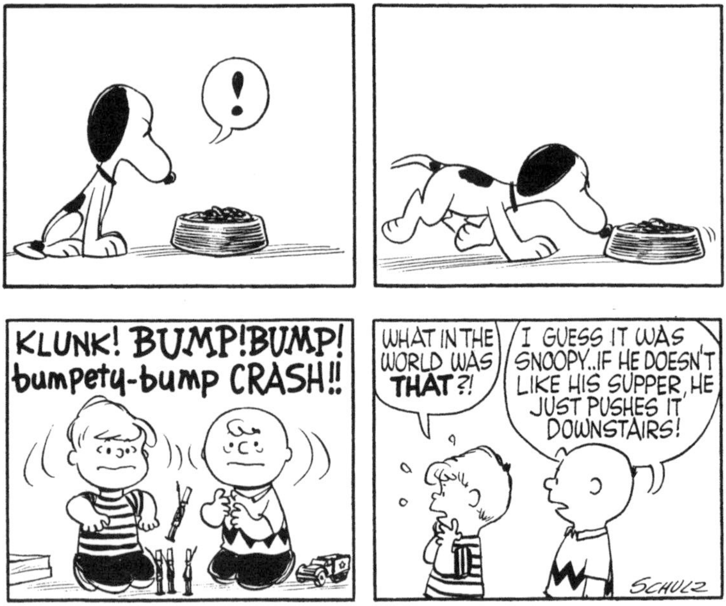
!
KLUNK! BUMP!BUMP! bumpety-bump CRASH!!
WHAT IN THE WORLD WAS **THAT**?!
I GUESS IT WAS SNOOPY..IF HE DOESN'T LIKE HIS SUPPER, HE JUST PUSHES IT DOWNSTAIRS!
SCHULZ

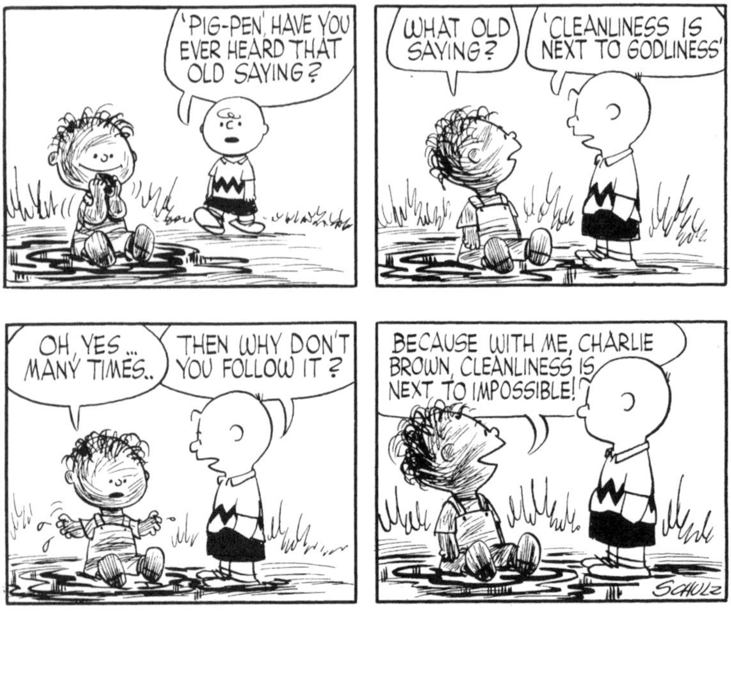
'PIG-PEN,' HAVE YOU EVER HEARD THAT OLD SAYING?
WHAT OLD SAYING?
'CLEANLINESS IS NEXT TO GODLINESS'
OH, YES... MANY TIMES..
THEN WHY DON'T YOU FOLLOW IT?
BECAUSE WITH ME, CHARLIE BROWN, CLEANLINESS IS NEXT TO IMPOSSIBLE!
SCHULZ

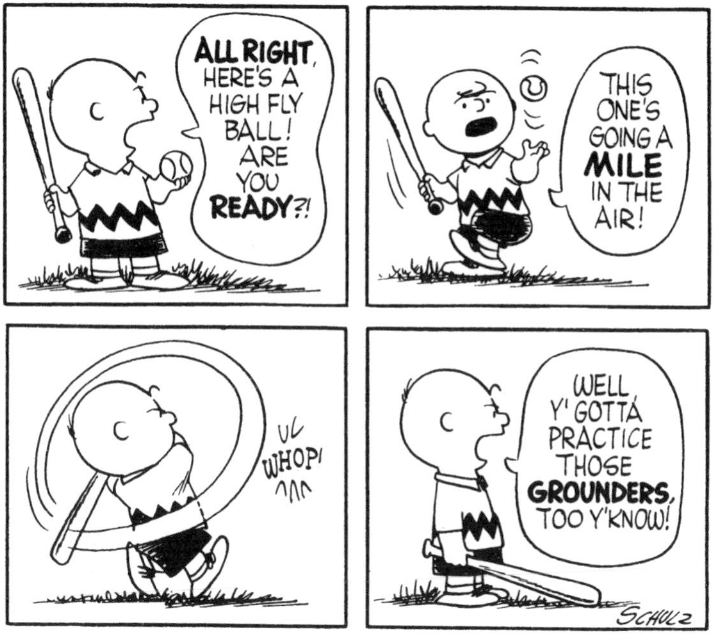
ALL RIGHT, HERE'S A HIGH FLY BALL! ARE YOU READY?!
THIS ONE'S GOING A MILE IN THE AIR!
WHOP!
WELL Y' GOTTA PRACTICE THOSE GROUNDERS, TOO Y'KNOW!
SCHULZ

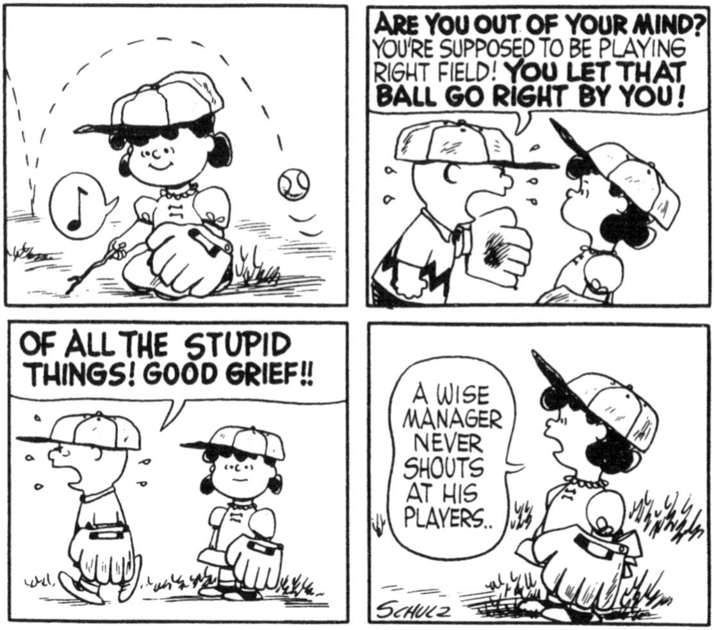
ARE YOU OUT OF YOUR MIND? YOU'RE SUPPOSED TO BE PLAYING RIGHT FIELD! YOU LET THAT BALL GO RIGHT BY YOU!
OF ALL THE STUPID THINGS! GOOD GRIEF!!
A WISE MANAGER NEVER SHOUTS AT HIS PLAYERS..
SCHULZ

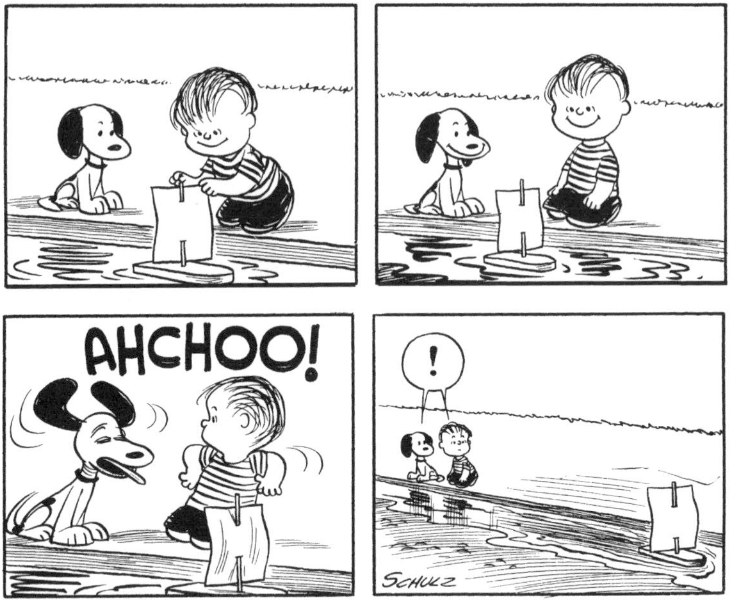
AHCHOO!
!
SCHULZ

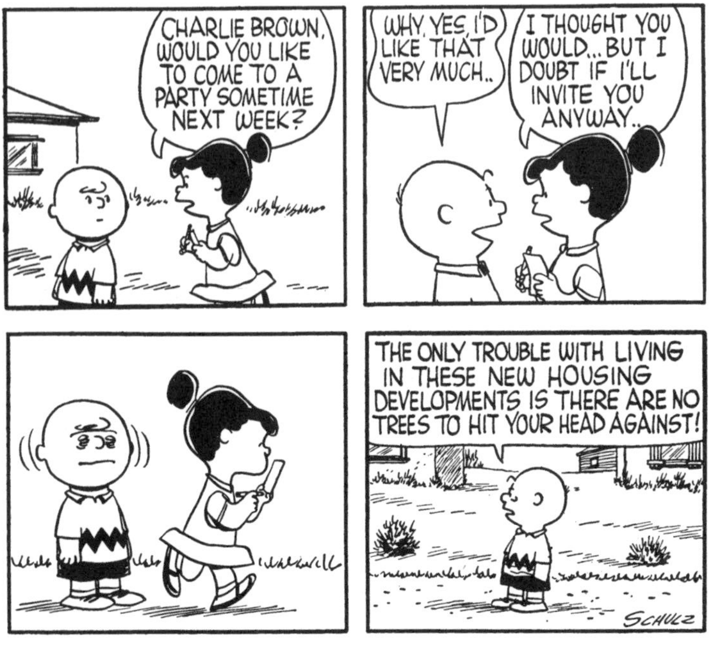
CHARLIE BROWN, WOULD YOU LIKE TO COME TO A PARTY SOMETIME NEXT WEEK?
WHY, YES, I'D LIKE THAT VERY MUCH..
I THOUGHT YOU WOULD... BUT I DOUBT IF I'LL INVITE YOU ANYWAY..
THE ONLY TROUBLE WITH LIVING IN THESE NEW HOUSING DEVELOPMENTS IS THERE ARE NO TREES TO HIT YOUR HEAD AGAINST!
SCHULZ

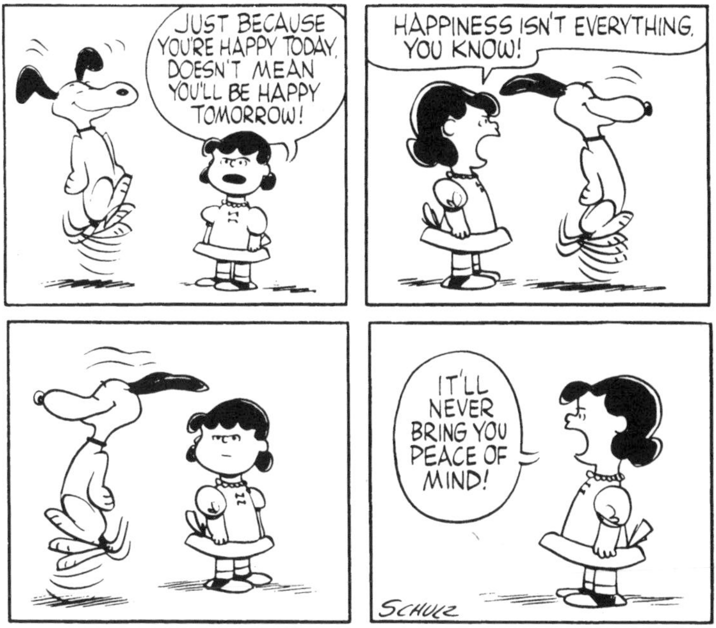
JUST BECAUSE YOU'RE HAPPY TODAY, DOESN'T MEAN YOU'LL BE HAPPY TOMORROW!
HAPPINESS ISN'T EVERYTHING, YOU KNOW!
IT'LL NEVER BRING YOU PEACE OF MIND!
SCHULZ

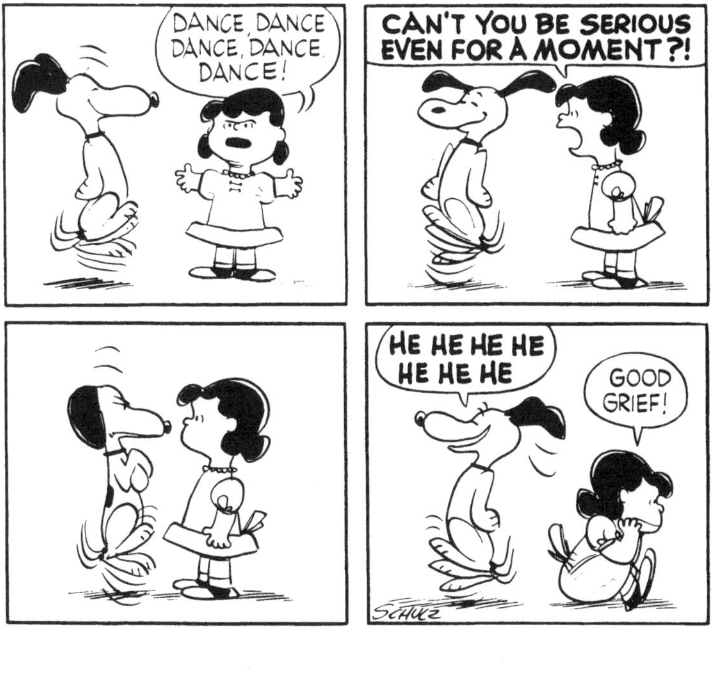
DANCE, DANCE DANCE, DANCE DANCE!
CAN'T YOU BE SERIOUS EVEN FOR A MOMENT?!
HE HE HE HE HE HE HE
GOOD GRIEF!
SCHULZ

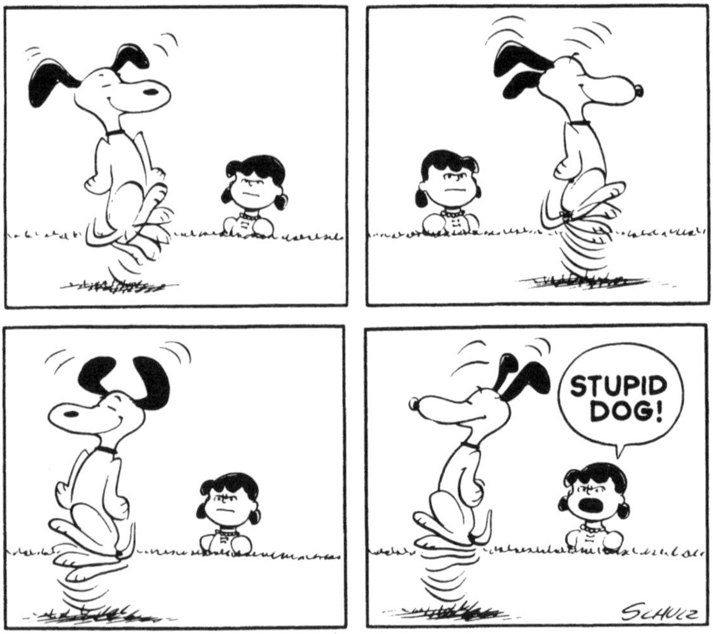
STUPID DOG!
SCHULZ

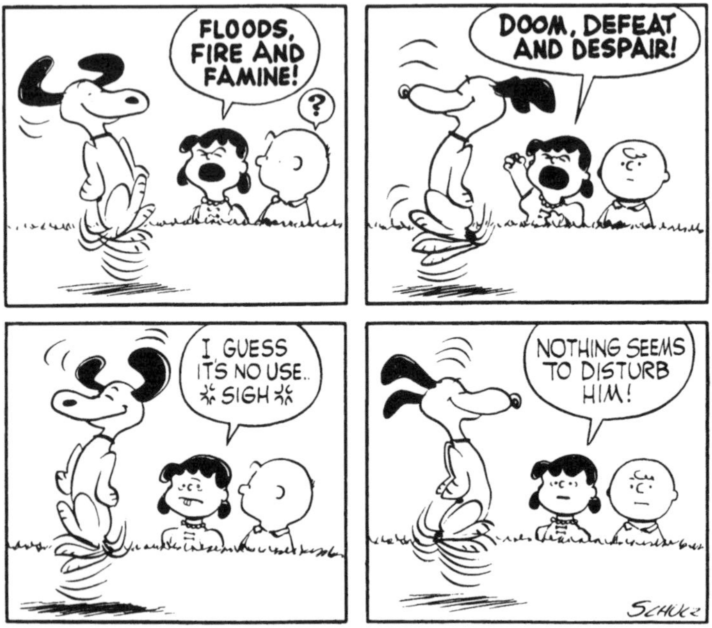
FLOODS, FIRE AND FAMINE!
?
DOOM, DEFEAT AND DESPAIR!
I GUESS IT'S NO USE..
SIGH
NOTHING SEEMS TO DISTURB HIM!
SCHULZ

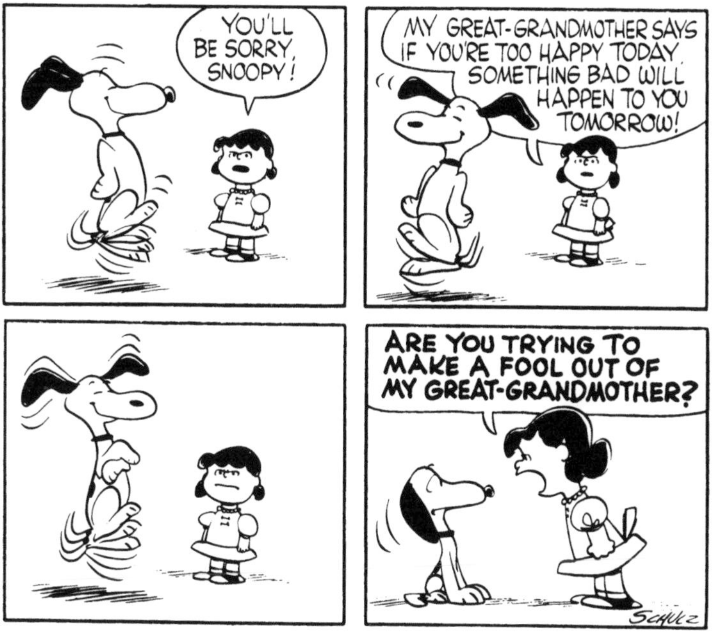
YOU'LL BE SORRY, SNOOPY!
MY GREAT-GRANDMOTHER SAYS IF YOU'RE TOO HAPPY TODAY SOMETHING BAD WILL HAPPEN TO YOU TOMORROW!
ARE YOU TRYING TO MAKE A FOOL OUT OF MY GREAT-GRANDMOTHER?
SCHULZ

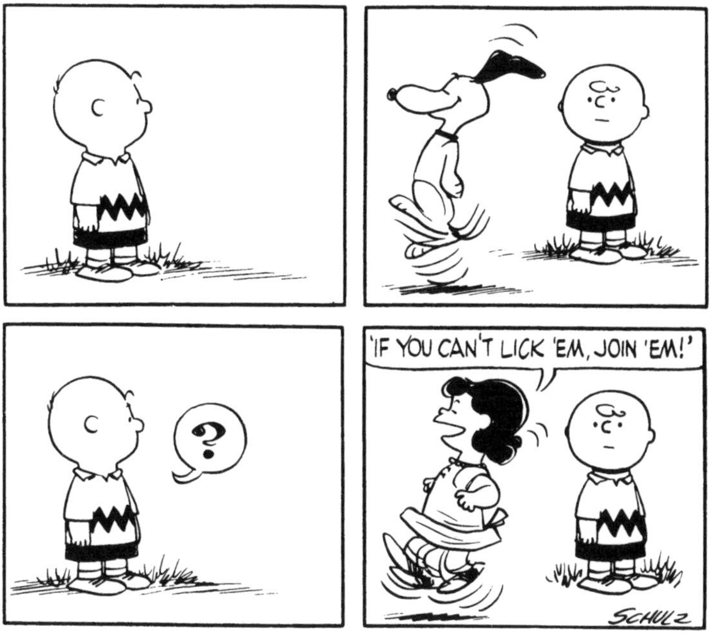
?
'IF YOU CAN'T LICK 'EM, JOIN 'EM!'
SCHULZ

GEE! IT DIDN'T EVEN BREAK..

NOW, YOU KNOW WHAT YOU'RE GOING TO DO TOMORROW NIGHT, DON'T YOU?

SURE..I JUST GO UP TO THESE DIFFERENT HOUSES, RING THEIR DOORBELLS AND THEN SHOUT, "**TRICKS OR TREATS!**"

SAY, BY THE WAY.. THERE'S NO LAW AGAINST THAT, IS THERE?

OF COURSE NOT..

I WOULDN'T WANT TO DO ANYTHING THAT MIGHT AROUSE THE F.B.I.!

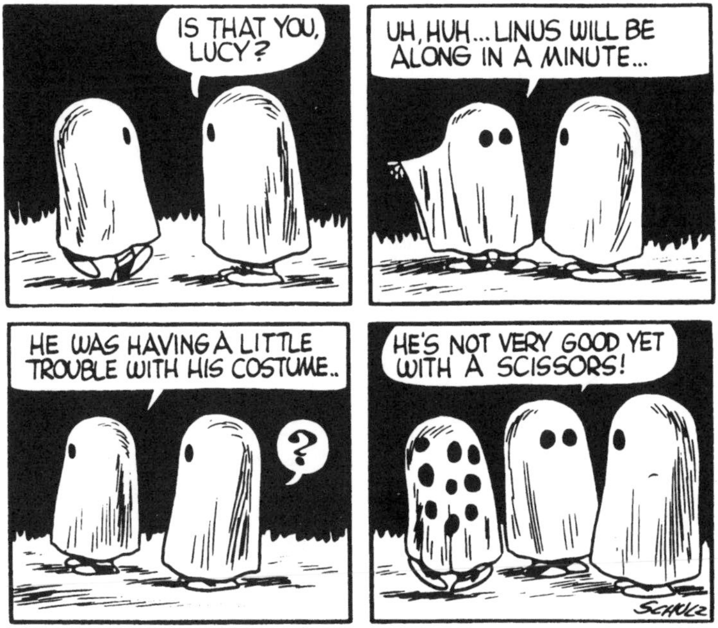
IS THAT YOU, LUCY?
UH, HUH... LINUS WILL BE ALONG IN A MINUTE...
HE WAS HAVING A LITTLE TROUBLE WITH HIS COSTUME..
?
HE'S NOT VERY GOOD YET WITH A SCISSORS!
SCHULZ

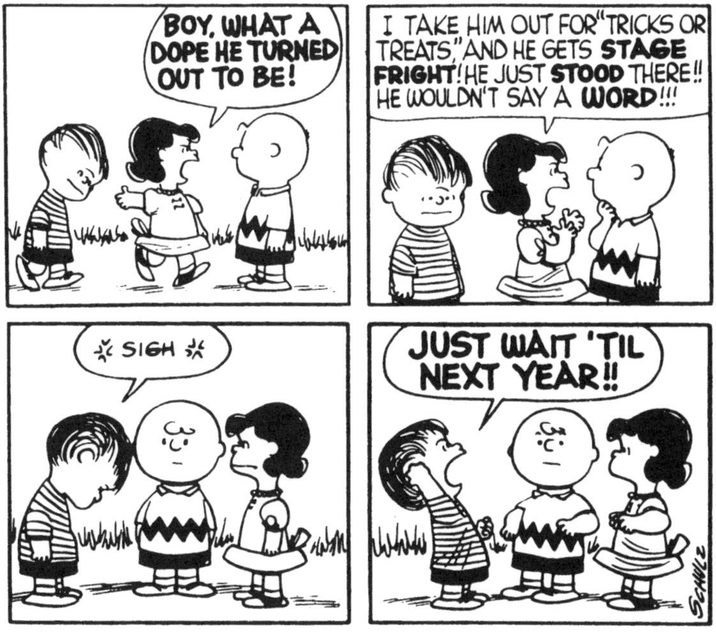
BOY, WHAT A DOPE HE TURNED OUT TO BE!
I TAKE HIM OUT FOR "TRICKS OR TREATS," AND HE GETS STAGE FRIGHT! HE JUST STOOD THERE!! HE WOULDN'T SAY A WORD!!!
SIGH
JUST WAIT 'TIL NEXT YEAR!!
SCHULZ

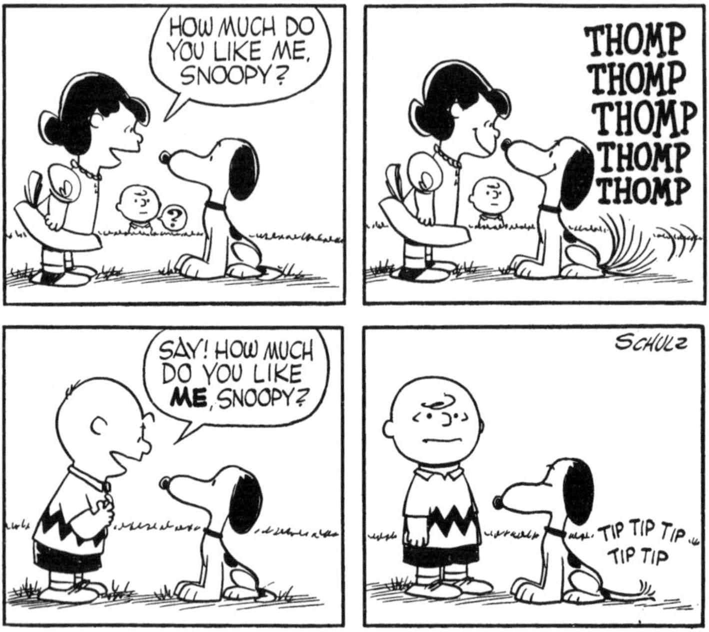
HOW MUCH DO YOU LIKE ME, SNOOPY?
?
THOMP THOMP THOMP THOMP THOMP
SAY! HOW MUCH DO YOU LIKE **ME**, SNOOPY?
SCHULZ
TIP TIP TIP TIP TIP

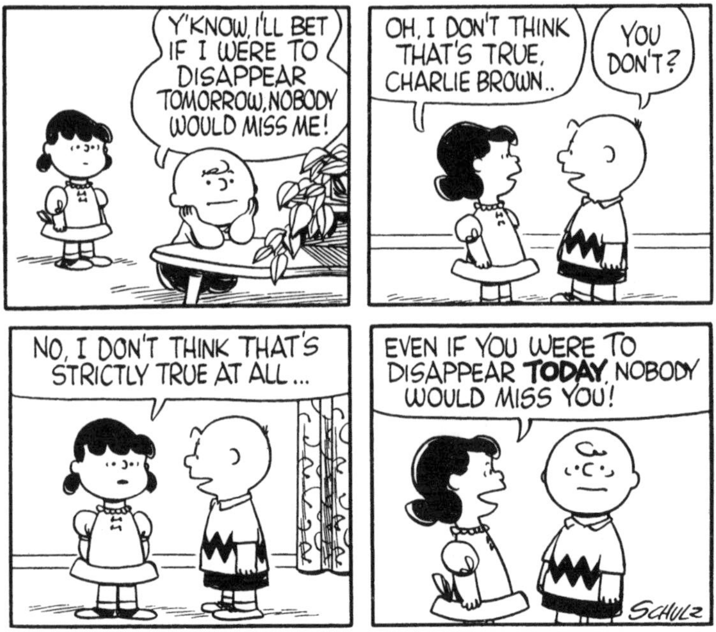
Y'KNOW, I'LL BET IF I WERE TO DISAPPEAR TOMORROW, NOBODY WOULD MISS ME!
OH, I DON'T THINK THAT'S TRUE, CHARLIE BROWN..
YOU DON'T?
NO, I DON'T THINK THAT'S STRICTLY TRUE AT ALL...
EVEN IF YOU WERE TO DISAPPEAR **TODAY**, NOBODY WOULD MISS YOU!
SCHULZ

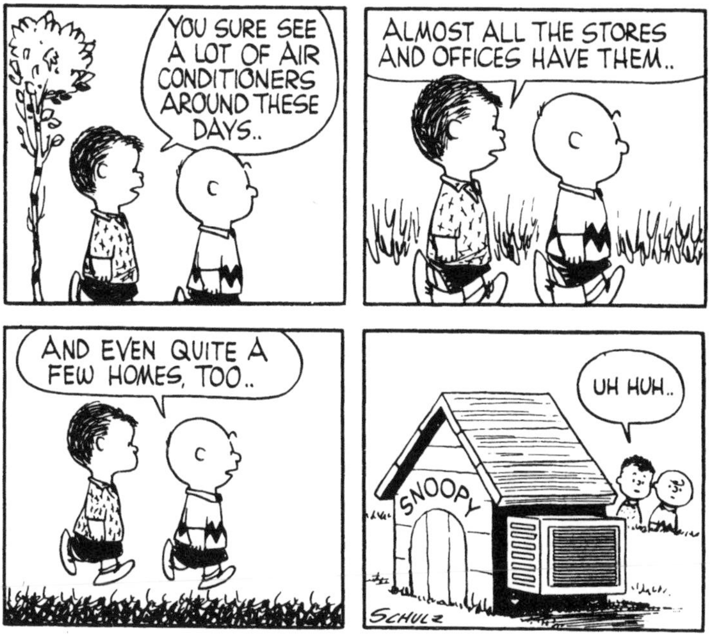
YOU SURE SEE A LOT OF AIR CONDITIONERS AROUND THESE DAYS..
ALMOST ALL THE STORES AND OFFICES HAVE THEM..
AND EVEN QUITE A FEW HOMES, TOO..
UH HUH..
SNOOPY
SCHULZ

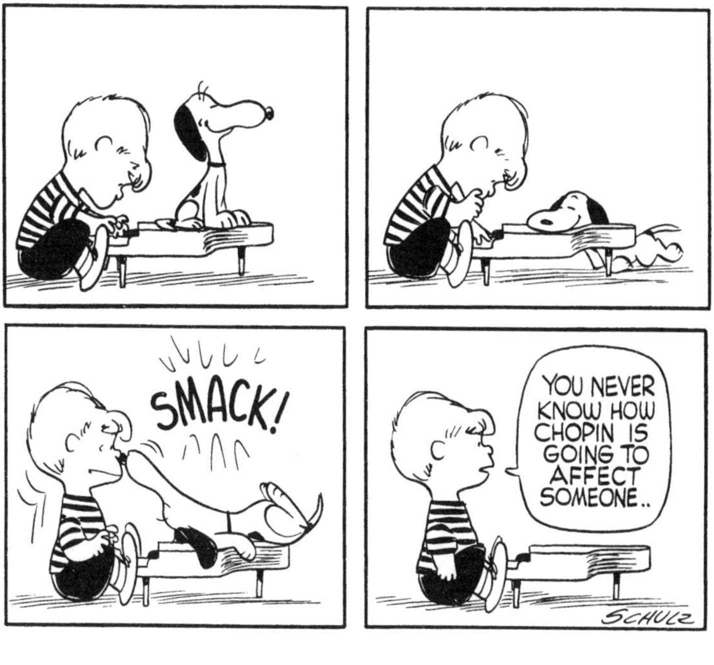
SMACK!
YOU NEVER KNOW HOW CHOPIN IS GOING TO AFFECT SOMEONE..
SCHULZ

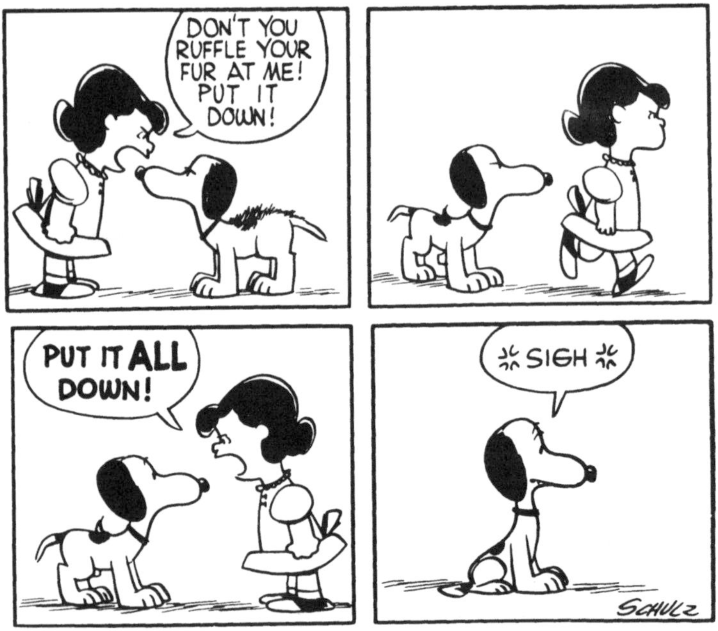
DON'T YOU RUFFLE YOUR FUR AT ME! PUT IT DOWN!
PUT IT ALL DOWN!
SIGH
SCHULZ

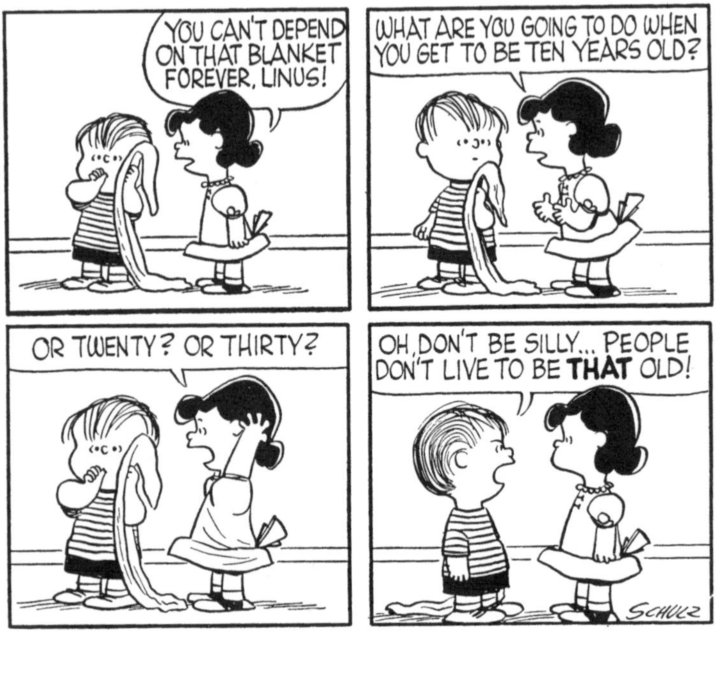
YOU CAN'T DEPEND ON THAT BLANKET FOREVER, LINUS!
WHAT ARE YOU GOING TO DO WHEN YOU GET TO BE TEN YEARS OLD?
OR TWENTY? OR THIRTY?
OH, DON'T BE SILLY... PEOPLE DON'T LIVE TO BE THAT OLD!
SCHULZ

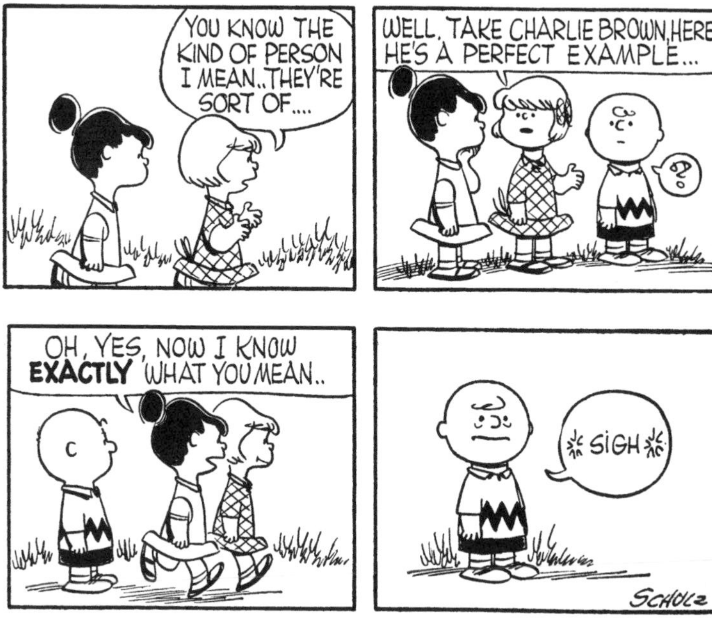
YOU KNOW THE KIND OF PERSON I MEAN..THEY'RE SORT OF....
WELL, TAKE CHARLIE BROWN, HERE, HE'S A PERFECT EXAMPLE...
?
OH, YES, NOW I KNOW **EXACTLY** WHAT YOU MEAN..
SIGH
SCHULZ

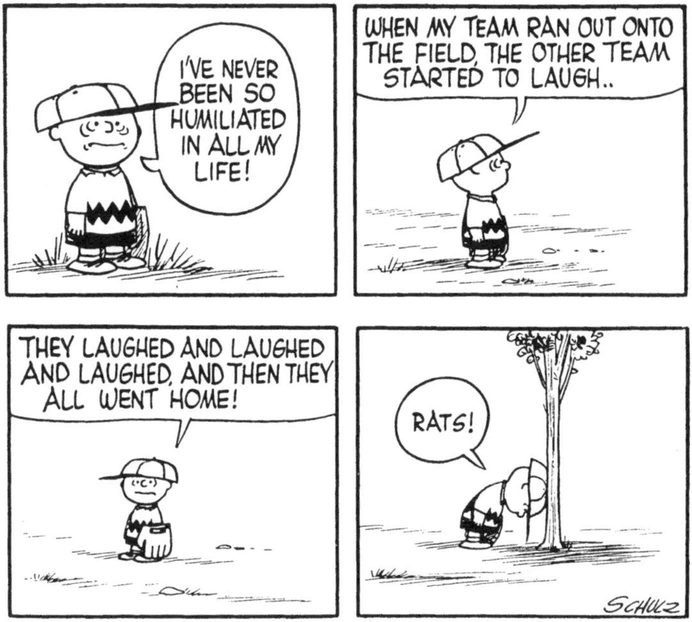
I'VE NEVER BEEN SO HUMILIATED IN ALL MY LIFE!
WHEN MY TEAM RAN OUT ONTO THE FIELD, THE OTHER TEAM STARTED TO LAUGH..
THEY LAUGHED AND LAUGHED AND LAUGHED, AND THEN THEY ALL WENT HOME!
RATS!
SCHULZ

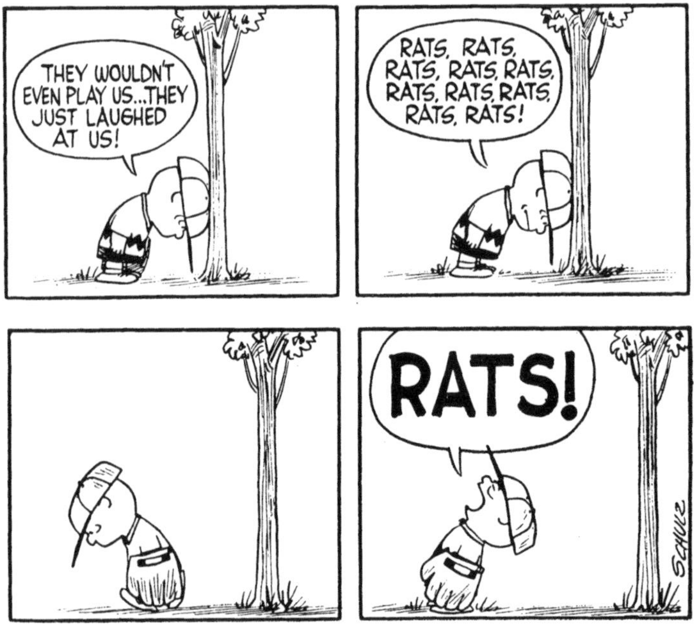
THEY WOULDN'T EVEN PLAY US...THEY JUST LAUGHED AT US!
RATS, RATS, RATS, RATS, RATS, RATS, RATS, RATS, RATS, RATS!
RATS!
SCHULZ

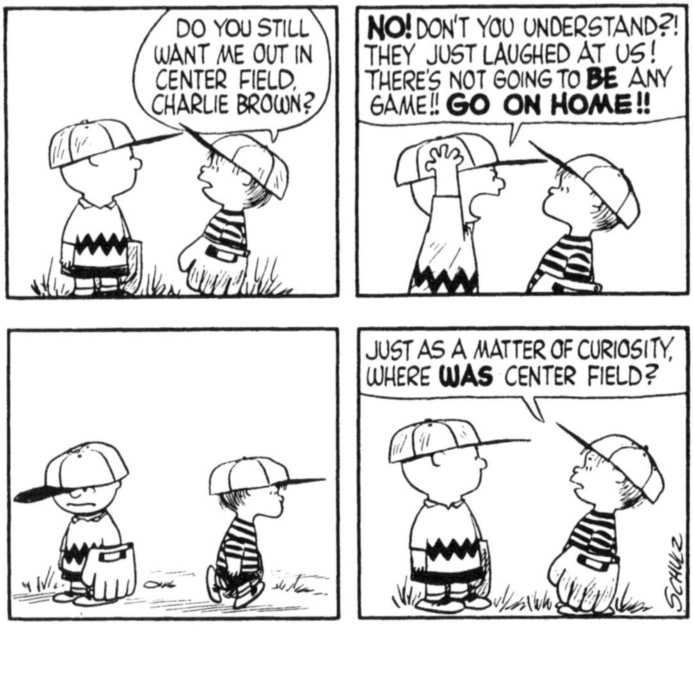
DO YOU STILL WANT ME OUT IN CENTER FIELD, CHARLIE BROWN?
NO! DON'T YOU UNDERSTAND?! THEY JUST LAUGHED AT US! THERE'S NOT GOING TO BE ANY GAME!! GO ON HOME!!
JUST AS A MATTER OF CURIOSITY, WHERE WAS CENTER FIELD?
SCHULZ

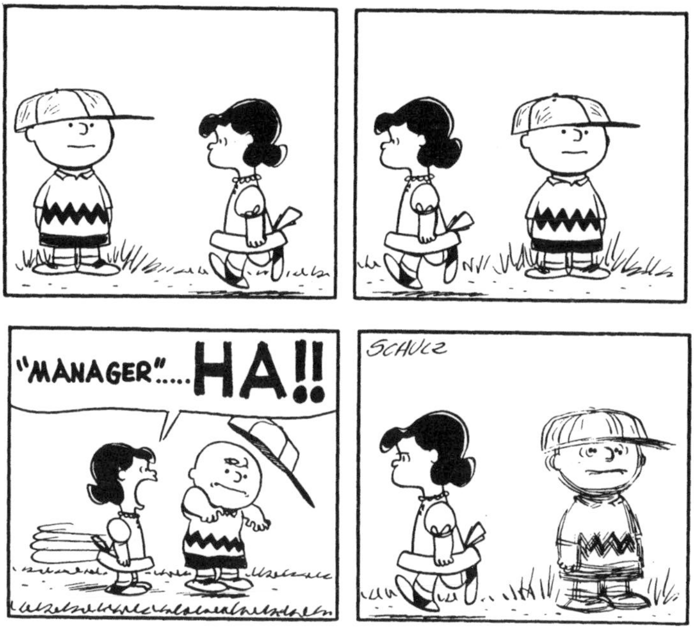
"MANAGER"..... HA!!
SCHULZ

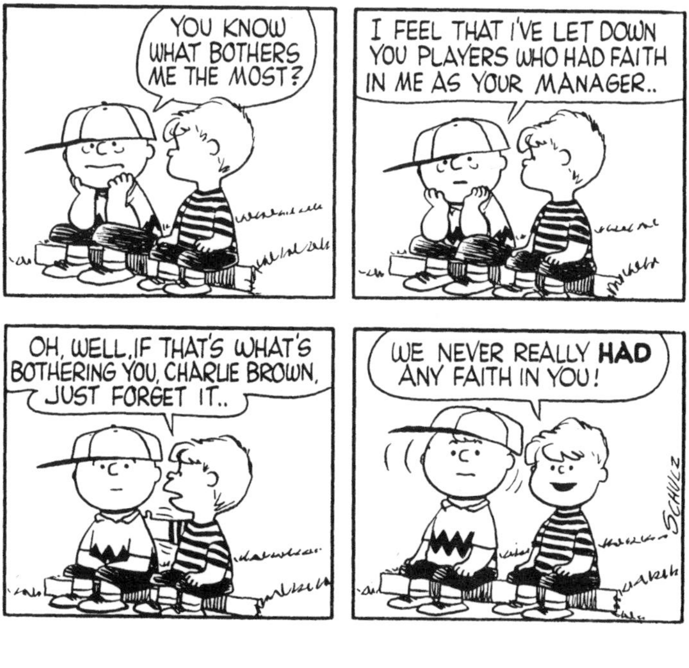
YOU KNOW WHAT BOTHERS ME THE MOST?
I FEEL THAT I'VE LET DOWN YOU PLAYERS WHO HAD FAITH IN ME AS YOUR MANAGER..
OH, WELL, IF THAT'S WHAT'S BOTHERING YOU, CHARLIE BROWN, JUST FORGET IT..
WE NEVER REALLY **HAD** ANY FAITH IN YOU!
SCHULZ

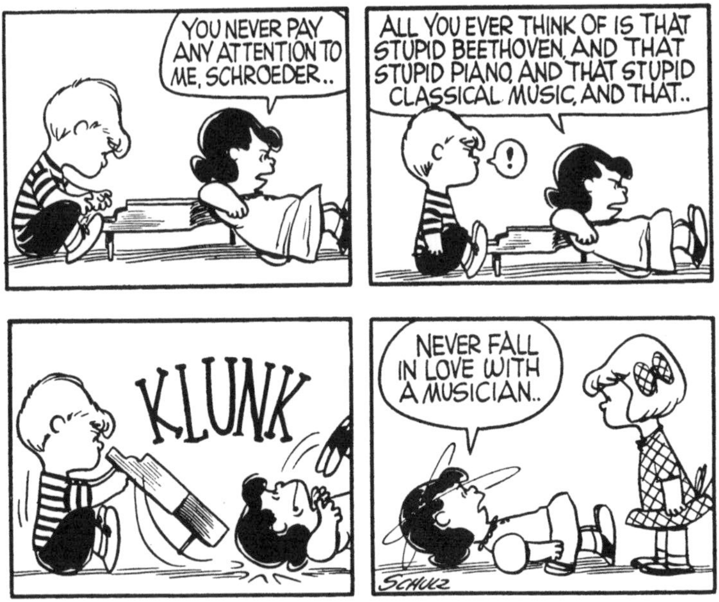
YOU NEVER PAY ANY ATTENTION TO ME, SCHROEDER..
ALL YOU EVER THINK OF IS THAT STUPID BEETHOVEN, AND THAT STUPID PIANO, AND THAT STUPID CLASSICAL MUSIC, AND THAT..
!
KLUNK
NEVER FALL IN LOVE WITH A MUSICIAN..
SCHULZ

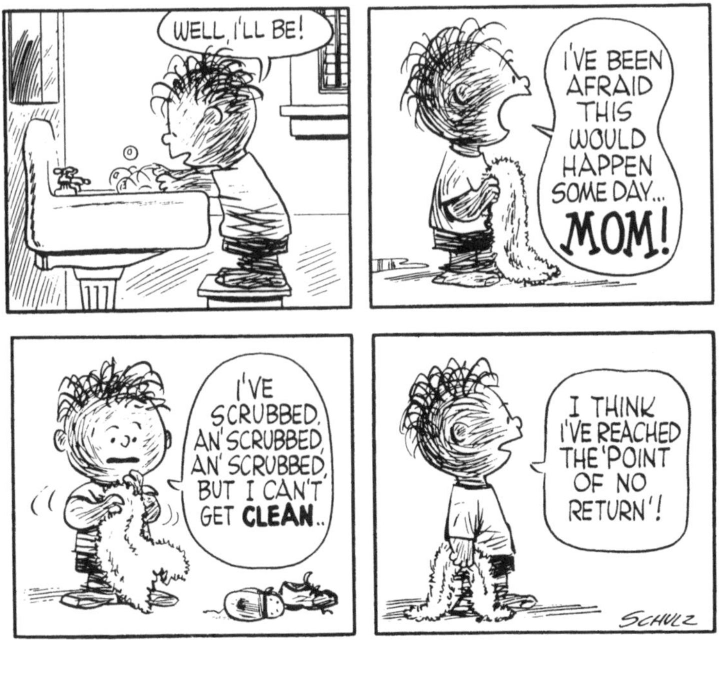
WELL, I'LL BE!
I'VE BEEN AFRAID THIS WOULD HAPPEN SOME DAY... MOM!
I'VE SCRUBBED, AN' SCRUBBED, AN' SCRUBBED, BUT I CAN'T GET CLEAN..
I THINK I'VE REACHED THE 'POINT OF NO RETURN'!
SCHULZ

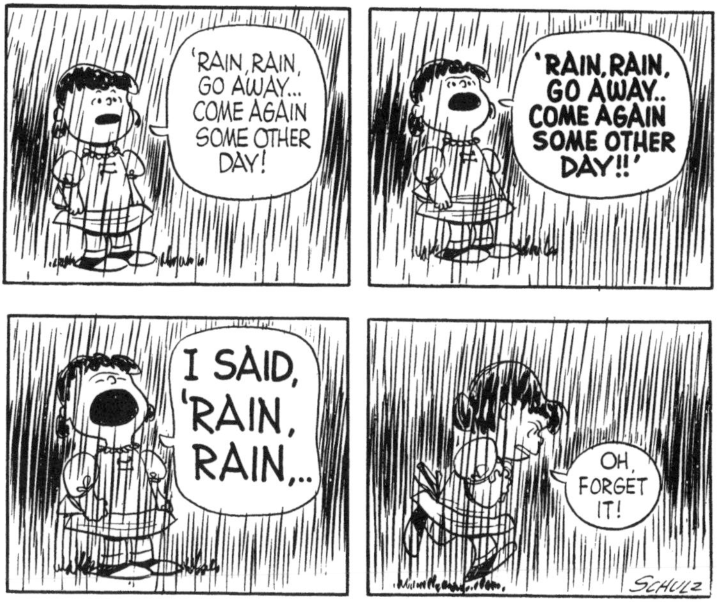
'RAIN, RAIN, GO AWAY... COME AGAIN SOME OTHER DAY!
'RAIN, RAIN, GO AWAY.. COME AGAIN SOME OTHER DAY!!'
I SAID, 'RAIN, RAIN,...
OH, FORGET IT!
SCHULZ

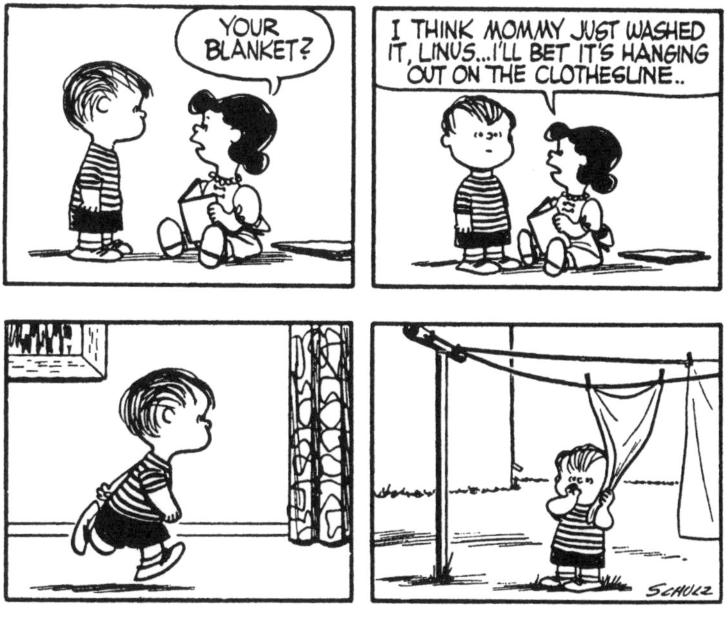
YOUR BLANKET?
I THINK MOMMY JUST WASHED IT, LINUS...I'LL BET IT'S HANGING OUT ON THE CLOTHESLINE..
SCHULZ

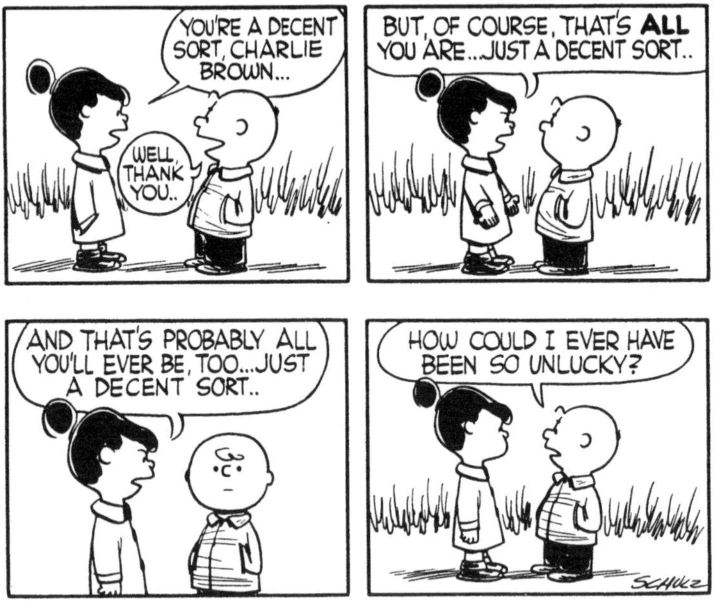
YOU'RE A DECENT SORT, CHARLIE BROWN...
WELL, THANK YOU..
BUT, OF COURSE, THAT'S **ALL** YOU ARE...JUST A DECENT SORT..
AND THAT'S PROBABLY ALL YOU'LL EVER BE, TOO...JUST A DECENT SORT..
HOW COULD I EVER HAVE BEEN SO UNLUCKY?
SCHULZ

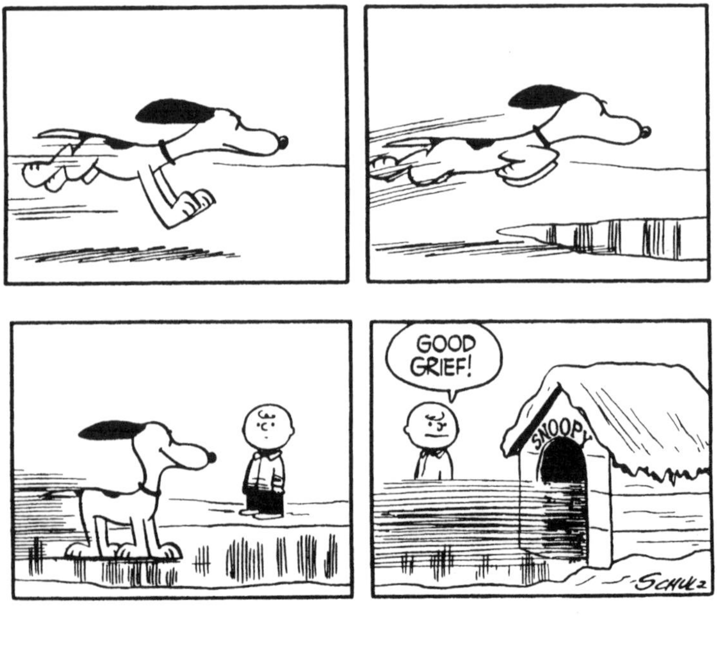
GOOD GRIEF!
SNOOPY
SCHULZ